Fix It!
Grammar

Frog Prince, or Just Deserts

TEACHER'S MANUAL BOOK 3

Pamela White

THIRD EDITION

Also by Pamela White

Fix It! Grammar: The Nose Tree Teacher's Manual Book 1
Fix It! Grammar: The Nose Tree Student Book 1
Fix It! Grammar: Robin Hood Teacher's Manual Book 2
Fix It! Grammar: Robin Hood Student Book 2
Fix It! Grammar: Frog Prince, or Just Deserts Student Book 3
Fix It! Grammar: Little Mermaid Teacher's Manual Book 4
Fix It! Grammar: Little Mermaid Student Book 4
Fix It! Grammar: Chanticleer Teacher's Manual Book 5
Fix It! Grammar: Chanticleer Student Book 5
Fix It! Grammar: Sir Gawain and the Green Knight Teacher's Manual Book 6
Fix It! Grammar: Sir Gawain and the Green Knight Student Book 6

The purchase of this book entitles its owner to a free download of the *Frog Prince* student Blackline Masters.

Go to: IEW.com/FIX-3-E

(See the blue page for complete download instructions.)

Institute for Excellence in Writing, L.L.C.
8799 N. 387 Road
Locust Grove, OK 74352

800.856.5815

info@IEW.com

IEW.com

Printed in the United States of America

IEW® is a registered trademark of the Institute for Excellence in Writing, L.L.C.

Accessing Your Downloads

The purchase of this book entitles its owner to a free download of the following:

- *Fix-It! Student Book 3* e-book (132 pages*)
- *Mastery Learning* e-audio
- *But, but, but ...What about Grammar?* e-audio

To download these e-resources, please follow the directions below:

1. Go to our website: IEW.com.
2. Log in to your online customer account. If you do not have an account, you will need to create one.
3. After you are logged in, go to this web page: IEW.com/FIX-3-E.
4. Click the red arrow, and then click the checkboxes next to the names of the files you wish to place in your account.
5. Click the "Add to my files" button.
6. To access your files now and in the future, click on "Your Account" and click on the "Files" tab (one of the gray tabs).
7. Click on each file name to download the files onto your computer.

Please note: You are free to download and print the student e-book as needed for use within *your immediate family or classroom*. However, this information is proprietary, and we are trusting you to be on your honor not to share it with anyone. Please see the copyright page for further details. Thank you.

  * If you would prefer to purchase *Fix It! Student Book 3* as a preprinted, spiral-bound book, it is available at this web page: IEW.com/FIX-3-SB.

If you have any difficulty receiving these downloads after going through the steps above, please call 800.856.5815.

Institute for Excellence in Writing
8799 N. 387 Road
Locust Grove, OK 74352

Introduction

Welcome to *Fix It!*

Welcome to the third book of *Fix It! Grammar: Frog Prince, or Just Deserts*.

If you are wondering about the spelling of *deserts*, it is correct because the title is an intentional pun. You will understand why when you get to the end of this delightful retelling of "The Frog Prince." When someone receives his just deserts, he is getting what he deserves (his deserts) for good or ill, not sweet delicacies.

As your students enjoy reading a sentence or two of this adaptation of a classic fairy tale each day, they will learn to apply grammar rules to the writing. Over the course of the year, they will explore how sentences are structured and learn how to apply punctuation rules to that structure.

This book builds on the work that was started in the first two *Fix It!* stories: *The Nose Tree* and *Robin Hood*. If you find that this book moves too quickly, it may be better to go back and work through *Robin Hood*.

This is not a traditional grammar program, so it will not feel as if you are really learning grammar. Instead, you and your students will be internalizing the tools necessary for editing their own compositions, which is the main goal of grammar.

The Method: Modeling Proper Grammar within Stories

The traditional method of teaching grammar is to present a grammar rule and then have students apply it in a series of contrived exercises. When that grammar rule is learned, another is taught and practiced in the same manner.

Although students often do well on these traditional worksheets, the learning does not usually transfer to their own writing and editing. Why? The grammar involved in real-life sentences is usually much more complicated than what is in the grammar exercise book, so students are often unable to edit their own work.

Fix It! Grammar overcomes these difficulties by teaching grammar at the point of need. Instead of a page full of grammar exercises, students will tackle real-life sentences with limited instruction. Thus, students will learn to think about their writing and incrementally learn how to apply the grammar rules to written work. Moreover, it is this daily practice of editing that will help instill the habit of editing anything they write.

For this to work, you as the teacher need to approach this book as a series of modeling exercises. Discuss each rule as it is presented, and then model for your students how to label the sentences and make the corrections. As your students gain confidence, they will often complete the labels and corrections accurately, but that is not always the case. Consider that mistakes are an opportunity to learn. If your students mismark a word or miss a correction, laugh! Show them what they missed, revisit the grammar rule involved, and encourage them that they can catch it next time.

After all, everyone needs an editor. Even professional writers and editors miss errors. The important thing is to understand the process and catch as much as you can. Knowing the reasons behind the fixes will make your students much better editors in the long run, and you will also gain the expertise to evaluate your students' papers better when they are older.

Weekly Classes

If you are using this course with a writing class that meets weekly, we recommend having each family purchase the Teacher's Manual. Ask the parents to go over the passages at home with their children. That frees you up to focus on just some of the concepts so it does not take up too much class time.

Get Ready

This book provides 33 weeks of grammar instruction and practice. The process should take about fifteen minutes a day, four days a week.

Follow the instructions on the blue page in the front of this manual to download the student book. Print out one copy per student. You can purchase a spiral-bound version of the student book if desired at the IEW website: IEW.com/FIX-3-SB.

Your student will need a binder with four tabs organized as follows:

- **Fix Its**   The first part of the book includes the weekly instruction, passages, and grammar cards. Put all of the first part except the weekly fixes behind this tab. Each week as you hand your students the next week's fixes, they can keep adding them to this section and not be tempted to read ahead and spoil the surprise.
- **Grammar Glossary**   The rest of the student book, the Grammar Glossary, should be placed behind this tab.
- **Rewrite**   Place a few pages of lined paper here for your student to use when rewriting the passage.
- **Vocabulary**   Provide more lined paper for your student to keep a list of the vocabulary words along with their meanings.

Get Started

Begin the program by reading the directions presented on page 3 of the student book (page 7 of this Teacher's Manual). Tell your student that this program works like a puzzle. It is a series of daily games to practice the elements of grammar that they will learn over many weeks.

Your students will likely miss many of the fixes and markings as they work through the program, so stress that "a mistake is an opportunity to learn." They can use their mistakes to learn grammar better. Thus, keep the lessons light and fun, and teach your students to laugh and learn from the elements they miss.

Learn It

Start the week by reading through the "Learn It" section of the student book. Cut out the related grammar cards located near the back of the student book. Your student may keep these cards handy throughout the year and reference them as needed.

Next, show your student how to apply the lesson to the Day 1 passage. Model how to make the editing marks and grammar notations. Since all the markings are illustrated in this Teacher's Manual, you can easily guide your student.

The explanations below the edited text are for the teacher. The discussion notes provide you with the reasons behind each of the fixes as well as some of the other elements of grammar that may come up in your discussion. Notice that they are organized into two

The Layout

Sentences. At the beginning of each lesson is the student passage with corrections.

Fixes. These notes often provide a dialogue for you to explore the reasons behind the fixes with your students. Ensure that your students not only fix the errors but can explain why.

You do not have to discuss everything. Limit the discussion each day to fifteen minutes. If you do not get to something in one passage, it will appear in another and you can address it then.

Grammar Notations. Use these notes to check your students' grammar markings before discussing the punctuation fixes.

Style. This enhances vocabulary by identifying certain dress-ups and appears on Day 4 each week.

Week 5

DAY 4

¶ shaking her head in dismay, [lady constance one day clucked to lady bertha], " [its/it's no wonder (that child has turned out so blemished)].

Fixes

INDENT ¶ because of a new speaker.

CAPITALIZATION. Shaking, Lady Constance, Lady Bertha, It's (capitalized as the first word of a quoted sentence).

USAGE. Use the contraction *It's*, meaning *it is*. **It's** no wonder.

COMMAS AND OTHER PUNCTUATION.
- **#4 -ing openers** take commas. Fix: **Shaking her head in dismay,** Lady Constance.... Ask: Is Lady Constance the one doing the shaking? Answer: Yes, so this is a legal #4.
- **Quotations.** Fix: Lady Constance one day clucked to Lady Bertha, "It's no wonder.... Rules: 1) When a speaking verb (*clucked*) sets up a direct quotation, add a comma right before the quotation. 2) Use quotation marks with direct quotations but no close quotation marks because she is not finished speaking.

Grammar Notations

PREPOSITIONAL PHRASES. in dismay; to Lady Bertha. *See* ✎ **1.**

CLAUSES, PHRASES, AND OPENERS. Subjects and verbs are bolded to make them easy to see.
- **#4 -ing participial phrase opener:** Shaking her head in dismay. *See* ✎ **2.**
- MC: **Lady Constance** one day **clucked** to Lady Bertha.
- MC: **It's** no wonder. If students miss the *is* in *it's*, ask them to find a *be* verb using the verb card list. If they have trouble recognizing that this is a main clause, explain that pronouns (*it*) can function as subjects.
- DC: that **child has turned** so blemished. *See* ♡.

Style

If desired, have students identify the strongest of the vocabulary dress-ups from this week. Discuss their answers. Suggestions:
- **Strong verbs.** recalled, cuddled, gratify (a verbal), clucked, blemished.
- **Quality adjectives.** unsurprising, tractable, contented, assorted.
- **-ly adverbs.** hopelessly.

blemished: marred or spoiled by imperfections

✎ **1. Teacher's note.** *Out* is an adverb here, not a preposition, and is part of the verb phrase. *Turned out* (ended up, proven to be) has a different meaning from *turned.*

✎ **2. Teacher's note.** *Shaking her head in dismay* is a phrase and not a clause because there is no subject and helping verb to make *shaking* a verb. It functions as an adjective phrase describing the subject (*Lady Constance*) after the comma.

♡ **Grammar lovers.** This is a disguised noun clause with *that* understood, not a main clause: It is no wonder *that* that child has turned out so blemished. The first (and hidden) *that* is a relative pronoun setting up the clause; the second is a demonstrative pronoun modifying *child* (which child? *that* child).

38   Institute for Excellence in Writing

Vocabulary words. These and their definitions are printed in the sidebar.

Teacher's notes. Additional information is included in the sidebar to further your understanding of the grammar involved.

---

sections: Fixes and Grammar Notations. You will likely need to reference the grammar notations in order to make the corrections, so do not feel that you have to follow the discussion notes in order. Simply use them as a reference as you work through the passage.

Fix It

On the remaining three days of the week, follow the process detailed on page 7 of this Teacher's Manual to fix and mark the passage. Students may do some of the lesson on their own, such as looking up the vocabulary word and attempting to fix and mark the passage. However, it can also be done together.

Use the discussion notes as needed to explain the fixes and discuss the grammar involved. Use the questions to help your student understand the grammar better, but do not feel compelled to read them all to your student. The discussion part should not take more than fifteen minutes per day. The principles will be repeated, so there is plenty of time to learn. The daily discussion and practice will bring mastery, so keep this part of the lesson light and fun.

In addition to the regular discussion of grammar, the discussion notes include advanced concepts, teacher's notes, and tidbits for the grammar lovers among you. These additions, set off with icons, are primarily for the teacher's information to explain something that might be confusing in the discussion. If a student is curious, go ahead and discuss those concepts. However, they are generally above the scope of this course and can be just for a teacher's enjoyment and training.

ADVANCED

✐ Teacher's note

♡ Grammar lovers

Rewrite

Finally, the rewrite is the key to success. By rewriting the passage and paying attention to detail, your student will internalize the corrections. For your convenience, the corrected passage rewrite is printed in the Teacher's Manual at the end of each week's fixes.

Pacing

Adjust the pace of the teaching as needed. If your student is not understanding all the details, then do not require him to add new markings until the previous ones are easy. This mastery learning approach should be fun and low stress. If your students start to groan when you say, "Time for *Fix It!*" something is wrong.

For more on a mastery learning approach to teaching, listen to Andrew Pudewa's "Mastery Learning" talk. It has been included as a free download with your *Fix It!* purchase. See the blue page in the front of this manual for download instructions.

Grammar Glossary

The Grammar Glossary is a tool that can be used for all six *Fix It! Grammar* books. It summarizes most of the information that is taught in the books. Reference it if you want a little more information than was provided with the passage. It will also be a handy grammar guide for your student to use in the future.

Grading

This course is intended to be used as a teaching tool and thus should not be graded. If you must assign a grade, assess the students' rewrite of the passage. You can simply choose one of the passages from the week to evaluate. The passage can be worth ten points. Deduct one point for each error.

Find Help

The scope and sequence for this book is on pages 210–212.

If you would like to see a demonstration of how to do the *Fix It!* lessons, please watch the webinar on the IEW website. It is on the *Fix It!* Overview page. See IEW.com/Fix.

The Institute for Excellence in Writing also provides teacher forums for those using our materials. It is a great place to meet other IEW teachers and find answers to specific writing and grammar questions. To join, see IEW.com/forum.

Instructions

Instructions

Welcome to *Fix It! Grammar*. This year you can enjoy learning grammar by seeing how it works in a real-life story.

GET READY

To organize your work, you will need a two-pocket notebook with three-hole fasteners and a single-subject spiral notebook. If you have the spiral-bound *Fix It!* student book, then all you need is a single subject spiral notebook.

Use the center of the two-pocket notebook to collect the lesson and *Fix It!* pages as your teacher distributes them each week. Rewrite the passage in the front of the spiral notebook and use the back of the book to write down the vocabulary words and their definitions, working from the back forward.

Grammar cards are located in the back of the student book after page 72 and before the Grammar Glossary section. These may be cut out as they are needed and stored in a resealable plastic pouch or taped to a piece of card stock, as illustrated at right. The cards may be kept in the notebook pocket or tucked into the spiral-bound student book.

LEARN IT

With your teacher, read through the "Learn It" section for the week. This will show you what you will be looking for that week and for weeks to come.

To help you remember and review what you learned, use the grammar card(s) for the week. Keep them handy each time you work on *Fix It!* so that the information is at your fingertips.

FIX IT

Each day complete the following tasks.

Every Day	Read the sentence. Look up the bolded word in a dictionary. Decide which definition best fits the meaning of the word in this sentence. In the vocabulary section of your notebook, write a brief definition (using key words) labeled with the appropriate week. Add to this list every day.
Day 1	Read the instructions for the week with your teacher. Mark and fix the first passage with your teacher's help. Discuss what you missed with your teacher, and then complete the rewrite after fixing.
Days 2–4	Use your grammar cards to help you remember how to mark the passages as taught in the weekly instructions. Your teacher will help you with anything you miss. Remember, a mistake is an opportunity to learn.
Rewrite	After marking, correcting, and discussing the passage with your teacher each day, copy the corrected passage into a separate notebook so that you end up with a handwritten copy of the complete story. Your teacher can show you an example of the rewrite in the teacher's book.

- Be sure to double-space.
- Do not copy the markings, just the story.
- Be careful to indent where indicated and use capital letters properly.
- Carefully copy the punctuation and use end marks.

Page 3, *Fix It! Grammar: Frog Prince, or Just Deserts*, Student Book 3

Read this introductory page with your students.

Help your students set up their Fix It notebook as described in the Get Ready section.

Notice that the first day of each week is a teaching day. Read through the Learn It part with your students and then show them exactly what to do using the Day 1 passage.

On the remaining days your students can complete the fixes independently before you go over them to ensure understanding.

Week 1

Review

In the back of this book just before the Grammar Glossary is a set of grammar cards. Find the ones that say Week 1 and cut them out. Read over the cards to refresh your memory of **indents**, **capitalization**, **homophones and usage**, **apostrophes**, **comparative and superlative adjectives**, and **verbs**. Use them for reference if you need a quick review of any of the concepts. Here are some additional directions:

Indent ¶. For each sentence in the passage, decide if it needs to begin a new paragraph. If so, place a paragraph symbol in front of the sentence to remember to indent when you rewrite the passage.

Capitalization. You will not see any capital letters in your student book sentences. Show where capitals are needed by drawing three short lines directly underneath letters that should be capitalized. In your copy work, be sure to use capital letters where needed instead of those three lines.

Homophones and Usage. When you see a list of words underlined in the passage, simply draw a line through the incorrect choices. If you notice a word misused, simply cross off the incorrect word in the passage and write the appropriate one above it. In addition to the words listed on the grammar cards, other words may be misused or misspelled without any warning, so watch out for them.

LEARN IT

Prepositional Phrases	Mark prepositional phrases with an underline. Start the line under the preposition and end with the noun. Think: <u>prep + noun</u> (no verb). Refer to the list of prepositions on the Prepositional Phrases grammar card to check the first word.
Subjects and Verbs	If you completed the first two books of *Fix It! Grammar*, you will find that this book requires less marking. This week all you have to mark are subject-verbs and prepositional phrases. The easiest way to identify subjects is to find the verbs first and mark them with a *V*. Use the verb card to help you identify the verbs. With each verb ask, "Who or what is doing this action?" That is the subject. Mark subjects with a capital *S*. Use the Subjects and Verbs grammar card to remember how to mark these.
Commas with Prepositional Phrases	If the prepositional phrase starts a sentence and is five or more words, it needs a comma. If it is shorter than five words, the comma is optional, but let the pause test be your guide: if a pause is needed, add a comma. Prepositional phrases that appear later in the sentence do not take commas. Use the grammar card to remember the comma rules.
Other Punctuation	This book will help you become an expert in punctuation, especially commas. The passages often contain unneeded punctuation marks such as commas and apostrophes, which you will have to omit or move. End marks and commas will often be missing or used incorrectly. Your teacher will help you find and correct the ones you missed.

Follow the process detailed on page 3 to complete this week's fixes. Use the Fix It and Rewrite It grammar card to remember the steps.

The most important thing to remember as you work through this course is that a mistake is an opportunity to learn. You are not expected to find everything, but do try your best. Once you have fixed and marked the sentences as best as you can, your teacher will go through and show you anything you missed and discuss the reasons behind the grammar. Then you can copy the correct version into your notebook.

If desired, read the sections from the Grammar Glossary that are introduced in this week's fixes. The Grammar Glossary includes both "need to know" concepts and extra information for those who wish to learn more.

Page 4, *Fix It! Grammar: Frog Prince, or Just Deserts*, **Student Book 3**

DAY 1

V   S

¶ in the recent past in an obscure kingdom tucked away among the alps reigned a **decorous** king,

S   V

ruling monarch in a line of monarchs that stretched back to the middle ages.

Fixes

Before checking the fixes, discuss the Grammar Notations, which are explained in the notes after the fixes. When to use commas and other punctuation depends heavily on the structure of the sentence. Taking time now to understand how sentences are constructed will reap great rewards later.

INDENT. Have students put a ¶ in front of the sentence to remind them to indent when they begin their rewrite. This sentence is indented because of a new topic—the first!

> ✏ **Teacher's note.** In stories, indentation rules are somewhat flexible, so your student's choice to indent the remaining sentences may be different from what is recommended in this book. That is fine! As long as students can explain how their choice fulfills a rule for indentation, they are good to go. In the remaining notes, indentation will be discussed when it is needed or negotiable.

CAPITALIZATION.
- In, Alps (proper noun), Middle Ages (proper noun for a specific time period).
- Do not capitalize *king* or *monarch(s)*. Titles are common nouns when not coupled with someone's name, like King Morton.

COMMAS AND OTHER PUNCTUATION.
- **ADVANCED. Long #2 prepositional openers.** When multiple prepositional phrases begin a sentence, treat them like one long opener with no commas separating each short prepositional phrase. Usually, long #2 prepositional openers (five or more words) take a comma at the end of the opener, but not when a verb (*reigned*) instead of the subject follows the opener. The original is correct: **In the recent past in an obscure kingdom tucked away among the Alps reigned a decorous king.**

Grammar Notations

PREPOSITIONAL PHRASES. Check that students properly underlined all these phrases.

Guide students to see the pattern: **preposition + noun (no verb).** These phrases begin with a preposition, end with a noun, and have no verbs. There may be other words between the preposition and its object (the noun), but never a verb.

- In the recent past: *In* (prep) + *the* (article) + *recent* (adjective) + *past* (noun). No verb.
- in an obscure kingdom: *in* (prep) + *an* (article), *obscure* (adjective) + *kingdom* (noun). No verb.
- among the Alps: *among* (prep) + *the* (article) + *Alps* (noun). No verb.
- in a line: *in* (prep) + *a* (article) + *line* (noun). No verb.
- of monarchs: *of* (prep) + *monarchs* (noun). No verb.
- to the Middle Ages: *to* (prep) + *the* (article) + *Middle Ages* (noun). No verb.

SUBJECTS AND VERBS. Check that students correctly identify the subject-verb in each clause. Clauses are listed below with the subject-verb in boldface. See ✏ **1.**

- **reigned** a decorous **king.** If students are confused, explain that sometimes—especially after introductory prepositional phrases—the usual S-V order is reversed.
- **that stretched** back to the Middle Ages. See ✏ **2.**

---

decorous: with proper dignity in conduct and manners

✏ **1. Teacher's note.** If your students marked *tucked* as a verb, just tell them it is not one here. It is actually a past participle starting an adjective phrase. Participles are not verbs except when there is a subject and helping verb right before them. See Grammar Glossary: Parts of Speech: Verbals.

✏ **2. Teacher's note.** This is an essential *that* clause, which describes the line of monarchs. *That* substitutes for *which* in essential *which* clauses, as here, and it functions as the subject of its own clause. Students will later be introduced to the concept of essential elements, but they will not need to master it in this book.

DAY 2

> S   V   S   V   V
>
> king morton esteemed values. he would have none of this **drivel** of dropping "sir" and "ma'am" when
>
> V   ,   V   S   V   S
>
> addressing ones elders, nor could he tolerate modern jargon, especially outdated jargon. "awesome"
>
> V   V   S   V   S   V
>
> should refer to thing's that actually inspire; "cool" ought to ~~two/too~~ mean the temperature.

Fixes

INDENT. A new paragraph is arguable. Since King Morton was just introduced in the first sentence, turning to what he values can stay in the same paragraph or start a new one. Follow the basic principles, but allow students some flexibility on issues like new topics.

ADVANCED. Words as words, like *sir, ma'am, awesome,* and *cool,* should be put in quotation marks or italics (italics preferred in print). Students copying by hand will find quotation marks easier. Words are referred to as words (or names as names) if you can insert "the word(s)" in front. For example, dropping *the words* "sir" and "ma'am"; *the word* "cool" ought to mean the temperature. *See* ✎ **1.**

HOMOPHONES AND USAGE. to mean. *See* ✎ **2.**

COMMAS AND OTHER PUNCTUATION.

- **Apostrophes** for possession. Fixes: **one's** elders; **things**. Do not use apostrophes for plural nouns (*things*) unless they are also possessive. *See* ✎ **3.**
- **ADVANCED. Semicolon.** The semicolon is correctly used to join two main clauses that express one idea. Semicolons are especially effective when the two MCs have similar sentence structure, like these.

Grammar Notations

PREPOSITIONAL PHRASES. Continue to guide students to see the pattern in each phrase: preposition + noun (no verb). These phrases begin with a preposition, end with a noun, and have no verb. Other words may come between the preposition and its object (the noun), but never a verb.

Do not have students underline infinitives (*to* + verb) like *to mean*. Although infinitives use a preposition, *to*, they do not follow the usual prepositional phrase pattern.

- of this drivel: *of* (prep) + *this* (adjective) + *drivel* (noun). No verb.
- of dropping "sir" and "ma'am": *of* (prep) + *dropping "sir" and "ma'am"* (noun). No verb.

  > ✎ **Teacher's note.** *dropping* is not a verb here. It is a verbal serving as a noun: *dropping "sir" and "ma'am"* is the thing that the king abhorred.
  >
  > If students mark *to things*, let them! Technically, the words that go together are *refer to*, which make sense together, not *to things that actually inspire*. Therefore, *to* is an adverb with *refer* instead of a preposition starting its own phrase. The difference is not important, however, since it does not affect punctuation.

SUBJECTS AND VERBS. Check that students correctly identify the subject-verb in each clause. If students do not recognize the helping verbs, show them the Verb grammar card from the Week 1 cards and ask them if any of those helping verbs are in the passage.

drivel: nonsense; meaningless talk or thinking

✎ **1. Teacher's note.** Remember, advanced concepts are optional, included to help you answer questions as they arise, to prepare you for concepts students will eventually need to know, or to give added challenge to older and stronger students. You do not need to cover them now.

✎ **2. Teacher's note.** *To* is the preposition at the start of an infinitive: *to mean.*

✎ **3. Teacher's note.** You do not need to pre-teach every concept. Teach at the point of need.

- **King Morton esteemed** values.
- **He would have** none of this recent drivel of dropping "sir" and "ma'am." *Would* is a helping verb; *have* is an action verb here.
- **when addressing** one's elders. The subject and helping verb, *one was*, are implied.
- **could he tolerate** modern jargon. This subject comes between the helping verb (*could*) and the verb.
- **"Awesome" should refer** to things. *Should* is a helping verb.
- **that** actually **inspire**.
- **"cool" ought** to refer to the temperature.
    - ✏ **Teacher's note.** *to refer* is another infinitive, and infinitives never function as verbs.

DAY 3

¶ he became livid on the subject of modern gadgets—just so much **folderol**, in his opinion. downloading movies on iPhones would guarantee eye problems when children reached his distinguished age.

---

folderol: foolish talk or ideas; nonsense

Fixes

INDENT ¶ because of a new topic, King Morton's dislike of modern gadgets.

CAPITALIZATION. He, Downloading.

COMMAS AND OTHER PUNCTUATION.
- **Em dash.** Show the em dash (—) between *gadgets* and *just*. Explain that em dashes are used to draw attention to something or to signal a break in thought. Ask: Which is its purpose here? Answer: Draws attention to what follows. *See* ✏.
- **ADVANCED. Transitional phrases** should be set off with commas. The original is correct: just so much folderol, **in his opinion.**

✏ **Teacher's note.** When typing, an em dash is created by using two hyphens or typing option-shift-hyphen. It is called an em dash because it is the length of the capital letter M.

Grammar Notations

PREPOSITIONAL PHRASES. Continue to guide students to see the pattern in each phrase: preposition + noun (no verb). These phrases begin with a preposition, end with a noun, and have no verb. Other words may come between the preposition and its object (the noun), but never a verb.
- on the subject: *on* (prep) + *the* (article) + *subject* (noun). No verb.
- of modern gadgets: *of* (prep) + *modern* (adjective) + *gadgets* (noun). No verb.
- in his opinion: *in* (prep) + *his* (possessive pronoun) + *opinion* (noun). No verb.
- on iPhones: *on* (prep) + *iPhones* (noun). No verb.

SUBJECTS AND VERBS. Check that students correctly identify the subject-verb in each clause.
- **He became** livid on the subject of modern gadgets. Also a #1 subject opener.
- **ADVANCED. Downloading** movies on iPhones **would guarantee** eye problems. Also a #1 subject opener because *downloading movies* is doing the action in the sentence—it is the thing that would guarantee eye problems. If you have taught the #4 -ing opener, mention that this sentence is an imposter #4 because *Downloading* is not a verb but the subject of the sentence. *See* ♡.
- when **children reached** his distinguished age.

♡ **Grammar lovers.** Sometimes -ing words function as nouns, as *downloading* does here. They are called *gerunds* then.

DAY 4

V , S V S V V ?
moreover, didn't they realize that cell phones were intended for use outside the home, only yesterday the

S V V S *two* V
palace accountant had **vehemently** complained to ~~two / too~~ him that the younger of his ~~2~~ daughters had

V *one thousand*
accumulated ~~1000~~ text messages on her cell phone, in a single week!

Fixes

vehemently:
forcefully; with strong emotion

USAGE. Comparative versus superlative form: **younger** of his two daughters. Notice the use of -er (comparative) with two, instead of -est (superlative) with the most of three or more.

NUMBERS. Fix: two daughters, **one thousand** text messages. Use this passage to remind your students of the rule: Spell out numbers that can be written in one or two words.

COMMAS AND OTHER PUNCTUATION.

- **Apostrophes** for contractions. Fix: **didn't.** Contractions work well in fiction, especially in dialogue or people's thoughts, since they mimic our speech patterns, but they should be avoided in academic writing.

- **ADVANCED. Introductory transitions** take commas. The original is correct: **Moreover,** didn't they realize.

- **Mid-sentence prepositional phrases** do not take commas. Guide your students to drop the comma after *phone.* Fix: text messages **on her cell phone in a single week.**

- **End marks.**

    Question mark. The first sentence asks a question so ends with a question mark. Fix: didn't they realize that cell phones were intended for use outside the home?

    Exclamation mark. The second sentence shows strong emotion, so it may end with an exclamation mark or a period. Fix: in a single week!

Grammar Notations

PREPOSITIONAL PHRASES. Continue to guide students to see the pattern in each phrase: preposition + noun (no verb). These phrases begin with a preposition, end with a noun, and have no verb. Other words may come between the preposition and its object (the noun), but never a verb.

- for use: *for* (prep) + *use* (noun). No verb.
- outside the home: *outside* (prep) + *the* (article) + *home* (noun). No verb.
- to him: *to* (prep) + *him* (a personal pronoun). No verb.
- of his two daughters: *of* (prep) + *his* (possessive pronoun) + *two* (adjective) + *daughters* (noun). No verb.
- on her cell phone: *on* (prep) + *her* (possessive pronoun) + *cell phone* (noun). No verb.
- in a single week: *in* (prep) + *a* (article) + *single* (adjective) + *week* (noun). No verb.

SUBJECTS AND VERBS. Check that students correctly identify the subject-verb in each clause.

- **didn't they realize.** *Not* is an adverb, not part of the verb. *Did* is a helping verb: they *did* realize.

- that **cell phones were intended** for use outside the home. The *be* verb *were* is a helping verb here.
- the palace **accountant had** vehemently **complained** to him. Check that students mark the helping verb *had* as well as the action verb *complained*.
- that the **younger** of his two daughters **had accumulated** one thousand text messages on her cell phone in a single week. The helping verb is *had*. See ✎.

Style

If you have been doing IEW writing, have students take a few moments to identify the strongest of the three vocabulary dress-ups from this week's sentences. Dress-ups should create a strong image or feeling, so encourage your students to choose the strongest verb, adjective, or -ly word, not just any. Discuss their answers. Suggestions:

- **Strong verbs.** tucked away, reigned, esteemed, tolerate, accumulated.
- **Quality adjectives.** obscure, decorous, livid, distinguished.
- **-ly adverbs.** vehemently.

✎ **Teacher's note.** If students mark *daughters* as the subject, explain that *daughters* is the object of the preposition *of*. A noun cannot have two different functions (subject; object of preposition) at the same time. It is the younger who had accumulated.

STUDENT REWRITE

To ensure that the editing sticks, have your student rewrite the passage in a separate section of the notebook. Below is what that rewrite should look like.

In the recent past in an obscure kingdom tucked away among the Alps reigned a decorous king, ruling monarch in a line of monarchs that stretched back to the Middle Ages. King Morton esteemed values. He would have none of this drivel of dropping "sir" and "ma'am" when addressing one's elders, nor could he tolerate modern jargon, especially outdated jargon. "Awesome" should refer to things that actually inspire; "cool" ought to mean the temperature.

He became livid on the subject of modern gadgets—just so much folderol, in his opinion. Downloading movies on iPhones would guarantee eye problems when children reached his distinguished age. Moreover, didn't they realize that cell phones were intended for use outside the home? Only yesterday the palace accountant had vehemently complained to him that the younger of his two daughters had accumulated one thousand text messages on her cell phone in a single week!

Week 2

Review MC and DC

Cut out the Week 2 grammar cards and review the list of **coordinating conjunctions** (cc's) from the acronym FANBOYS. Also review the related comma rules: **items in a series (a, b, and c _or_ a and b)**, **MC cc 2nd verb**, and **MC, cc MC**.

LEARN IT

✏ **Teacher's note.** Remind students to first make grammar notations.

After checking the grammar notations, use the marked sentence to check students' work. Read through the added discussion in the _Fix It_ section as needed to ensure students understand the concepts.

Clauses

Last week you marked subjects and verbs. This week you will also mark main and dependent clauses. Use the Week 2 grammar cards to help you remember these concepts.

Main Clause (MC)

A main clause is a clause that can stand alone as a sentence. Like all clauses, it must have a subject and a verb. Use square brackets [ ] to surround main clauses and label them MC. Example: ^{MC} [**King Morton esteemed** values].

Main clauses usually start with a subject or with an article (_a, an, the_) plus subject: a princess. Often an adjective will come between the article and the subject: the insensitive princess. Occasionally the subject-verb will be switched: ^{MC} [There **huddled** the **courtiers**].

If there is an adverb or prepositional phrase at the beginning, do not include it in the brackets. End the clause at the most logical place after the S-V pair. If you pick up prepositional phrases or needed DCs that go with the first clause, that is fine, but you only need to mark the basic part of the clauses. Examples: ^{MC} [The king loathed modern gadgets]. In addition ^{MC} [he could not tolerate modern jargon]. Surely ^{MC} [the king dined with relish].

Dependent Clause (DC)

A dependent clause cannot stand alone as a sentence. It looks like a main clause, but one or more words in front of it turn the main clause into something that leaves us hanging. Use parenthesis ( ) to surround dependent clauses and label them DC.

who, which, that. A _who, which,_ or _that_ clause is one example of a dependent clause. It cannot stand alone. Examples: ^{DC} (**which** delighted the princess), ^{DC} (**who** texted incessantly), ^{DC} (**that** stood in the garden). Use _who_ for people and _which_ or _that_ for things.

www.asia.b (www words). These words can be used to start a dependent clause and often begin an adverb clause. Officially, these words are called _subordinating conjunctions_ because they begin a subordinate clause, but you do not have to worry about the terminology. For now, just learn the list of words included on the grammar card. Additional www words are included on the back of the card. Add to the list as you find more.

> ✏ **Teacher's note.** Concepts are cumulative, so each week students will continue to practice concepts from prior weeks. Sometimes the instructions will have them work on those concepts in different ways, so go over their instructions with them weekly.
>
> As you progress through these lessons, you will find many things to address in each passage. You do not need to cover them all! Keep it light and make it a game. Over time with repetition, mastery will come.

Page 6, _Fix It! Grammar: Frog Prince, or Just Deserts_, **Student Book 3**

DAY 1

Worse MC S V V   DC S
∨   *who* V
~~worst~~, [she was texting <u>for amusement</u> <u>to</u> ~~two, too~~ <u>her own sister</u>], <u>maribella</u>, (~~that~~ lived <u>in the same</u>

          DC   S   V   MC S   V   V
<u>place</u>)! (<u>when</u> he demanded it back), [dorinda had **inarticulately** mumbled something about not being

able to locate it]**.**

Discuss the Grammar Notations before discussing the Fixes. Proper punctuation use depends heavily on the structure of the sentence. Taking time now to understand sentence structure will reap great rewards later.

inarticulately: unable to express herself clearly

Fixes

USAGE.

- **Comparative and superlative adjectives.** Use *worse* since only two things are compared. See ✎ **1.**
- **Who, which or that.** Use *who* with people, *that* or *which* with things: her own sister, Maribella, **who** lived.

COMMAS AND OTHER PUNCTUATION.

✎ **Teacher's note.** Since comma placement is often a struggle for teachers and students alike, this section of the fixes attempts to cover any comma and other punctuation issues that may come up. The points marked *advanced* are for your information and can be discussed if your students ask or if you wish to cover that point of grammar.

Remember, it helps to work through the clause construction before addressing these commas. See Grammar Notations below.

- **ADVANCED. Nonessential elements** take commas. The commas around *Maribella* are correct. Her name adds information but does not specify any further who is meant since Dorinda has only one sister: her sister, **Maribella,** who lived. See ♡.
- **ADVANCED. #5 clausal openers.** Explain that when a www word begins a sentence, its clause is *always* followed by a comma: AC, MC. This rule will be taught next week. The original is correct: **When he demanded it back,** Dorinda had inarticulately mumbled something.

Grammar Notations

PREPOSITIONAL PHRASES. for amusement; to her own sister; in the same place. Continue to guide students to see that these fit the pattern, especially for any they miss: preposition + noun (no verb). See ✎ **2.**

CLAUSES. Check that students correctly mark the clauses as indicated in the fixed passage above. For your convenience, they are labeled below with the subject-verb pairs in bold.

- MC: **she was texting** for amusement to her own sister. If students do not catch *was*, ask them to find one of the *be* verbs using the Verb grammar card from Week 1.
- DC (*who-which* clause): **who lived** in the same place. Explain: the subject of a *who-which* clause is usually *who* or *which*.
- DC (adverb clause): When **he demanded** it back.
- MC: **Dorinda had** inarticulately **mumbled** something about not being able to locate it. *Had* is a helping verb here.

✎ **1. Teacher's note.** *Worse* is an idiom that is short for *what was worse,* that is, the greater of two evil things. Do not mark idioms.

♡ **Grammar lovers.** This is known as an appositive, a noun that renames the noun before it. Appositives are often nonessential, but not always.

✎ **2. Teacher's note.** Prepositional phrases, while needed for content, often muddy the basic structure of a sentence, making it harder for students to punctuate sentences correctly. By marking them, students will more easily grasp the underlying structure and therefore be able to punctuate their sentences. Marking prepositional phrases helps get the noise out of the way!

DAY 2

younger

¶ his ~~youngest~~ daughter—now [there ~~their/they're~~ was another topic] (that brought red to his face).

unlike her only sister, [princess dorinda had been an **obstinate** child from toddlerhood].

Fixes

obstinate: stubborn; inflexible

INDENT ¶ because of a new topic, the king's problems with his daughter Dorinda.

CAPITALIZATION. His, Unlike, Princess Dorinda (capitalize titles when used with names).

HOMOPHONES AND USAGE. Use the comparative adjective when comparing two (only two sisters): **younger.**

COMMAS AND OTHER PUNCTUATION.

- **Em dash.** Ask: Is this long dash used 1) to indicate a break in thought or 2) to draw attention to what follows? Answer: 1) to indicate a break in thought.

  ✏ **Teacher's note.** Em dashes are easy to teach at the point of need. No need to pre-teach.

- **Short #2 prepositional openers** (under five words): commas are usually optional, but one is needed after *sister* to avoid misreading. Fix: **Unlike her only sister,** Princess Dorinda had been an obstinate child.

  ✏ **Teacher's note.** Without the comma, it sounds as if her sister is Princess Dorinda, and then we expect a subject after *Dorinda.* Instead, *Dorinda* is the subject.

Grammar Notations

PREPOSITIONAL PHRASES. to his face; Unlike her only sister; from toddlerhood. Continue to guide students to see that these fit the pattern, especially for any they miss: preposition + noun (no verb).

CLAUSES. Check that students correctly mark the clauses as indicated in the fixed passage above.

- MC: there **was** another **topic.**

  ADVANCED. In sentences starting with *there is, there are, there was,* or *there were,* the true subject is not *there;* instead, the subject comes after the verb.

- DC (*that* clause): **that brought** red to his face. If students have trouble identifying this subject, explain that pronouns can function as subjects. *See* ♡ **1.**

- MC: **Princess Dorinda had been** an obstinate child from toddlerhood. *Had* is a helping verb here. If students miss *been,* have them find a *be* verb using the Verb grammar card list. *See* ♡ **2.**

♡ **1. Grammar lovers.** This is an essential *which* clause because the clause specifies what topic is meant: not any topic but one that embarrassed him. *That* is preferred over *which* in essential clauses. Essential clauses (including all *that* clauses) never take commas.

♡ **2. Grammar lovers.** *Been* is a linking verb here, linking the subject complement (that is, predicate nominative), *child,* back to the subject, *Princess Dorinda.*

DAY 3

never one to obey anyone, to say nothing of her royal father himself, [she would escape from the
MC S · V · V

nursery to find mischief] (wherever she could). once, [she stole into the throne room, ~~swinging~~ on the
DC · S · V · MC S · V · swung (V)

chandeliers, and landed at the feet of the scandalized **courtiers**].
V

Fixes

COMMAS AND OTHER PUNCTUATION.

- **ADVANCED. Nonessential elements** take commas. The original is correct: Never one to obey anyone, **to say nothing of her royal father himself,** she would escape.
- **ADVANCED. Transitional words** usually take commas. The original is correct: **Once,** she stole. *See* ♡ **1.**
- **Items in a series.** Three items in a series—*stole, swung,* and *landed*—take commas and need rewording. This one is a little complicated, so guide your students.

  Explain that it does not make sense to say she stole into the throne room swinging on the chandeliers, as if that is how she made her entrance. These are consecutive actions so need to be set up as items in a series, all of which must use the same part of speech. *See* ♡ **2.**

  In this case, all three items are past tense verbs, connected by the cc *and.* Fix: change **swinging** to the past tense **swung.**

  Now that the items in a series are all the same part of speech, guide students to add commas to separate them since there are three or more: she stole … , swung … , and landed. Pattern: a, b, and c.

Grammar Notations

PREPOSITIONAL PHRASES. of her royal father; from the nursery; into the throne room; on the chandeliers; at the feet; of the scandalized courtiers. *See* ♡ **3.**

CLAUSES. Check that students correctly mark the S-V pairs and the clauses as indicated in the fixed passage above.

- MC: **she would escape** from the nursery to find mischief.
- DC (adverb clause): wherever **she could.**

  🖉 **Teacher's note.** This is a regular adverb clause dress-up using a different subordinating conjunction than those in the www.asia.b list. Notice that *wherever* is included on the back of the clause starters card.

  If students ask, *could* is a helping verb, but the action verb and object, *find mischief,* are implied: *wherever she could find mischief.* You do not need to teach this.

- MC (fixed): **she stole** into the throne room, **swung** on the chandeliers, and **landed** at the feet of the scandalized courtiers.

courtiers: people in attendance at the court of a king

♡ **1. Grammar lovers.** *Once* is sometimes a subordinating conjunction (clausal starter) meaning *after.* Here it means *one time* and is an adverb. This matters because as an adverb, *once* starts a main clause, whereas as a clausal starter, it starts a dependent clause. Without the comma, we might misread *once* as a clausal starter: Once (after) she did this, she did something else.

♡ **2. Grammar lovers.** When items in a series do not use the same part of speech or grammatical construction (such as three prepositional phrases or three participial phrases), we say that the items are not parallel. The error is known as *faulty parallelism.*

♡ **3. Grammar lovers.** *to find mischief* is an infinitive, not a regular prepositional phrase.

DAY 4

MC S V
on another occasion, [she upset the **prestigious** new employee in the kitchen], the iron chef himself.

MC S V V   DC   S   V
[he was experimenting with sturgeon roe ice cream] (when she sneaked a taste), making a wry face at

the concoction.

Fixes

CAPITALIZATION. On, Iron Chef (title of a specific TV character and therefore a proper noun), He.

SPELLING. *Sneaked* is preferred but *snuck* is also correct. Some verbs have alternate spellings for past tense.

COMMAS AND OTHER PUNCTUATION. See ✐ 1.

- **Short #2 prepositional openers** (under five words): commas are optional. The current trend is to eliminate unnecessary commas, but use your own judgment. *On another occasion* is correct with or without a comma.

- **ADVANCED. Nonessential elements** take commas. The original is correct: new employee in the kitchen, **the Iron Chef himself.**

  ✐ **Teacher's note.** The comma before *the Iron Chef himself* is used to set off a nonessential appositive. Appositives are nouns that rename the noun that comes before them. In IEW writing, this is sometimes called an invisible *who-which* because *who was* is implied but invisible. It is not actually a clause because there is no subject-verb, but the idea of an invisible *who-which* is friendlier than the term *appositive.*

  Usually (but not always) appositives are nonessential and therefore need commas. If they are essential, they specify which particular person or thing. Although it adds important information, *the Iron Chef* is nonessential because presumably there is only one new employee in the kitchen, so the appositive is not needed in the sentence to identify which person she upset.

  Remember that advanced concepts and Teacher's Notes do not need to be taught. Later in *Frog Prince*, students will be introduced to the concept of essential and nonessential elements, but they will not be expected to master them in this book.

- **ADVANCED. Mid-sentence adverb clauses** do not take commas. Rule: MC AC, which will be addressed next week. The original is correct: He was experimenting with sturgeon roe ice cream **when she sneaked a taste.**

Grammar Notations

PREPOSITIONAL PHRASES. On another occasion; in the kitchen; with sturgeon roe ice cream; at the concoction.

CLAUSES. Check that students correctly mark the clauses as indicated in the fixed passage above.

- MC: **she upset** the prestigious new employee in the kitchen.
- MC: **He was experimenting** with sturgeon roe ice cream. If students miss *was*, have them find a *be* verb using the Verb grammar card from Week 1.
- DC (adverb clause): when **she sneaked** a taste.

prestigious: respected; distinguished; honored

Sturgeon roe are the eggs (roe) of sturgeon, a type of fish prized for its caviar—not a tasty flavoring in ice cream!

✐ **1. Teacher's note.** It helps to work through the clause construction before addressing punctuation. See Grammar Notations below.

- -ing phrase: making a wry face at the concoction. Students do not need to mark this.

  ✏ **Teacher's note.** Start familiarizing your students with participial phrases to the degree they are ready. Present participles (-ing words) are verbs only when they do not have a subject and helping verb in front of them. Contrast "she was making a wry face," which has a subject-verb pair. "Making a wry face" is a phrase, not a clause, because it has no subject-verb.

  Participial phrases function as adjectives modifying the subject before them (*she*, in this case). They are like #4 openers except that they come later in the sentence.

  The nice thing about participial phrases is that they almost always take commas, whether they come at the beginning of the sentence as a #4 opener or later in the sentence.

Style

If desired, have students identify the strongest of the vocabulary dress-ups from this week. Discuss their answers. Suggestions:

- **Strong verbs.** mumbled.
- **Quality adjectives.** obstinate, scandalized, prestigious, wry.
- **-ly adverbs.** inarticulately.

STUDENT REWRITE

Worse, she was texting for amusement to her own sister, Maribella, who lived in the same place! When he demanded it back, Dorinda had inarticulately mumbled something about not being able to locate it.

His younger daughter—now there was another topic that brought red to his face. Unlike her only sister, Princess Dorinda had been an obstinate child from toddlerhood. Never one to obey anyone, to say nothing of her royal father himself, she would escape from the nursery to find mischief wherever she could. Once, she stole into the throne room, swung on the chandeliers, and landed at the feet of the scandalized courtiers. On another occasion she upset the prestigious new employee in the kitchen, the Iron Chef himself. He was experimenting with sturgeon roe ice cream when she sneaked a taste, making a wry face at the concoction.

Week 3

Openers and Mid-Sentence Adverb Clauses

Cut out this week's grammar cards and use them to refresh your memory of **quotations**, **transitions**, and **interjections**. The other cards will help with the following.

LEARN IT

Sentence Openers	The IEW method of organizing sentence openers is especially helpful to sort out the comma rules. This week, you will explore all but the #3 opener.
#1 Subject Opener	If a sentence begins with a subject or things related to the subject (an article and adjective, for example), then mark it a #1 subject opener. If the subject-verb is reversed, still mark it a #1.
#2 Prepositional Opener	If the sentence begins with a prepositional phrase, mark it a #2 prepositional opener. Long #2 openers (five or more words) take commas. Commas are optional for short #2 openers.
#4 -ing Opener	This one may be new to you. A #4 opener is a participial phrase opener. A participial phrase starts with an -ing word, like these: Bouncing her ball; Racing through the castle; Muttering. Legal (grammatical) #4 openers always take a comma after the phrase.

The #4 opener has an important rule you should learn: the thing after the comma must be the thing doing the -inging. Examples:

- **Legal:** *Racing through the castle,* Dorinda knocked over a priceless vase.

- **Illegal** (wrong): *Racing through the castle,* the antique vase was smashed to smithereens.

In the illegal example it sounds as if the antique vase was running through the castle. The technical term for an illegal #4 opener is dangling modifier, but you do not need to worry about that. Just follow the rule and you will not have any danglers!

#5 Clausal Opener	When a clause begins with a www.asia.b word (*when, while, where, as, since, if, although, because*), it usually starts an adverb clause, so instead of marking it a DC, mark it with an AC. When an adverb clause begins a sentence, a comma is always needed after the clause. Rule: AC, MC. Example: When Dorinda smashed the vase, she did not even notice.
#6 vss	The vss is the very short sentence. It must be two to five words and must contain a verb. Example: Dorinda scurried out the door. The servants relaxed.
Mid-sentence Adverb Clauses	When a www.asia.b word starts an adverb clause in the middle or end of a sentence, it does not take commas. Rule: MC AC. There are a few exceptions, which will be pointed out as they show up in the fixes. Use the grammar card to remember the comma rules with adverb clauses.

Page 8, *Fix It! Grammar: Frog Prince, or Just Deserts,* **Student Book 3**

Teacher's note. From this week forward, discuss the clauses, phrases, and openers first and then the commas and other punctuation. Punctuation makes most sense in the context of structure.

Teacher's note. Tip: #1 sentences always begin with a main clause.

The #3 sentence opener will be addressed next week.

Tip: The #6 opener must be a legal sentence, which means it needs a verb and can stand alone. Dependent clauses contain a verb but cannot stand alone.

DAY 1

#1 MC   S   V   V   **two**

¶ [king mortons greatest **mortification** had occurred 2 years earlier, at a dinner party for the

#4

ambassador of nordicland]. taking an instant dislike to the ambassador's son, (who was truthfully a bit   DC S   V

MC S   V   DC S   V

of a brat), [dorinda squirted mouthwash from a travel bottle (she carried in her purse) into his

sturgeon roe soup].

Details about the phrases, clauses, and sentence openers are in the Grammar Notations below. Check your students' markings and discuss as needed. Clause and phrase markings are especially helpful in understanding comma usage.

mortification: a feeling of humiliation or shame

Fixes

INDENT ¶ because this goes back in time. In literature, this is called a flashback.

CAPITALIZATION. King Morton's, Ambassador of Nordicland (capitalize honorific titles), Taking, Dorinda.

NUMBERS. Spell out numbers written as one or two words: **two** years earlier.

COMMAS AND OTHER PUNCTUATION. *See* ✎ **1.**

- **Apostrophes** for possession. Fix: King **Morton's** mortification; **ambassador's** son.
- **Mid-sentence prepositional phrases** do not take commas. Fix: two years earlier **at a dinner party for the Ambassador of Nordicland.**

  ✎ **Teacher's note.** This prepositional phrase rule also explains why there are no commas around any of the other prepositional phrases unless one is needed for a different reason. That is, when a phrase or clause should not be set off with commas but one is needed before or after for a different part of the sentence, the need for a comma overrules the need for no comma.

- **#4 -ing openers** take commas. Fix: **Taking an instant dislike to the ambassador's son, who was truthfully a bit of a brat,** Dorinda squirted mouthwash.

  Teach this concept: For #4 openers to be legal (grammatical), the thing (subject) after the comma has to be the thing doing the -inging. Here, Dorinda (the subject) is the one who is taking, so this is legal.

  ✎ **Teacher's note.** This opener includes the *who* clause (*who was truthfully a bit of a brat*), which also needs commas because it is nonessential. Except for #1 subject and #6 vss, openers include everything up to the main clause.

Grammar Notations

PREPOSITIONAL PHRASES. at a dinner party; for the Ambassador; of Nordicland; to the ambassador's son; of a brat; from a travel bottle; in her purse; into his sturgeon roe soup.

CLAUSES, PHRASES, AND OPENERS. Check that students correctly mark the openers and clauses as indicated in the fixed passage above.

- MC: #1 King Morton's greatest **mortification had occurred** two years earlier at a dinner party for the Ambassador of Nordicland. *See* ✎ **2.**

✎ **1. Teacher's note.** Remember, it helps to work through the clause and phrase construction before addressing these commas. See Grammar Notations below.

✎ **2. Teacher's note.** If students are confused about what the subject is, explain that *King Morton's* is possessive. The true subject is *mortification* because that is what *had occurred.* It does not make sense to say *King Morton had occurred two years earlier.*

- #4 -ing participial phrase opener: Taking an instant dislike to the ambassador's son. *See* ♡.
- DC (*who-which* clause): **who was** truthfully a bit of a brat.
- MC: **Dorinda squirted** mouthwash from a travel bottle (she carried in her purse) into his sturgeon roe soup.
- **ADVANCED.** DC: **she carried** in her purse. This DC is included in the MC above. It is a dependent clause because *that* is implied.

♡ **Grammar lovers.** *Taking* functions as an adjective here modifying the subject after the comma (*Dorinda*). It is not a verb because there is no subject and helping verb with it, as in *Dorinda was taking a dislike to him*. This means that this opener is a phrase and not a clause.

DAY 2

#2   **,**   *MC S   V*   #2
despite the youngsters **queasiness,** [she had no mercy]. during the obligatory dance/ after the dinner, [she

         V   *MC S V   V*
rapidly twirled him around]. last seen, [he was rushing to ~~two/too~~ the royal restrooms], noticeably green.

Fixes

HOMOPHONES. Use the preposition: **to** the royal restrooms.

COMMAS AND OTHER PUNCTUATION.

- **Apostrophes** for possession. Fix: **youngster's** queasiness.
- **#2 prepositional openers.** Commas after short #2s are optional but required for long ones. There are two in this passage.

  The first is under five words, but the words are long and the phrase needs a pause. Fix: **Despite the youngster's queasiness,** she had no mercy.

  The second has two phrases back to back. When the opener includes two or more phrases, save the comma for the end of all of them. Drop the one after *dance*. Fix: **During the obligatory dance after the dinner,** she rapidly twirled him around.

queasiness: nausea; the feeling of sickness to the stomach

✎ **1. Teacher's note.** Check that students correctly mark the openers and clauses as indicated in the fixed passage above. Help them see that these are clauses only when they have a subject-verb pair. If they do not have both, they are phrases.

Grammar Notations

PREPOSITIONAL PHRASES. Despite the youngster's queasiness; During the obligatory dance; after the dinner; to the royal restrooms.

CLAUSES, PHRASES, AND OPENERS. *See* ✎ **1.**

- #2 prepositional phrase opener: Despite the youngster's queasiness. Ask: How do we know this is a phrase and not a clause? Answer: no verb.
- MC: **she had** no mercy. This is a case where *had* is an action verb expressing ownership, not a helping verb, because there is no second verb after it.
- #2 prepositional phrase opener: During the obligatory dance after the dinner. Ask: Can you find a verb in this opener? Answer: No, so it is not a clause. *During* is always a preposition, and prepositions always start a phrase.
- MC: **she** rapidly **twirled** him around.
- Strange opener: Last seen. In compositions, students need to mark only the sentence openers on their checklist. If they do not know what an opener is, they do not need to mark it. *See* ♡.
- MC: **he was rushing** to the royal restrooms. *See* ✎ **2.**

♡ **Grammar lovers.** *Last seen* is an elliptical construction, short for *When he was last seen*.

✎ **2. Teacher's note.** This is a case where an -ing word functions as a verb; -ing words are verbs only when there is a subject (*he*) and helping verb (*was*) stated in the sentence before the -ing participle.

DAY 3

#4   *MC*   *S*   *V*

¶ threatening to **sever** diplomatic ties**,** [the ambassador quit the palace the following morning/ in a fury].

#5 *AC*   *S*   *V*   *MC*   *S*   *V*   *V*   *AC*   *S*   *V*   *V*

(as he expressed it to his attaché)**,** "[the king can hardly run a country] (if he can't rule his own

daughter)**."**

Fixes

sever: break off or dissolve; cut off

INDENT ¶ because of a new topic, turning to the ambassador's reaction. The second sentence can stay in the same paragraph since the first sets it up, but if students want to put it in a new paragraph because of the speech, that is fine.

CAPITALIZATION.

- Capitalize the first word of sentences: Threatening, As.
- Capitalize the first word of quoted sentences even when they do not begin the full sentence: As he expressed it to his attaché, "**The** king … ."
- Use lowercase for titles without names: the king, as opposed to King Morton.
- Do not capitalize *ambassador* because it is a common noun that could be used with any ambassador, not an honorific title for the ambassador of a particular country.

COMMAS AND OTHER PUNCTUATION. Remember to cover the Grammar Notations before addressing punctuation.

- **#4 -ing openers** take commas. Pattern: -ing phrase + **comma** + subject doing the -inging + verb. Fix: **Threatening to sever diplomatic ties,** the ambassador quit the palace.
- **Mid-sentence prepositional phrases** do not take commas. Fix: the ambassador quit the palace the following morning **in a fury.**
- **#5 clausal openers** take commas. Rule: AC, MC. The comma goes at the end of the clause, not after the www word. Fix: **As he expressed it to his attaché,** "The king … ." See ✎ **1.**

✎ **1. Teacher's note.** This comma is also needed because a speaking verb, *expressed*, sets up the quotation.

- **Quotation marks** are needed to enclose direct quotations: "The king … daughter." Check that students placed the period inside the closing quotes.
- **Mid-sentence adverb clauses.** Ask: Is a comma needed before the www word *if* in the quotation? Answer: No, mid-sentence adverb clauses do not take commas. Rule: MC AC (no comma). The original is correct: "The king can hardly run a country **if he can't rule his own daughter.**"

Grammar Notations

PREPOSITIONAL PHRASES. in a fury; to his attaché.

CLAUSES, PHRASES, AND OPENERS. Check that students correctly mark the openers and clauses as indicated in the fixed passage above.

- #4 -ing participial phrase opener: Threatening to sever diplomatic ties.
  Ask: is the ambassador (the subject after the comma) the one doing the threatening? Answer: Yes, so this is a legal #4.
- MC: the **ambassador quit** the palace the following morning in a fury.
- #5 clausal opener and AC (adverb clause): As **he expressed** it to his attaché.

- MC: The **king can** hardly **run** a country. If students did not catch the helping verb, *can*, show them the list of helping verbs from the Verb grammar card and ask them to find two in this passage (see next item).
- AC (adverb clause): if **he can't rule** his own daughter. *See* ✏ **2.**

✏ **2. Teacher's note.** *Not* is an adverb, not part of the verb, in the contraction *can't* (cannot).

DAY 4

#1 MC   S   V   AC   S   V   #1 MC   S   V
¶ [king morton still reddened], (when he recalled that day). [it took several months' of **diplomatic**

                                                    Worse   MC   S   V   DC   S   V
negotiations to smooth over the episode]. ~~worst~~, [dorinda never seemed to understand] (that she was

responsible).

Fixes

INDENT ¶ because of a new topic, pulling out of a character's speech.

CAPITALIZATION. King Morton, It, Worse (in corrected sentence), Dorinda.

USAGE. Comparative adjectives. Use the comparative form *worse* (meaning *what was worse*) since this compares only two things: Dorinda's irresponsibility and the diplomacy required. Use the superlative *worst* for the most bad of three or more things.

COMMAS AND OTHER PUNCTUATION. Teach advanced concepts only if desired.

- **Mid-sentence adverb clauses.** Ask: Do we need a comma to set off the dependent clause starting with *when*, and why? Answer: No, mid-sentence adverb clauses do not take commas. Pattern: MC AC (no comma). Fix: King Morton still reddened **when he recalled that day.**
- **Apostrophe.** *Months* should be plural, not possessive: It took several **months**.
- **ADVANCED. Introductory transitional expressions** take commas. The original is correct: **Worse,** Dorinda never seemed to understand.
- **ADVANCED.** *That* **clauses** do not take commas. The original is correct: Dorinda never seemed to understand **that she was responsible.** *See* ♡ **1.**

Grammar Notations

PREPOSITIONAL PHRASES. of diplomatic negotiations.

> ✏ **Teacher's note.** *To smooth over* and *to understand* are infinitives, not prepositional phrases.
>
> If students mark *over the episode* as a prepositional phrase, you could let it go since *over* sometimes is a preposition. However, *over* is an adverb here. What makes sense together is *smooth over*, not *over the episode*. It may help to point out that *smooth over* has a different meaning (to make seem less disagreeable) than *smooth* (to free from roughness or difficulties).

CLAUSES, PHRASES, AND OPENERS. Check that students correctly mark the openers and clauses as indicated in the fixed passage above.

- #1 subject opener and MC: **King Morton** still **reddened.**
- AC (adverb clause): when **he recalled** that day. *See* ✏.
- #1 subject opener and MC: **It took** several months of diplomatic negotiations to smooth over the episode.

diplomatic: skillful in handling negotiations and other relations with foreign countries

♡ **1. Grammar lovers.** This *that* clause is a noun clause because it follows a verbal (*understand*) and answers the question *what*.

✏ **Teacher's note.** When a DC comes after an MC, it does not matter whether students group them together, ending the main clause at the end of the dependent clause (e.g., King Morton still reddened when he recalled that day), or group them separately, as here.

The important thing is to identify the clauses and recognize that a S-V pair makes a clause. *Fix It!* groups them together when the dependent clause is needed to make sense of the main clause and marks them separately when not, but if students choose differently, that is fine.

- MC: **Dorinda** never **seemed** to understand.
- DC: that **she was** responsible. *See* ♡ **2.**

♡ **2. Grammar lovers.** This is a noun clause because it follows a verbal, the infinitive *to understand*. *Was* is a linking verb, linking the subject complement (a.k.a. predicate adjective), *responsible*, back to the subject, *she*.

Style

If desired, have students identify the strongest of the vocabulary dress-ups from this week. Discuss their answers. Suggestions:

- **Strong verbs.** squirted, twirled, rushing, quit, reddened.
  - ✏ **Teacher's note.** If students choose *sever*, praise them for marking a strong word that expresses action. Technically, infinitives do not function as verbs, but this is too advanced to explain now.
- **Quality adjectives.** obligatory.
- **-ly adverbs.** truthfully, rapidly, noticeably.

STUDENT REWRITE

King Morton's greatest mortification had occurred two years earlier at a dinner party for the Ambassador of Nordicland. Taking an instant dislike to the ambassador's son, who was truthfully a bit of a brat, Dorinda squirted mouthwash from a travel bottle she carried in her purse into his sturgeon roe soup. Despite the youngster's queasiness, she had no mercy. During the obligatory dance after the dinner, she rapidly twirled him around. Last seen, he was rushing to the royal restrooms, noticeably green.

Threatening to sever diplomatic ties, the ambassador quit the palace the following morning in a fury. As he expressed it to his attaché, "The king can hardly run a country if he can't rule his own daughter."

King Morton still reddened when he recalled that day. It took several months of diplomatic negotiations to smooth over the episode. Worse, Dorinda never seemed to understand that she was responsible.

Week 4

Teacher's note.
As you discuss each fix with your students and help them correctly mark the passage in their student book, keep the exercise light and fun. It should be like a game. If your student groans when you say, "Time for *Fix It!*" something is wrong.

#3 -ly Openers, Commas with Adjectives Before a Noun, "Be" Verbs, Run-On Sentences

LEARN IT

#3 -ly Openers

The last opener for review is the -ly adverb opener. Commas are optional with #3 openers; use the pause test to decide.

Commas with Adjectives Before a Noun

The rules for adjectives before a noun are a little tricky. Use the grammar card to help you remember how to punctuate these kinds of adjectives.

Coordinate adjectives need commas. Usually two or more adjectives before a noun are separated by commas, as in *dewy, silent leaves*. Coordinate adjectives describe the noun independently (*the leaves are dewy and also silent*). Since there is no coordinating conjunction (it is not *dewy and silent leaves*), this is not the same as items in a series.

Two tricks can help you tell if the two adjectives might be coordinate.

- Can you add *and* between them?
- Can you reverse their order and they sound right?

If both tests work, the adjectives are likely coordinate and will need a comma between them. If they fail the test, they are likely cumulative adjectives.

Cumulative adjectives do not take commas. Sometimes the last adjective pairs with the noun as a unit; the adjective before it describes the adjective-noun pair, as in *dry autumn leaves* (*autumn leaves* that are *dry*). These are called cumulative adjectives and do not take commas. Notice that *autumn, dry leaves* and *dry and autumn leaves* both sound odd, so these are not coordinate adjectives.

Teacher's note.
"Adjectives before a noun" refers to two or more adjectives that come before a noun. Students sometimes confuse this with items in a series, which is different. Items in a series uses *and* or another cc to connect the words; adjectives before a noun are not linked with *and*.

"Be" Verbs

Finding clauses depends on being able to find the verbs in a sentence. Since the "be" verbs are often overlooked, memorize the list of them printed on the back of the Verb grammar card.

Run-on Sentences

A common writing mistake is run-on sentences. This happens when two main clauses are connected with nothing stronger than a comma, which is always wrong because main clauses need something as strong as a period between them.

If two main clauses are joined by nothing, it is called a **fused sentence (MC MC)**. If there is only a comma between them, it is called a **comma splice (MC, MC)**. In both cases, something stronger is needed. The easiest way to fix them is to use a period, but your teacher can explore other options with you, which are also listed on the Stop Run-on Sentences! grammar card.

Teacher's note.
Sometimes discussion points under commas or punctuation will address something that is already correct but that some students may incorrectly change. You do not need to go over what students have not missed unless you think it will help their understanding.

Page 10, *Fix It! Grammar: Frog Prince, or Just Deserts*, **Student Book 3**

DAY 1

¶ older now, [the princess had earned a reputation for beauty] (that reached into the ~~furthest~~ *farthest* kingdoms).

#2

with the latest fad, a beauty spot, perched high on her cheek and her hair twisted into a powdered

pompadour, [princess dorinda fancied ~~her quiet~~ *herself quite* chic].

Fixes

INDENT ¶ because of a new time and a new topic, the princess's appearance.

CAPITALIZATION. Older, With, Princess Dorinda. Lowercase: the princess (title without a name).

USAGE. Superlative adjectives. the **farthest** kingdoms. Use *farthest* to refer to physical distance, *furthest* for anything else. Tip to help remember: *far* always means distance: we do not go "fur" down the road!

PRONOUN USAGE. When referring back to the subject of the same sentence, add *self* to the pronoun. Dorinda fancied **herself**. These are known as reflexive pronouns.

SPELLING. *quite*, not *quiet*.

COMMAS AND OTHER PUNCTUATION. *See* ✎ **1.**

- **ADVANCED. Essential elements** do not take commas. The original is correct: the princess had earned a reputation for beauty **that reached into the farthest kingdoms**. *See* ♡.

- **ADVANCED. Nonessential elements** take commas. The original is correct: the latest fad, **a beauty spot**, perched high. It is just additional information about the latest fad, so it should be set off with commas. *See* ✎ **2.**

- **ADVANCED. Items in a series.** No comma after *cheek* is correct because *and* joins only two items, both objects of the preposition *with*: *fad* and *hair*. Each of these has an adjective phrase describing it (*perched high on her cheek* and *twisted into a powdered pompadour*), but *and* still connects only two items in a series. It may help to simplify the sentence and add another *with* mentally: With the latest fad … and *with* her hair twisted.

- **Long #2 prepositional openers.** This phrase begins with *With* and has two objects; it does not end until *pompadour*. Ask: Does this opener need a comma, and why? Answer: Yes, because long prepositional openers (five or more words) take commas. Fix: **With the latest fad … perched high on her cheek and her hair twisted into a powdered pompadour,** Princess Dorinda fancied herself quite chic.

Grammar Notations

PREPOSITIONAL PHRASES. for beauty; into the farthest kingdoms; With the latest fad, a beauty spot, perched high on her cheek and her hair twisted into a powdered pompadour; on her cheek; into a powdered pompadour.

✎ **Teacher's note.** The double underlines in the fixed sentences above are deliberate: they indicate the phrases within the phrase.

pompadour: woman's hairstyle in which her hair is raised over her forehead in a roll; a puffy hairstyle

✎ **1. Teacher's note.** Remember, the points marked *advanced* are for your information and can be discussed if your students ask or if you wish to cover that point of grammar for an older or stronger student.

♡ **Grammar lovers.** This clause is an essential adjective clause because it modifies the noun *reputation*. It uses *that* in place of *which*.

✎ **2. Teacher's note.** This is a nonessential appositive, a noun renaming the noun just before it (*the latest fad*). Since presumably there is only one "latest fad," the added information does not specify *fad* any further so is nonessential and therefore needs commas. See Grammar Glossary: Commas: Essential-Nonessential elements.

CLAUSES, PHRASES, AND OPENERS. Check that students correctly mark the openers and clauses as indicated in the fixed passage. In the notes below, the subject-verb pairs are bolded. Students should indicate MC, DC, or AC. The type of dependent clause is listed in parentheses for teacher reference.

- **ADVANCED.** Invisible #4 -ing opener: Older now. The word *being* is implied (*being older now*), but it sounds better without it. Students do not need to mark Invisible #4s yet.
- MC: the **princess had earned** a reputation for beauty.
- DC (adjective clause): **that reached** into the farthest kingdoms.
    - ✒ **Teacher's note.** The words *who, which,* and *that* usually start adjective clauses, which usually follow nouns or pronouns.
- #2 prepositional phrase opener: With the latest fad, a beauty spot, perched high on her cheek and her hair twisted into a powdered pompadour. *See* ✒ **3.**
- MC: **Princess Dorinda fancied** herself quite chic.

✒ **3. Teacher's note.** Students may think this should be a clause because *perched* and *twisted* look like verbs. These past participles (known as verbals because they derive from verbs) function as adjectives, however, modifying the nouns before them (*fad, hair*).

DAY 2

```
#3            MC       S      V     V
¶ lamentably, [her beauty was flawed by her reputation for fastidiousness⌐ and self-centeredness]. time
            MC    S      V      V
after time, [king morton had urged her to consider some young suitor]⌐; time after time, [she had
    V
refused all the eligible⌐young men].
```

Fixes

INDENT ¶ because of a new topic, Dorinda's negative traits.

CAPITALIZATION. Lamentably, Time, King Morton.

COMMAS AND OTHER PUNCTUATION.

- **#3 -ly adverb openers.** Determine commas after #3 openers with the pause test. Do you need a pause after *Lamentably*? Yes, so add a comma. This is the simple way to test for commas after #3 openers. *See* ✒.
- **Items in a series.** No comma before *and* to join two items in a series: a and b. Fix: fastidiousness **and** self-centeredness (two nouns).
- **Run-on sentence** (comma splice MC, MC). The comma after *suitor* is not strong enough to hold two main clauses together. The easiest solution is a period, but a semicolon works better here. Use semicolons to join MCs that are inextricably linked together. Semicolons work especially well when main clauses have a parallel structure.

    Fix, with main clauses italicized: Time after time, *King Morton had urged her to consider some young suitor*; time after time, *she had refused all the eligible young men*.

- **ADVANCED. Transitional openers** take commas. The comma after *time after time* is correct both times. *Time after time* is an idiom meaning repeatedly.
- **Cumulative adjectives** do not take commas. Fix: **eligible young** men.

    Apply the two tests to tell if these adjectives are coordinate (comma) or cumulative (no comma): 1) Does it work to say *young eligible men*? No, it sounds awkward. 2) What about *eligible and young men*? Also awkward. This means the adjectives are cumulative and do not take commas.

lamentably: regrettably; unfortunately

fastidiousness: the condition of being hard to please and excessively demanding

✒ **Teacher's note.** Technically, we need the comma because *lamentably* modifies the entire sentence, not just the verb. What is lamentable is that her inner character does not match her outer, which is the idea of the whole main clause.

✎ **Teacher's note.** With cumulative adjectives, the first one modifies the second adjective plus the noun. The tests depend on a quick response; not all students will hear that these are awkward. The more you think about it, the harder it is to tell!

Tip: With cumulative adjectives, the last adjective will deal with time/age or color, or it will form a compound noun. *Young* deals with age, so this is further evidence it is cumulative.

Grammar Notations

PREPOSITIONAL PHRASES. by her reputation; for fastidiousness and self-centeredness; after time (twice). Guide students to see the pattern in each: preposition + noun (no verb).

CLAUSES, PHRASES, AND OPENERS.

- #3 -ly adverb opener: Lamentably.

  ✎ **Teacher's note.** Dress-ups never start a sentence, so this counts as an opener, not as a dress-up.

- MC: her **beauty was** flawed by her reputation for fastidiousness and self-centeredness. *See* ♡.
- MC: **King Morton had urged** her to consider one or another young suitor.
- MC: **she had refused** all the eligible young men.

♡ **Grammar lovers.** Grammarians will argue over whether words like *flawed* are predicate adjectives or part of the verb phrase, but it does not affect grammar or punctuation so is not important. It is treated as a subject complement (predicate adjective) here because it is not her reputation that flaws her; hers is a flawed beauty because of her poor reputation. That makes *was* a linking verb instead of a helping verb. This is beyond the scope or need of students of any age!

DAY 3

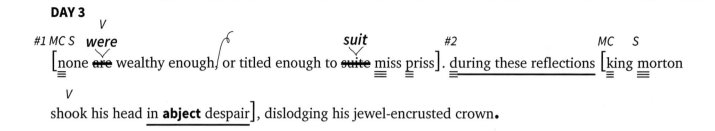

V

#1 MC S *were*   *suit*   #2   MC   S

[none ~~are~~ wealthy enough⸍ or titled enough to ~~suite~~ miss priss]. during these reflections [king morton

V

shook his head in **abject** despair], dislodging his jewel-encrusted crown.

Fixes

CAPITALIZATION. None, Miss Priss, During, King Morton.

VERB TENSE. Keep the same tense throughout a story. This one is told in the past tense, so do not switch to present. Fix: None **were**. *See* ✏.

SPELLING. Fix: to **suit** Miss Priss, i.e., to satisfy. Students often confuse *suite*, pronounced like *sweet*, with *suit*, which rhymes with *boot*. Besides the similar spelling, part of the confusion is that *suite* can be pronounced the same as *suit* when it means a collection of bedroom furniture.

COMMAS AND OTHER PUNCTUATION.

- **Items in a series.** No comma before the cc *or* to join two items in a series, in this case adjectives. Pattern: a or b. Fix: wealthy enough **or** titled enough.
- **Short #2 prepositional openers** (under five words): commas are optional. The original is correct: **During these reflections** King Morton shook his head in abject despair.
- **ADVANCED. Nonessential elements** take commas. The original is correct: in abject despair, **dislodging his jewel-encrusted crown.** *See* ♡.
- **ADVANCED. Hyphens.** Notice the hyphen in *jewel-encrusted*. When words function as a single adjective before a noun, connect them with a hyphen: **jewel-encrusted** crown.

Grammar Notations

PREPOSITIONAL PHRASES. During these reflections; in abject despair. Guide students to see the pattern: preposition + noun (no verb).

CLAUSES, PHRASES, AND OPENERS.

- #1 subject opener and MC: **None were** wealthy enough or titled enough to suit Miss Priss. If students miss *none*, explain that pronouns sometimes function as subjects. If they miss *were*, ask them to find a *be* verb using the verb card list.
- #2 prepositional phrase opener: During these reflections. Ask: Why is this a phrase and not a clause? Answer: There is no verb. *During* is always a preposition.
- MC: **King Morton shook** his head in abject despair.
- **ADVANCED.** Show the participial phrase: dislodging his jewel-encrusted crown. It follows the pattern of a #4 -ing opener but comes at the end. It is not a clause because there is no subject and helping verb before *dislodging*.

abject: utterly hopeless; miserable

Miss Priss is a common label for a girl who looks down on others.

✏ **Teacher's note.** *None were* is correct because *none* can be treated as a singular or plural noun. It is plural here because it refers back to the plural *men* of the previous sentence.

♡ **Grammar lovers.** Most participial (-ing) phrases are nonessential and therefore need commas.

DAY 4

#1 MC S   V   one   #1
                                                                                        MC   S
¶ [he wasn't the only ~~+~~ clucking his tongue, in **consternation** over princess dorinda]. [lady constance,

                    V   V
her elder companion since childhood, had virtually given up on training her young charge in true,

courtly behavior].

Fixes

consternation: dismay; alarm

INDENT ¶ because of a new topic, Lady Constance and her attitude toward Dorinda.

CAPITALIZATION. He, Princess Dorinda, Lady Constance.

NUMBERS. Spell out numbers written as one or two words: the only **one**.

COMMAS AND OTHER PUNCTUATION.

- **Mid-sentence prepositional phrases** do not take commas. Fix: clucking his tongue **in consternation.**

- **Run-on sentence** (comma splice MC, MC, which is always wrong). A comma is not strong enough to hold together two main clauses.

  Fix, with MCs italicized: *He wasn't the only one clucking his tongue in consternation over Princess Dorinda. Lady Constance … had virtually given up on training her young charge.*

- **ADVANCED. Nonessential elements** take commas. The original is correct: Lady Constance, **her elder companion since childhood,** had virtually given up. *See* ♡.

- **Cumulative adjectives** do not take commas: **true courtly** behavior. Test: 1) *courtly true behavior* is awkward; 2) *true and courtly behavior* is also awkward. Since the tests fail, the adjectives are cumulative and should not have a comma.

  - ✏ **Teacher's note.** They are cumulative because *true* describes *courtly behavior*. The two adjectives do not independently modify *behavior*. That is, it is not *true behavior and courtly behavior*, but *true courtly-behavior*.

Grammar Notations

PREPOSITIONAL PHRASES. in consternation; over Princess Dorinda; since childhood; on training; in true courtly behavior.

Guide students to see the pattern in each: preposition + noun (no verb). Students may be confused about two of these:

- *Since* is usually a subordinating conjunction starting adverb clauses (www word), but it is a preposition when there is no subject-verb after it. *Since childhood* has only a noun, *childhood*, after *since*, so this is a prepositional phrase (preposition + noun), not an adverb clause (clause starter + subject + verb).

- **ADVANCED.** Some students may mark *up* as a preposition, but as a phrase, *up on training* does not make sense, whereas *given up* and *on training* by themselves do. This means that *up* is an adverb that goes with the verb, not a preposition starting a phrase. *See* ✏ **1.**

♡ **Grammar lovers.** This is an appositive, a noun or noun phrase that renames the noun (Lady Constance) that comes before it. Since Lady Constance is identified specifically by her name, the appositive adds information but is not necessary for us to know who is meant. It is therefore nonessential and takes commas.

✏ **1. Teacher's note.** *Up* is an adverb here but part of the verb phrase because some verbs require a certain adverb. *Given up* has a different meaning from *given*.

CLAUSES, PHRASES, AND OPENERS.

- #1 subject opener and MC: **He was**n't the only one clucking his tongue in consternation over Princess Dorinda. *See* ✐ **2**.
- #1 subject opener and MC: **Lady Constance** … **had** virtually **given up** on training her young charge in true courtly behavior.

Style

If desired, have students identify the strongest of these three dress-ups from this week. Discuss their answers. Suggestions:

- **Strong verbs.** perched, twisted, fancied, flawed, urged, dislodging, clucking.
    - ✐ **Teacher's note.** It is OK at this level to allow students to count verbals (*perched, twisted, clucking,* and *dislodging*) as strong verbs. In their own writing, encourage them to choose action verbs over verbals for the strong verb dress-up, but only as they are ready.
- **Quality adjectives.** chic, eligible, abject, jewel-encrusted.
- **-ly adverbs.** virtually.
    - ✐ **Teacher's note.** *Courtly* is an adjective because it describes a noun, *behavior*. If students mark it as an -ly adverb, guide them to see that it does not describe a verb or adjective but a noun, so it is an imposter -ly adverb. They could count it as a quality adjective, but consider whether it is "quality" enough to count as a dress-up.

✐ **2. Teacher's note.** *Clucking* is a verbal, not a true verb. It can count as an invisible *who*: one *who was clucking his tongue*. Present participles (-ing) function as verbs only when a subject and helping verb come before them, as in *she was clucking her tongue*. Here, *clucking* functions as an adjective describing *one*. See Style on this page.

STUDENT REWRITE

Older now, the princess had earned a reputation for beauty that reached into the farthest kingdoms. With the latest fad, a beauty spot, perched high on her cheek and her hair twisted into a powdered pompadour, Princess Dorinda fancied herself quite chic.

Lamentably, her beauty was flawed by her reputation for fastidiousness and self-centeredness. Time after time, King Morton had urged her to consider some young suitor; time after time, she had refused all the eligible young men. None were wealthy enough or titled enough to suit Miss Priss. During these reflections King Morton shook his head in abject despair, dislodging his jewel-encrusted crown.

He wasn't the only one clucking his tongue in consternation over Princess Dorinda. Lady Constance, her elder companion since childhood, had virtually given up on training her young charge in true courtly behavior.

Week 5

Continue to have students mark the subjects and verbs of clauses and discuss with them the ones they missed. A lot of practice recognizing subjects and verbs will help students in many ways with punctuation and grammar.

Transitional Expressions and Interjections

LEARN IT

Transitions   Transitional words and expressions can occur anywhere in a sentence. These words help connect ideas or show relationships between them. The Commas with Transitional Expressions and Interjections grammar card from Week 3 will help you remember the following:

Punctuation (usually commas) is needed on both sides of mid-sentence words or phrases that interrupt the flow of the sentence.

- As the king's daughter, **however,** she was not often reprimanded.
- She could tear down the halls and get away with it, **too.**
- **Of course,** the king would eventually assign a consequence to her misdemeanors.

#T Transitional Opener   When a transitional word or expression occurs at the beginning of a sentence, mark it with a #T and set it off with a comma. Use the Transitional Opener grammar card to remember the rules.

#T **Moreover,** didn't they realize cell phones were intended for emergencies only?

#T **Not only that,** her sister was just across the room.

#T **Now,** isn't that a reasonable expectation?

Interjections   When an interjection expresses a strong emotion, use an exclamation mark. If the emotion is less strong, just use a comma.

- **Alas,** Dorinda's recklessness resulted in the destruction of her favorite figurine.
- **"Oh!** Why did I dash through the hall?"

Page 12, *Fix It! Grammar: Frog Prince, or Just Deserts*, **Student Book 3**

DAY 1   *#1 MC S*

#T   MC S   V   effect   Lady Constance

indeed, [years of indulgence had the unsurprising ~~affect~~ of hopelessly spoiling dorinda]. [~~she~~

V   Dorinda's   DC   S   V   V

recalled a time in ~~her~~ childhood], however, (when her charge had seemed a lovable, **tractable,** and

contented child).

Fixes

tractable: easily controlled; manageable; willing

CAPITALIZATION. Indeed, Dorinda. In the corrected version also capitalize *Lady Constance* and *Dorinda's.*

USAGE. the unsurprising **effect**. Students often confuse *affect* and *effect*. Since there is an article (*the*), we need the noun *effect*, not the verb *affect*.

ANTECEDENTS. A pronoun should clearly refer back to one noun, its antecedent. If what it refers to is not clear, use the person's name instead. Confusing: years of indulgence had the effect of spoiling Dorinda. **She** [Dorinda? Lady Constance?] recalled a time in **her** [Dorinda's? Lady Constance's?] childhood when … .

Fix: years of indulgence had the effect of spoiling Dorinda. **Lady Constance** recalled a time in **Dorinda's** childhood … .

COMMAS AND OTHER PUNCTUATION.

- **Transitions** take commas because they interrupt the flow of the sentence. Fixes: 1) **Indeed,** years of indulgence … . 2) Lady Constance recalled a time in Dorinda's childhood, **however,** when … .
- **Run-on sentence** (fused sentence MC MC, which is always wrong). This needs a period after *Dorinda*. Fix, with MCs italicized: *years of indulgence had the effect of spoiling Dorinda. Lady Constance recalled a time.*
- **Items in a series.** Use commas with three or more adjectives in a series: *lovable, tractable,* and *contented* child.

Grammar Notations

PREPOSITIONAL PHRASES. of indulgence; of hopelessly spoiling; in Dorinda's childhood. Guide students to see the pattern: preposition + noun (no verb).

> ✎ **Teacher's note.** If students are confused by *of hopelessly spoiling*, explain that verbals like -ing words are not always verbs but can function as nouns (called *gerunds* then). *Spoiling* is the object of the preposition *of.*

CLAUSES, PHRASES, AND OPENERS. Subjects and verbs are bolded.

- #T transitional opener: Indeed.
- MC: **years** of indulgence **had** the unsurprising effect of hopelessly spoiling Dorinda.

  If students mark *indulgence* as the subject, explain that it is the object of the preposition *of* and cannot double as the subject. The true subject is *years.*
- #1 subject opener and MC: **Lady Constance recalled** a time in Dorinda's childhood.
- DC (www clause): when her **charge had seemed** a lovable, tractable, and contented child. *See* ✎ *and* ♡.

✎ **Teacher's note.** If students mark this as an adverb clause (AC), let it go. The following explanation is advanced even for high schoolers.

♡ **Grammar lovers.** Usually *when* and *where* begin an adverb clause but not when they follow a noun. Here, *when* starts an essential adjective clause because it describes *time* and specifies what particular time: she recalled a *time when* Dorinda had been lovable. To complicate matters, the commas needed around *however* trump the no-comma needed for the essential *when* clause. If *however* were not there, no comma would set off the *when* clause, just like adverb clauses, only this time because it is essential.

DAY 2

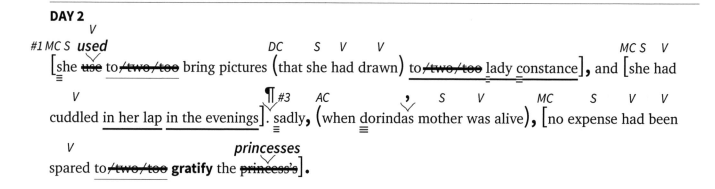

Fixes

INDENT ¶ with the second sentence, which switches to the topic of what spoiled Dorinda in the first place.

CAPITALIZATION. She, Lady Constance, Sadly, Dorinda's.

HOMOPHONES AND USAGE.

- Students sometimes write *use to* when they mean *used to*: She **used** to bring.
- Use the preposition *to*: She used **to** bring pictures ... **to** Lady Constance; **to** gratify the princesses. *See* ✏ **1.**

COMMAS AND OTHER PUNCTUATION.

- **ADVANCED.** *That* **clauses** do not take commas. The original is correct: She used to bring pictures **that she had drawn**. She brought the pictures she had drawn, not just any pictures, so the clause is essential (no comma).
- **Items in a series.** Put a comma before the cc *and* to connect two main clauses. Fix, with MCs in italics: *She used to bring pictures that she had drawn to Lady Constance,* **and** *she had cuddled in her lap in the evenings.*
- **#3 -ly adverb openers.** *Sadly* needs a comma after it because we pause there (simple pause test). *See* ✏ **2.**
- **AC, MC.** Fix: Sadly, **when Dorinda's mother was alive,** no expense had been spared. *See* ✏ **3.**
- **Apostrophes and plurals.** 1) Use *'s* to show possession. Fix: **Dorinda's** mother. 2) Do not use apostrophes when plural is meant. *The princess's* means belonging to the princess, which does not make sense. Fix: to gratify the **princesses**.

Grammar Notations

PREPOSITIONAL PHRASES. to Lady Constance; in her lap; in the evenings. Guide students to see the pattern in each prepositional phrase: preposition + noun (no verb).

CLAUSES, PHRASES, AND OPENERS. Subjects and verbs are bolded to make them easy to see.

- **#1 subject opener and MC: She used** to bring pictures (that she had drawn) to Lady Constance. This MC has inside it a dependent clause.
- DC: that **she had drawn. ADVANCED.** This is an adjective clause because it modifies the noun *pictures*.
- MC: **she had cuddled** in her lap in the evenings.
- #3 -ly adverb opener: Sadly.
- AC (adverb clause): when Dorinda's **mother was** alive.
- MC: no **expense had been spared** to gratify the princesses. Ask students to identify the helping verbs: *had been.*

gratify: indulge; give pleasure to

✏ **1. Teacher's note.**
The first and last of these are the *to* of infinitives; the middle one is in a regular prepositional phrase.

✏ **2. Teacher's note.**
Technical reason: *Sadly* modifies the idea in the main clause (that they spoiled Dorinda), not the verb by itself, so the comma is required. It is optional when it modifies just the main verb.

✏ **3. Teacher's note.**
In IEW's system, students count only the first opener of a sentence, but grammatically this sentence has two openers before the main clause, a #3 and a #5. Use the same punctuation rule you would if the -ly adverb were not there, a comma at the end of the #5 opener.

DAY 3

#6 MC   S   V   #1 MC   ,   S   V
[no **prodigality** was ~~to~~/~~two~~/too great]. [cinderellas castle became ~~there~~/their/~~they're~~ playground],

MC S   V
and [they each enjoyed ~~there~~/their/~~they're~~ own set of the american girl dolls/ with complete

wardrobes/ and assorted furniture].

prodigality: wasteful extravagance in spending

Fixes

CAPITALIZATION. No, Cinderella's (proper noun), American Girl (proper noun). *Cinderella's* is a proper noun so capitalized, but *castle* is a common noun so it is lowercase. *American Girl* is the name of a company so it is proper, but *dolls* is a common noun so lowercase.

HOMOPHONES.
- Use *too* meaning too much, excessively: no prodigality was **too** great.
- Use the possessive: **their** playground; **their** own set.

COMMAS AND OTHER PUNCTUATION.
- **Apostrophes** for possession. Fix: **Cinderella's** castle.
- **MC, cc MC.** Use commas before cc's to join two main clauses. Fix: Cinderella's castle became their playground, **and** they each enjoyed their own set of the American Girl dolls.
- **Mid-sentence prepositional phrases** do not take commas. Fix: the American Girl dolls with complete wardrobes.
- **Items in a series.** No comma before *and* to join two nouns. Pattern: a and b. Fix: complete **wardrobes** and assorted **furniture**.

Grammar Notations

PREPOSITIONAL PHRASES. of the American Girl dolls; with complete wardrobes and assorted furniture. Guide students to see the pattern in each prepositional phrase: preposition + noun (no verb). The second phrase has two objects of the preposition: *wardrobes* and *furniture*.

CLAUSES, PHRASES, AND OPENERS. Subjects and verbs are bolded to make them easy to see.
- #6 vss and MC: No **prodigality was** too great.
- #1 subject opener and MC: Cinderella's **castle became** their playground.
  If students mark *Cinderella's* as the subject, make a joke of it: Is Cinderella their playground? Explain that possessive names cannot be the subject.
- MC: **they** each **enjoyed** their own set of the American Girl dolls with complete wardrobes and assorted furniture.

DAY 4

#4   *MC*   *S*   *V*   *MC*   *S V*

¶ shaking her head in dismay, [lady constance one day clucked to lady bertha], " [~~its~~ it's no wonder]

DC   *S*   *V*   *V*

(that child has turned out so **blemished**).

Fixes

INDENT ¶ because of a new speaker.

CAPITALIZATION. Shaking, Lady Constance, Lady Bertha, It's (capitalized as the first word of a quoted sentence).

USAGE. Use the contraction *It's,* meaning *it is.* **It's** no wonder.

COMMAS AND OTHER PUNCTUATION.

- **#4 -ing openers** take commas. Fix: **Shaking her head in dismay,** Lady Constance … . Ask: Is Lady Constance the one doing the shaking? Answer: Yes, so this is a legal #4.
- **Quotations.** Fix: Lady Constance one day clucked to Lady Bertha, "It's no wonder … . Rules: 1) When a speaking verb (*clucked*) sets up a direct quotation, add a comma right before the quotation. 2) Use quotation marks with direct quotations but no close quotation marks because she is not finished speaking.

Grammar Notations

PREPOSITIONAL PHRASES. in dismay; to Lady Bertha. *See* ✏ **1.**

CLAUSES, PHRASES, AND OPENERS. Subjects and verbs are bolded to make them easy to see.

- #4 -ing participial phrase opener: Shaking her head in dismay. *See* ✏ **2.**
- MC: **Lady Constance** one day **clucked** to Lady Bertha.
- MC: **It's** no wonder. If students miss the *is* in *it's,* ask them to find a *be* verb using the verb card list. If they have trouble recognizing that this is a main clause, explain that pronouns (*it*) can function as subjects.
- DC: that **child has turned out** so blemished. *See* ♡.

Style

If desired, have students identify the strongest of the vocabulary dress-ups from this week. Discuss their answers. Suggestions:

- **Strong verbs.** recalled, cuddled, gratify (a verbal), clucked, blemished.
- **Quality adjectives.** unsurprising, tractable, contented, assorted.
- **-ly adverbs.** hopelessly.

Sidebar:

blemished: marred or spoiled by imperfections

✏ **1. Teacher's note.** *Out* is an adverb here, not a preposition, and is part of the verb phrase. *Turned out* (ended up, proven to be) has a different meaning from *turned.*

✏ **2. Teacher's note.** *Shaking her head in dismay* is a phrase and not a clause because there is no subject and helping verb to make *shaking* a verb. It functions as an adjective phrase describing the subject (*Lady Constance*) after the comma.

♡ **Grammar lovers.** This is a disguised noun clause with *that* understood, not a main clause: It is no wonder *that* that child has turned out so blemished. The first (and hidden) *that* is a relative pronoun setting up the clause; the second is a demonstrative pronoun modifying child (which child? *that* child).

STUDENT REWRITE

Indeed, years of indulgence had the unsurprising effect of hopelessly spoiling Dorinda. Lady Constance recalled a time in Dorinda's childhood, however, when her charge had seemed a lovable, tractable, and contented child. She used to bring pictures that she had drawn to Lady Constance, and she had cuddled in her lap in the evenings.

Sadly, when Dorinda's mother was alive, no expense had been spared to gratify the princesses. No prodigality was too great. Cinderella's castle became their playground, and they each enjoyed their own set of the American Girl dolls with complete wardrobes and assorted furniture.

Shaking her head in dismay, Lady Constance one day clucked to Lady Bertha, "It's no wonder that child has turned out so blemished.

Week 6

Once each day's passage has been marked, have your students copy it in their notebook without all the grammar notations, continuing where they left off last week. This rewrite cements the fixes in a student's mind.

Multiple Openers

LEARN IT

Sentences may have a variety of openers before the main clause. For example, there can be a string of prepositional phrases, an -ly adverb followed by a clausal, or an -ing opener followed by something else. Save commas for the end of them all unless needed for better understanding.

Label the sentence with the number of the opener that comes *first*.

#2 During inclement weather when no one ventured out of doors, the servants feared for the safety of the knick-knacks adorning the halls.

#4 Stabilizing the delicate vase as Dorinda sped by, the chambermaid sighed with exasperation.

#3 Cheerfully escaping to the garden, Dorinda spared the rest of the castle's finery from destruction.

#5 If the king could monitor Dorinda every moment of every day, her behavior would improve.

🖉 **Teacher's note.** Remember that you do not need to complete all the discussion notes with your student. They are there if you need them, but if your student has mastered a skill, you do not need to reinforce it daily.

Use the grammar notations to help your student gain mastery, but do not let this become a drudgery. Continue to make the entire process a game. Let your student tell you what he or she knows and laugh when something is missed or mismarked: a mistake is an opportunity to learn.

Page 14, *Fix It! Grammar: Frog Prince, or Just Deserts,* **Student Book 3**

DAY 1

#1 MC S   V   V   DC   S   V

[she merely stomped her foot and pouted] (that her entertainment center was **minuscule**), and

MC   S   V

[queen magnifica directed the palace accountant to ~~two/too~~ order her a new HDTV], complete

with surround sound speakers, ~~to/two/~~too."

Fixes

minuscule: very small

CAPITALIZATION. She, Queen Magnifica, HDTV. *See* ✏ **1.**

HOMOPHONES. *To, two,* or *too.* 1) The first is the preposition in infinitives: **to** order. 2) The second means *also*: complete with surround sound speakers, **too.**

COMMAS AND OTHER PUNCTUATION. *See* ✏ **2.**

- **Quotation:** Why are there no open quotation marks? Answer: This is a continuation of her speech. Ask: Where does her speech end and what should you do? Answer: After *too.* Add closing quotes after the period.

- **Items in a series.** Remind students that cc's must join the same parts of speech or grammatical structure (phrases, clauses). Ask: Where are cc's in this passage and what do they connect?

  The first *and* connects two verbs, *stomped* and *pouted.* Does it need a comma, and why? No, these are compound verbs that share the same subject, *she.* Pattern: a and b. The original is correct: stomped **and** pouted.

  The second *and* connects two MCs. Does it need a comma, and why? Yes, main clauses need a comma plus a cc to hold them together, not a comma alone (comma splice) or a cc alone. Pattern: MC, cc MC. Fix, with main clauses italicized: *She merely stomped her foot and pouted that her entertainment center was minuscule,* **and** *Queen Magnifica directed the palace accountant to order her a new HDTV.*

- **ADVANCED. Nonessential elements** take commas. The comma after *HDTV* is correct since *complete with surround sound speakers* is an invisible nonessential *which:* **which was** complete with surround sound speakers.

- **Transitional words** are usually set off with commas. Fix: surround sound speakers, **too.**

  If students did not catch this, ask: Can you find a transition in this passage? Answer: *too.* Does it need a comma to set it off? If they do not know, simply tell them the rule.

✏ **1. Teacher's note.** Acronyms, formed from the first letters of words in a phrase, are usually capitalized.

✏ **2. Teacher's note.** Ask questions to lead students to figure out the punctuation they missed and understand the punctuation they got right. The questions in the notes illustrate different ways to guide students, but do not feel bound by them. What is important is that students understand why the punctuation marks are there.

Grammar Notations

PREPOSITIONAL PHRASES. with surround sound speakers. Guide students to see the pattern: preposition + noun (no verb).

CLAUSES, PHRASES, AND OPENERS. Subjects and verbs are bolded.

- #1 subject opener and MC: **She** merely **stomped** her foot and **pouted.**
- DC: that her **entertainment center was** minuscule. (*Entertainment center* is a compound noun.) *See* ✏ **3.**
- MC: **Queen Magnifica directed** the palace accountant to order her a new HDTV.
- **ADVANCED.** Adjective phrase: complete with surround sound speakers. If students wonder, *complete* is an adjective in this sentence, not a verb, so the words after *HDTV* are just phrases.

✏ **3. Teacher's note.** You do not need to teach this, but this is a noun clause beginning with the relative pronoun *that.* As students will later learn, *that* clauses are never set off with commas.

DAY 2

#5 AC   S   V   V   MC   ,   S   V

¶ (although they agonized, and **fretted**), [princess dorindas companions found no remedy]. one crisp,

DC   S   V   V   MC   S   V

spring morning (when the cherry blossoms were just beginning to appear), [princess dorinda was

V

distracted by her latest plaything], a golden ball.

Fixes

fretted: felt worry or annoyance

INDENT ¶s: 1) new topic pulling out of Lady Constance's speech; 2) time has passed.

CAPITALIZATION. Although, Princess Dorinda's, One, Princess Dorinda.

Lowercase: *spring*. Teach at point of need: capitalize calendar items (days of the week, months) but not seasons.

COMMAS AND OTHER PUNCTUATION. Ask questions to help students understand the punctuation. Some are suggested below.

- **Items in a series.** No comma before *and* to join two verbs: **agonized and fretted**. Pattern a and b.

  Ask: Can you find a compound verb (two verbs joined with *and*)? Answer: *agonized and fretted*. How many items is this cc joining? Answer: Two. Do you need a comma when a cc joins only two items in a series? Answer: No, only with three or more (or with two main clauses).

- **#5 clausal openers** take commas: AC, MC. Fix: **Although they agonized and fretted,** Princess Dorinda's companions … . Ask: What opener is this? Does it require a comma? Answer: #5, yes, comma at the end.

- **Apostrophe** for possession. Fix: **Dorinda's** companions.

- **Adjectives before a noun.** Ask students if the adjectives before *morning* are coordinate (comma) or cumulative (no comma). Apply the two tests: 1) Does *spring crisp morning* sound right? No, it is awkward. 2) What about *crisp and spring morning*? No, we would not say that. Since both tests fail, these are cumulative adjectives, so no comma. Fix: **crisp spring** morning. See ✏ **1.**

- **Multiple openers. One crisp spring morning when the cherry blossoms were just beginning to appear,** Princess Dorinda was distracted.

  Ask: Do we need a comma after the opener *One crisp spring morning*? Answer: No. Save the comma for the end of all the openers.

  Ask: Do we need a comma after *appear*? Answer: Yes, introductory www clauses take commas: One crisp spring morning **when the cherry blossoms were just beginning to appear,** Princess Dorinda was distracted. See ✏ **2.**

- **ADVANCED. Nonessential elements** take commas. The original is correct: her latest plaything, **her golden ball.** This is an invisible *which*: her latest plaything, *which was* her golden ball.

✏ **1. Teacher's note.** When the last adjective deals with time, like *spring*, they are cumulative.

✏ **2. Teacher's note.** This is not a #5 sentence opener because an invisible #2 opener comes first, but since the www clause precedes the main clause, it is treated like an opener with a comma after it: AC, MC.

✏ **3. Teacher's note.** The subject of this clause is not *Princess Dorinda* but *companions*. *Princess Dorinda's* is possessive.

Grammar Notations

PREPOSITIONAL PHRASES. by her latest plaything.

CLAUSES, PHRASES, AND OPENERS. Subjects and verbs are bolded.

- #5 clausal opener and AC: Although **they agonized** and **fretted**.
- MC: Princess Dorinda's **companions found** no remedy. See ✏ **3.**

- **ADVANCED.** Invisible #2 opener. One crisp spring morning. This is not literally a prepositional phrase, but it functions like one and has a prepositional idea implied in front of it, such as *During* or *In* that time period. Sentences that start with some kind of time frame before the main clause can count as #2s.
- DC (www adjective clause): when the **cherry blossoms were** just **beginning** to appear.
  - ✏ **Teacher's note.** Students may label this either AC or DC. Determining whether a www word is starting an adverb clause or some other kind of clause is not something they need to learn at this level. See ♡. Also, *cherry blossoms* is a compound noun; students may mark either *blossoms* or *cherry blossoms*.
- MC: **Princess Dorinda was distracted** by her latest plaything.

♡ **Grammar lovers.** When *when* or *where* follows a noun that it also describes (the morning when this happened), it starts an adjective clause, which can be essential or nonessential, instead of an adverb clause. Since this adjective clause is essential, it does not take a comma. This is too advanced to teach this level.

DAY 3

$$V$$
#1 MC S   V   ♂ AC S *wandered among*
[she tossed it up], (as she ~~wondered~~ ~~between~~ the exotic) botanical species in the regal conservatory),

DC *where*   S   V   V
(~~were~~ her father had found **haven** from his royal cares).

Fixes

haven: a place of shelter and safety; asylum

CAPITALIZATION. She. Keep *father* lowercase except when used as a name in a noun of direct address: May I leave, Father? My father is well.

USAGE AND SPELLING.

- She **wandered**, not *wondered*.
- Use *between* with two items but *among* with three or more. Presumably there are many different species of plants in the royal gardens. Fix: she wandered **among** the exotic botanical species.
- The www word is spelled with an *h*: **where** her father had found haven. Some students confuse *where* with the *be* verb *were*.

COMMAS AND OTHER PUNCTUATION.

- **Mid-sentence adverb clauses.** Ask: Do we need a comma before *as she wandered*? Answer: No, adverb clause dress-ups do not take commas. Rule: MC AC. Fix: She tossed it up **as she wandered.** *See* ✏.
- **Adjectives before a noun.** Ask: Do we need a comma between *exotic* and *botanical*? To find out, apply the tests: 1) *botanical exotic species* sounds awkward; 2) *exotic and botanical species* sounds awkward. Since neither works, these are cumulative adjectives, so no comma.

✏ **Teacher's note.** Adverb clause dress-ups (mid-sentence adverb clauses) are the same as adverb clause openers except they do not begin the sentence.

Grammar Notations

PREPOSITIONAL PHRASES. among the exotic botanical species; in the regal conservatory; from his royal cares. Guide students to see the pattern in each phrase: preposition + noun (no verb).

CLAUSES, PHRASES, AND OPENERS.

- #1 subject opener and MC: **She tossed** it up.
- AC (adverb clause): as **she wandered** among the exotic botanical species in the regal conservatory.
- DC (www clause): where her **father had found** haven from his royal cares. If students mark this as an adverb clause (AC), let it go. The comma before *where* is correct.
  - ♡ **Grammar lovers.** Like the *when* clauses in earlier passages, this *where* clause is an adjective clause because it follows a noun that it describes (*the conservatory, where*). Adjective clauses are either essential (no commas, like adverb clause dress-ups) or nonessential (commas). This one is nonessential because we can remove it without changing the meaning of the rest of the sentence. Dorinda still wandered among the species in the conservatory. This concept is too advanced for this level, however.

DAY 4

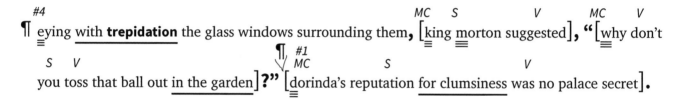

Fixes

trepidation: alarm; agitation

INDENT ¶s because of a new speaker and new topic.

CAPITALIZATION. Eying, King Morton, Why (first word of quoted sentence), Dorinda's.

COMMAS AND OTHER PUNCTUATION.

- **#4 -ing openers** take commas. Fix: **Eying with trepidation the glass windows surrounding them,** King Morton suggested. Ask: Is King Morton the one doing the -inging (*eying*)? Answer: Yes, so this is a legal #4.
- **Quotations.** Fix: King Morton suggested, "Why don't you toss that ball out in the garden?" Rules: 1) Use commas before quotes set up by a speaking verb: speaking verb + comma + quotation. 2) Use quotations marks with direct quotations. 3) Close with a question mark inside the closing quotes.

Grammar Notations

PREPOSITIONAL PHRASES. with trepidation; in the garden; for clumsiness. Guide students to see the pattern: preposition + noun (no verb).

CLAUSES, PHRASES, AND OPENERS. Ask students questions to help them figure out things they miss.

- #4 -ing participial phrase opener: Eying with trepidation the glass windows surrounding them. See ✏.
- MC: **King Morton suggested.**
- MC: Why **don't you toss** that ball out in the garden? We do not count this as an opener because it comes in the middle of a sentence. Check that students marked the helping verb, *do*, as well as the main verb, *toss*.
- #1 subject opener and MC: Dorinda's **reputation** for clumsiness **was** no palace secret. If students are confused about the subject, explain that it is not Dorinda who was no palace secret but her reputation.

Style

If desired, have students identify the strongest of the vocabulary dress-ups from this week. Discuss their answers. Suggestions:

- **Strong verbs.** pouted, directed, agonized and fretted (nice example of dual verbs), distracted.
- **Quality adjectives.** minuscule, crisp, exotic.
- **-ly adverbs.** merely.

✏ **Teacher's note.**
Eying functions as an adjective modifying the subject after the comma (King Morton). It is not a verb unless it has a subject and helping verb with it, so #4 openers are phrases, not clauses.

STUDENT REWRITE

She merely stomped her foot and pouted that her entertainment center was minuscule, and Queen Magnifica directed the palace accountant to order her a new HDTV, complete with surround sound speakers, too."

Although they agonized and fretted, Princess Dorinda's companions found no remedy.

One crisp spring morning when the cherry blossoms were just beginning to appear, Princess Dorinda was distracted by her latest plaything, a golden ball. She tossed it up as she wandered among the exotic botanical species in the regal conservatory, where her father had found haven from his royal cares.

Eying with trepidation the glass windows surrounding them, King Morton suggested, "Why don't you toss that ball out in the garden?"

Dorinda's reputation for clumsiness was no palace secret.

Week 7

Sentence Fragments

LEARN IT

A fragment is usually an error in which a sentence has phrases and/or dependent clauses but no main clause.

In fiction, fragments that do not leave the reader hanging and that fit the flow of the paragraph are dramatic and effective. *Fix It!* stories permit such fragments, especially in dialogue when complete sentences would sound unnatural. The key is whether or not the fragment leaves the reader feeling as if something more is needed.

- "Would you like me to rescue your ball?"

- "Oh, yes, I would like you to rescue my ball." (unnatural response)

- "Oh, yes!" (acceptable fragment)

- The frog leaped into the well after the bauble. Splashing loudly. (unacceptable fragment)

Some teachers forbid the use of any fragment in formal writing because students often use them ineffectively.

As you run across fragments in this story, discuss with your teacher which ones work well and which ones do not.

> ✏ **Teacher's note.** Keep these lessons short and fun. Make the notations more of a game than an exercise. You cannot help too much! The goal is daily repetition to move your students gently toward mastery.
>
> 🔊 **Listen.** For more on the process of mastery learning, see the blue page of this book for a free mp3 download entitled "Mastery Learning."

Page 16, *Fix It! Grammar: Frog Prince, or Just Deserts*, **Student Book 3**

Institute for Excellence in Writing

DAY 1

¶ "awesome," [princess dorinda answered], not noticing her father's grimace. "[~~its~~ it's nice enough outside], you know, [i was, like, ~~to two~~ too warm in here]. "precisely". [How else could he respond to such **twaddle**]?

Fixes

INDENT two ¶s because of new speakers.

CAPITALIZATION. Awesome, Princess Dorinda, It's, I, Precisely, How.

HOMOPHONES. 1) Use the contraction *it's* to mean *it is*: **It's** nice enough outside. 2) Use *too* to mean excessively: I was **too** warm.

SENTENCE FRAGMENT. "Precisely." Sentence fragments can work effectively in stories because we often speak in incomplete sentences, as here. This one-word response to Dorinda does not leave us hanging. *See* ✏ **1.**

COMMAS AND OTHER PUNCTUATION.

- **Quotations.** Fixes: "Awesome," Dorinda answered. " … warm in here." "Precisely." Rules: 1) What punctuation is needed after *awesome*, and why? Answer: a comma because a speaking verb (*answered*) sets up the quote. 2) Where do commas and periods go in relation to closing quotes? Answer: Inside! *See* ✏ **2.**
- **Apostrophes** for possession. Fix: **father's** grimace.
- **ADVANCED. Nonessential elements** take commas. The original is correct: Princess Dorinda answered, **not noticing her father's grimace.** Note: -ing participial phrases are almost always nonessential and therefore set off with commas. Without this comma, it could also be confusing where *not* goes: *answered not* or *not noticing*?
- **Run-on sentence** (comma splice MC, MC). Ask: Which two main clauses are joined with only a comma? Answer: *It's nice enough outside, you know,* and *I was, like, too warm in here.*

  Ask: What punctuation should we use instead? Answer: A period. It may help to show students the main clauses without the interrupters. Fix: *It's nice enough outside. I was too warm in here.*
- **End mark.** The narrator asks a question, so end with a question mark.

Grammar Notations

PREPOSITIONAL PHRASES. to such twaddle. **ADVANCED.** in here.

  ✏ **Teacher's note.** *Here* is usually an adverb but can be a noun meaning *this place*, as it is used in this phrase. If students do not catch this one, it is fine to let it go.

CLAUSES, PHRASES, AND OPENERS.

- MC: **Princess Dorinda answered.** If students include "Awesome," that is fine.
- **ADVANCED.** -ing participial phrase (students do not label): not noticing her father's grimace. This is like a #4 participial phrase, but it comes later in the sentence.

twaddle: trivial, silly talk; drivel

✏ **1. Teacher's note.** Allow these kinds of fragments in the *Fix It!* stories, but use them as an opportunity to discuss when sentence fragments are or are not appropriate. In academic writing, many teachers forbid any fragments; all teachers forbid fragments that leave us expecting more in a sentence.

✏ **2. Teacher's note.** This "speaking verb + comma + quote" concept is worth emphasizing throughout *Fix It!* When older students start merging quotations from sources into their text, it helps to have taught well that commas are needed with quotations only when a speaking verb sets them up. In upper-level academic writing, quotations usually merge into text with no punctuation or sometimes a colon.

- #1 subject opener and MC: **It's** nice enough outside.

  ✏ **Teacher's note.** The subject and verb are *it is*. If students do not catch this, remind them that *it* can function as a subject. Have them find a *be* verb using the verb card list.

  You know is a transitional interrupter rather than a regular main clause, which is why it is set off with commas. Students should not label it.

- #1 subject opener and MC: **I was,** like, too warm in here. Note that *like* is a meaningless interrupter, properly set off with commas.

- **ADVANCED.** #Q (question) and MC: How else **could he respond** to such twaddle?

DAY 2

#2   MC   S   V

¶ beyond the imperial patio, [princess dorinda **meandered** aimlessly, through the stately gardens],

tossing her ball up and down, and catching it repeatedly with slick confidence.

Fixes

meandered: rambled; took a winding course

INDENT ¶ because of a new scene.

CAPITALIZATION. Beyond, Princess Dorinda.

COMMAS AND OTHER PUNCTUATION.

- **#2 prepositional openers.** Ask: What is the rule for commas after #2 openers? Answer: Comma required if five or more words, optional if fewer. *Beyond the imperial patio* has only four words, but since one of the words is long, a pause is reasonable. Let your students decide!

- **Mid-sentence prepositional phrases.** Ask: Do you need a comma before the preposition *through*, and why? Answer: No, mid-sentence prepositional phrases do not take commas. Fix: meandered aimlessly **through the stately gardens**.

- **ADVANCED. Nonessential elements** take commas. Ask: Why is there a comma after *stately gardens*? Answer: To set off the nonessential participial phrase that follows: Dorinda meandered through the gardens, **tossing her ball up and down.** *See* ✏ **1.**

- **Items in a series.** Ask: What items does the second cc *and* join, and how many? Answer: two -ing phrases. Ask: Should there be a comma? Answer: No, this cc joins only two items in a series. Pattern: a and b. Fix: **tossing** her ball up and down **and catching** it. *See* ✏ **2.**

✏ **1. Teacher's note.** This phrase is nonessential because we can remove it without affecting the meaning of the rest of the sentence. Dorinda still meandered through the gardens.

✏ **2. Teacher's note.** Sharp-eyed students may notice that *up and down* follows the same pattern: no comma because *and* joins only two adverbs, not three or more.

Grammar Notations

PREPOSITIONAL PHRASES. Beyond the imperial patio; through the stately gardens; with slick confidence. Guide students to see the pattern in each: preposition + noun (no verb).

CLAUSES, PHRASES, AND OPENERS.

- #2 prepositional phrase opener: Beyond the imperial patio.
- MC: **Princess Dorinda meandered** aimlessly through the stately gardens.
- **ADVANCED.** Nonessential participial (-ing) phrase (students do not label): tossing her ball up and down and catching it repeatedly.

  ✏ **Teacher's note.** If students mark the -ing words as verbs, you could explain that they are verbs only when there is also a subject and helping verb with them. Contrast this: She (subject) was (helping verb) tossing (verb) her ball and catching (verb) it.

DAY 3

#2   MC   S   V   *#3*   MC S   V

at the corner of the well, however, [a most regrettable event **transpired**], carelessly [she tossed

                             MC   S V   *#1* MC   S   *sank*

her golden ball ~~to two~~ too high], and [down it fell with a splash]. [the heavy orb ~~sinked~~ to the bottom

of the well].

Fixes

transpired: took place; occurred

CAPITALIZATION. At, Carelessly, The.

USAGE AND SPELLING. 1) Use *too,* meaning excessively: **too** high. 2) *Sank* (or, alternatively, *sunk*) is the past tense of *to sink.*

COMMAS AND OTHER PUNCTUATION.

- **Long #2 prepositional openers** take commas. Fix: **At the corner of the well, however,** a most regrettable event transpired. If students put a comma after the first prepositional phrase (*At the corner*), remind them to save the comma for the end of all phrase openers when there is more than one.

- **Transitional words** take commas. Fix: At the corner of the well, **however,** a most regrettable event transpired.

- **Run-on sentence** (comma splice MC, MC, which is always wrong). Ask: Where do you see two main clauses joined with just a comma? Answer: between *transpired* and *carelessly.* Fix, with main clauses simplified: *A most regrettable event transpired.* **Carelessly** *she tossed her golden ball too high.*

- **#3 -ly adverb opener.** Ask: Do you need a comma after the #3 -ly adverb opener? Answer: It is optional but not necessary because we do not need a pause: **Carelessly** she tossed her golden ball too high. *See* ✏ **1.**

- **MC, cc MC.** Ask: Find *and;* then tell whether or not it needs a comma before it and why. Answer: It does because it joins two main clauses. Rule: MC, cc MC. Fix, with MCs italicized: *She tossed her golden ball too high,* **and** *down it fell with a splash.*

✏ **1. Teacher's note.** The comma is not needed because *carelessly* modifies the verb (*she carelessly tossed*), and commas are usually unneeded then.

Grammar Notations

PREPOSITIONAL PHRASES. At the corner; of the well; with a splash; to the bottom; of the well. Guide students to see the pattern in each: preposition + noun (no verb). *See* ✏ **2.**

CLAUSES, PHRASES, AND OPENERS.

- #2 prepositional phrase opener: At the corner of the well.
- MC: a most regrettable **event transpired.**
- #3 -ly adverb opener: Carelessly.
- MC: **she tossed** her golden ball too high.
- MC: down **it fell** with a splash.
- #1 subject opener and MC: The heavy **orb sank** to the bottom of the well.

✏ **2. Teacher's note.** *Down* is not a preposition but an adverb in *down it fell.* It modifies *fell,* and only adverbs modify verbs. Also, it does not have an object so does not fit the prepositional phrase pattern. *It* is the subject of the sentence (*it fell*) and cannot do double duty as an object.

DAY 4

#6 MC S V   *#1 MC S V*   ¶ *MC*

[tears flowed **copiously**], [huge drops splashed her golden dress]. "[oh, my golden baaall!"

S V #5 AC S V V MC S V V

dorinda wailed]. "(if only i could have my ball back), [i would bestow a handsome reward

on my **benefactor**]!"

Explain that *ball* is deliberately misspelled to mimic Dorinda's speech, emphasizing her overreaction.

copiously: abundantly; plentifully

benefactor: someone who confers a favor

Fixes

CAPITALIZATION. Tears, Huge, Oh, Dorinda, If, I, I.

INDENT ¶ in the second part because of a new speaker.

COMMAS AND OTHER PUNCTUATION.

- **Run-on sentence** (comma splice MC, MC, which is always wrong). Ask: Where is the comma splice? Answer: the comma between *copiously* and *huge*. Discuss different solutions.
  - MC, cc MC: Tears flowed copiously, and huge drops splashed her golden dress.
  - MC; MC: Tears flowed copiously; huge drops splashed her golden dress.
  - MC. MC: Tears flowed copiously. Huge drops splashed her golden dress.

  Ask: Which solution works best? Answer: All three options are fine, but choice *c* is nice because a vss can be more powerful than two main clauses in one sentence.

- **Run-on sentence** (fused sentence MC MC, which is always wrong). Look at the quoted parts alone to determine punctuation. Ask: Does "Oh, my golden baaall" stand alone as a thought even though it is a sentence fragment, or does it connect to the second quote?

  Answer: It stands alone; Dorinda's next words start a new thought and have an MC later in the sentence. Since *Dorinda wailed* sets up the first quote, add a period after *wailed* to correct this fused sentence. Fix: … Dorinda wailed. "If only I could have my ball back, I would bestow a handsome reward on my benefactor."

- **Quotation marks and end mark.** "Oh, my golden baaall!" Dorinda wailed. "If … benefactor!" Students may use either a period or an exclamation after *benefactor*, but it needs to go inside the closing quotes. Dorinda is an exclamatory kind of girl, so she can get away with lots of exclamation marks.

- **Introductory interjections.** Use commas after introductory interjections: **Oh,** my golden ball.

- **#5 clausal openers** take commas. Rule: AC, MC. Fix: **If only I could have my ball back,** I would bestow.

Grammar Notations

PREPOSITIONAL PHRASES. on my benefactor.

CLAUSES, PHRASES, AND OPENERS.

- #6 vss and MC: **Tears flowed** copiously.
- #1 subject opener and MC: Huge **drops splashed** her golden dress.
- MC: "Oh, my golden baaall!" **Dorinda wailed.** *See* ✏ **1**.

✏ **1. Teacher's note.** The subject and verb in the narrative (*Dorinda wailed*) set up the spoken words before them, so the whole MC includes her phrase. It is fine to mark just "Dorinda wailed" as the main clause, however.

- #5 clausal opener and AC: If only **I could have** my ball back.
- MC: **I would bestow** a handsome reward on my benefactor.

Style

If desired, have students identify the strongest of the vocabulary dress-ups from this week. Discuss their answers. Suggestions:

- **Strong verbs.** meandered, transpired, splashed, wailed, bestow.
- **Quality adjectives.** stately, slick, regrettable, handsome. *See* ✐ **2** *and* **3**.
- **-ly adverbs.** aimlessly, repeatedly, copiously. *See* ✐ **3**.

✐ **2. Teacher's note.** Sometimes words are strong in one context but not in another. A handsome man is clichéd, but a handsome reward is strong for a student this age.

✐ **3. Teacher's note.** *Stately* is an imposter -ly. It modifies a noun (*gardens*) so has to be an adjective, not an adverb.

STUDENT REWRITE

"Awesome," Princess Dorinda answered, not noticing her father's grimace. "It's nice enough outside, you know. I was, like, too warm in here."

"Precisely." How else could he respond to such twaddle?

Beyond the imperial patio, Princess Dorinda meandered aimlessly through the stately gardens, tossing her ball up and down and catching it repeatedly with slick confidence. At the corner of the well, however, a most regrettable event transpired. Carelessly she tossed her golden ball too high, and down it fell with a splash. The heavy orb sank to the bottom of the well. Tears flowed copiously. Huge drops splashed her golden dress.

"Oh, my golden baaall!" Dorinda wailed. "If only I could have my ball back, I would bestow a handsome reward on my benefactor!"

Week 8

Commas with NDAs, Hyphens

LEARN IT

Commas with NDAs

Commas are needed to set off nouns of direct address (NDAs). NDAs are usually names where someone is directly addressed by name or title. They can show up anywhere in the sentence (beginning, middle, end). Examples:

- Dorinda, please be more careful when you traipse through the hall.

- If you would permit me, madam, I should be honored to rescue your plaything.

- How is it you can talk, Mr. Frog?

Use the grammar card if needed to help you with NDAs.

Hyphens

Hyphens are often used in compound words and many numbers. Be sure to include them as needed. Here are the rules:

- Use hyphens in some compound nouns, such as lady-in-waiting. Consult a dictionary to check whether the compound noun should be written as one word (marksman), two words (apple tree), or a hyphenated word.

- Use hyphens with compound adjectives in front of a noun but usually not after a noun: jewel-encrusted crown, nineteenth-century author, well-attired people. Her crown was jewel encrusted. He lived in the nineteenth century. The people were well attired.

- Use hyphens with compound numbers from twenty-one to ninety-nine and with spelled out fractions like one-fourth.

- Use hyphens in phone numbers: 555-1212.

Teacher's note. Students should continue to underline subjects and verbs of all clauses and label prepositional phrases, main clauses, dependent clauses, and sentence openers.

DAY 1

#5 AC   S   V   V   MC S   V   V

¶ " (if you would permit me), madam, [i should be honored to ~~two/too~~ rescue your plaything], "

MC   S   V   ¶ #1   S   V   AC   S   V
                                  MC   , MC
[a **throaty** voice offered]. ~~and~~ [dorindas tears dried instantly], (as she looked around for the person

belonging to ~~two/too~~ the voice).

Fixes

INDENT both ¶s: 1) new speaker; 2) new topic, pulling out of the frog's speech.

CAPITALIZATION. If, I, Dorinda's. *See* ✎.

HOMOPHONES. to rescue; belonging **to** the voice.

COORDINATING CONJUNCTIONS. Avoid starting sentences with cc's. Not "*And* Dorinda's tears dried," which sounds awkward. Fix: **Dorinda's** tears dried.

> ✎ **Teacher's note.** cc's connect together two or more items. When they start a sentence, the effect can be abrupt since they are not connecting anything. Avoid this practice, especially in academic writing. The exception is in casual dialogue, which often begins with cc's like *and* or *but*.

COMMAS AND OTHER PUNCTUATION.

- **#5 clausal openers** and **NDAs** take commas. Ask students how they punctuated *madam* and why. Answer: commas on both sides of *madam* because it is a noun of direct address. The comma after it is also needed to end the #5 clausal opener. Fix: **If you would permit me, madam,** I should be honored.

- **Quotations.** Fix: "I should be honored to rescue your plaything," a throaty voice offered. Rules: 1) Use commas when a speaking verb (*offered*) sets up a quote. 2) Place periods and commas inside closing quotation marks.

- **Apostrophes** for possession. Fix: **Dorinda's** tears.

- **Mid-sentence adverb clauses.** Ask: Did you keep the comma before *as*, and why? Answer: No comma with mid-sentence adverb clauses (MC AC). Fix: Dorinda's tears dried instantly **as she looked around.**

Grammar Notations

PREPOSITIONAL PHRASES. for the person; to the voice.

> ✎ **Teacher's note.** *Around* is an adverb here. It is not followed by a noun, so it does not start a prepositional phrase. You can also tell because *around for the person* does not make sense. The words in prepositional phrases should make sense as a phrase by themselves.

CLAUSES, PHRASES, AND OPENERS.

- #5 clausal opener and AC: If **you would permit** me.
- MC: **I should be** honored to rescue your plaything. *See* ♡ **1.**
- MC: a throaty **voice offered.** Students may not recognize that *voice* is the subject. Remind them that articles (*a*) always introduce a noun. Ask what noun comes after *a* that is doing the offering. *Voice* is the only possibility since *throaty* cannot offer!
- #1 subject opener and MC: Dorinda's **tears dried** instantly.
- AC (adverb clause): as **she looked** around for the person belonging to the voice. *See* ♡ **2.**

throaty: husky; hoarse; guttural

✎ **Teacher's note.** *Sir* and *ma'am* (madam) are the only titles not capitalized when used as NDAs without a name. If students capitalize them, it is fine!

♡ **1. Grammar lovers.** Grammarians will debate whether to treat *honored* as a predicate adjective or part of the verb, but it is too advanced to teach and not important for punctuation or grammar. *Honored* is treated as a predicate adjective here because it means the honored frog more than the fact that someone is actively honoring him.

♡ **2. Grammar lovers.** *Belonging* is not a verb but a participle. It functions as an adjective describing *person*. This is a rare case where the participial phrase is essential and does not take a comma because it restricts the person to the one belonging to the voice. This is also an invisible *who*: the person who was belonging to the voice.

DAY 2

¶ a little flustered (when she ~~cited~~/sighted ~~/sited~~ no one), [dorinda inquired], "[pray tell]: [who

has **tendered** such a thoughtful offer], groomed in courtly speech, [she could talk like a princess],

(when convenient).

Fixes

INDENT ¶ because of a new speaker. The second sentence can stay in the same paragraph because it directly relates back to the words Dorinda just spoke.

CAPITALIZATION. A, Dorinda, Pray (capitalize the first word of a quoted sentence), Groomed.

> Lowercase: **princess**. It is not specifying a particular princess so is a common noun, not a proper noun.

HOMOPHONES AND USAGE. *Cited* means quoted a passage; *sited* means located; *sighted* means caught sight of. Fix: When she **sighted** no one.

COMMAS AND OTHER PUNCTUATION. As needed, review the Grammar Notations before addressing punctuation. Remember, the points marked *advanced* are for your information and can be discussed if your students ask or if you wish to cover that point of grammar for an older or stronger student.

- **ADVANCED. Invisible #4 -ing openers** take commas—twice! The original is correct: 1) **A little flustered when she sighted no one,** Dorinda inquired. 2) **Groomed in courtly speech,** Dorinda could talk.

  > ✎ **Teacher's note.** *Being* is implied before both openers. The first one also has an adverb clause in the opener, so save the comma for the end of both openers (after *no one*).

- **Quotation.** Fix: Dorinda inquired, "Pray tell: who has tendered such a thoughtful offer?" Rules: 1) Comma because of speaking verb (*inquired*) + comma + direct quote. 2) Quotations around direct quotes. 3) Question mark before close quotes since she is asking a question.

- **ADVANCED. Colons** follow main clauses and set up an example, list, or explanation. The colon after *Pray tell* is correct. It is a handy punctuation mark that effectively means "See what follows."

- **Mid-sentence adverb clauses.** Ask: Should there be a comma before the second *when* clause? Answer: No comma before adverb clause dress-ups. Rule: MC AC. Fix: she could talk like a princess **when convenient**.

  > ✎ **Teacher's note.** If students ask why this clause has no S-V pair, explain that it is implied: *when it was convenient*.

tendered: offered formally

Pray is an interjection here, not a verb, an archaic (no longer used) word meaning *please* or *I beg you*. *Pray tell* is an idiom meaning *Please tell me*.

Grammar Notations

PREPOSITIONAL PHRASES. in courtly speech, like a princess. As needed, guide students to see the pattern in each prepositional phrase: preposition + noun (no verb).

CLAUSES, PHRASES, AND OPENERS.

- **ADVANCED. Invisible #4 participial opener:** A little flustered.

  - ✏ **Teacher's note.** This is an invisible #4, with *being* implied: *Being a little flustered*. Do not expect students to catch this on their own; mention it only if they are ready. They do not need to label Invisible #4s yet.

- AC (adverb clause): when **she sighted** no one. *See* ♡ **1.**
- MC: **Dorinda inquired.**
- MC: Pray **tell.** Ask: What is the subject of *tell*? Answer: An implied *you.*

  - ✏ **Teacher's note.** This is in the imperative mood, used for requests or commands where *you* is understood.

- MC: **who has tendered** such a thoughtful offer? Dorinda is asking a question, so this is a question instead of a *who-which* adjective clause.
- **ADVANCED.** Invisible #4 participial opener with *being* implied: Groomed in courtly speech.
- MC: **she could talk** like a princess.
- AC (adverb clause): when convenient. *See* ♡ **2.**

♡ **1. Grammar lovers.** This *when* clause is an adverb clause. Since it does not follow a noun, it cannot be an adjective clause.

♡ **2. Grammar lovers.** This second *when* clause is another adverb clause. It follows a noun but does not describe that noun (she is not a "when-convenient princess"), so it is an adverb and not an adjective clause.

DAY 3

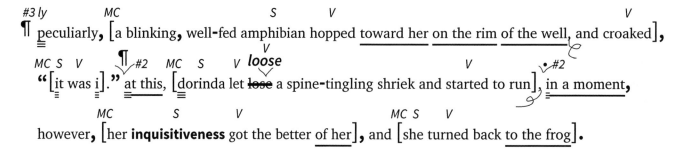

Fixes

INDENT ¶s: 1) new topic, the frog and his answer; 2) new topic pulling out of the frog's speech and turning to Dorinda's reaction.

CAPITALIZATION. Peculiarly, It (first word of quoted sentence), I, At, Dorinda, In.

SPELLING. Dorinda let **loose** (rhyming with *moose*), not *lose* (rhyming with *ooze*). *Let loose* is a verb phrase meaning to free from bonds or restraint.

HYPHENS. Use a hyphen to join words that function as a single adjective before a noun. Fix: **well-fed** amphibian, **spine-tingling** shriek.

COMMAS AND OTHER PUNCTUATION.

- **#3 -ly adverb openers.** Ask: Do you want a pause after *Peculiarly*? Answer: Yes, so add a comma.

  ADVANCED. This -ly adverb modifies the whole idea, not the verb alone (which would mean he hopped in a peculiar way). Modifying the whole sentence, *peculiarly* means it was peculiar that this frog hopped toward her and spoke.

- **Adjectives before a noun.** Ask: Do we need a comma between *blinking* and *well-fed*? To determine, apply the two tests. Do *well-fed, blinking amphibian* and *blinking and well-fed amphibian* work? Yes, so these are coordinate adjectives and need a comma.

  ✐ **Teacher's note.** Check that students do not add a comma between the last adjective and noun.

- **Items in a series.** Have students identify what specific words the three *and*'s join (the same parts of speech, phrases, or clauses).

  Guide them to use the rules for punctuating with cc's to determine whether or not commas are needed before each one. The words they join are bolded below and an explanation for the punctuation follows.

  Fix: **hopped** toward her on the rim of the well *and* **croaked**: no comma for a compound verb (two verbs with the same subject). Pattern: MC cc 2nd verb.

  The original is correct: Dorinda **let loose** a spine-tingling shriek *and* **started** to run: no comma for a compound verb: MC cc 2nd verb.

  Fix: **her inquisitiveness got the better of her,** *and* **she turned back**: comma because the cc joins two main clauses. A comma or a cc by itself is not strong enough to hold main clauses together. Rule: MC, cc MC.

- **Quotation.** … *and* **croaked,** "It was I." Rules: 1) Quotation marks enclose his words. 2) Add a comma after the speaking verb *croaked* to set up the quotation. 3) Put the period inside the closing quotations. *See* ♡.

- **ADVANCED. Short #2 prepositional openers** (under five words) do not need commas unless we need a pause. The original is correct: **At this,** Dorinda let loose. We need a pause because we might misread this as an adjective otherwise (this something) and get confused.

inquisitiveness: a state of active curiosity

♡ **Grammar lovers.** In "It was I," *I* is correct because it is a subject complement following a linking verb, which takes the subject pronoun *I*, not the object pronoun *me*. This is too advanced for this level.

- **Run-on sentence** (comma splice MC, MC). Ask: Where do we have two main clauses joined with only a comma? Answer: between *to run* and *in a moment*. Fix, with the MCs simplified and italicized for clarity: *Dorinda let loose a shriek and started to run. In a moment her inquisitiveness got the better of her.*
- **Transitional words** take commas. Fix: In a moment, **however,** her inquisitiveness.

Grammar Notations

PREPOSITIONAL PHRASES. toward her, on the rim, of the well, At this, In a moment, of her, to the frog.

✏ **Teacher's note.** In "turned back to the frog," *back* is an adverb modifying *turned*.

CLAUSES, PHRASES, AND OPENERS.

- #3 -ly adverb opener: Peculiarly.
- MC: a blinking, well-fed **amphibian hopped** toward her on the rim of the well and **croaked**.
- MC: **It was** I.
- #2 prepositional phrase opener: At this.
- MC: **Dorinda let loose** a spine-tingling shriek and **started** to run.
- #2 prepositional phrase opener: In a moment.
- MC: her **inquisitiveness got** the better of her.
- MC: **she turned** back to the frog.

DAY 4

MC   V S DC S   V   V   ¶/#1 MC S V   MC S V V

¶ " [how is it] (you can talk), mr. frog ?" " [its/it's a dull story], but maybe [i'll tell it to you one day],

#2   MC V S   V

for the present, [would you like me to **salvage** your ball] ?"

Fixes

salvage: to save from loss

INDENT ¶s because of new speakers.

CAPITALIZATION AND ABBREVIATIONS. How, Mr. Frog, It's, I'll, For. Check for a period after the abbreviation *Mr.*

HOMOPHONES. Use the contraction: **It's** (it is) a dull story.

COMMAS AND OTHER PUNCTUATION.

- **Quotations.** Fix: "How … frog?" and "It's … ball?" Rules: 1) Enclose speech in quotations. 2) End questions with question marks inside the closing quotations.
- **NDAs.** Ask: What is *Mr. Frog* and how is it used in the sentence? Answer: NDA (noun of direct address). What punctuation do NDAs need? Answer: comma. "How is it you can talk, **Mr. Frog**?"
- **MC, cc MC.** Does there need to be a comma before the cc *but,* and why? Yes, compound sentences take commas. Fix: *It's a dull story,* **but** *maybe I'll tell it to you.*
- **ADVANCED. Transitional #2 prepositional openers.** When short #2s function as transitions, they need a comma. Try reading the sentence with and without a pause to help advanced students hear the difference. The original is correct: **For the present,** would you like me to salvage your ball?
- **Run-on sentence** (comma splice MC, MC). Ask students to find the run-on. Remind them that dependent clauses and prepositional phrases can come between two clauses, but it is a run-on if there is nothing stronger than a comma somewhere between them. This is a comma splice after *one day.*

  Fix, with MCs italicized: "maybe *I'll tell it to you one day.* For the present, *would you like me to salvage your ball?*"

Grammar Notations

PREPOSITIONAL PHRASES. to you; For the present.

CLAUSES, PHRASES, AND OPENERS.

- **ADVANCED.** #Q (question) and MC: How **is it**.
- **ADVANCED.** DC: **you can talk.** This is a dependent clause with the relative pronoun *that* implied.
- #1 subject opener and MC: **It's** a dull story. S-V: It is.
- MC: **I'll tell** it to you one day. S-V: I will tell.
- #2 prepositional phrase opener: For the present.
- MC: **would you like** me to salvage your ball? *See* ✎.

✎ **Teacher's note.**
If students mark *salvage* as a verb, just explain that infinitives (*to* + the verb) do not function as verbs.

Style

If desired, have students identify the strongest of the vocabulary dress-ups from this week. Discuss their answers. Suggestions:

- **Strong verbs.** permit, honored, inquired, tendered, salvage (verbal). Verbals are allowed at this level because the goal is recognizing strong vocabulary.
- **Quality adjectives.** throaty, flustered, convenient, spine-tingling.
- **-ly adverbs.** instantly.

STUDENT REWRITE

"If you would permit me, madam, I should be honored to rescue your plaything," a throaty voice offered.

Dorinda's tears dried instantly as she looked around for the person belonging to the voice.

A little flustered when she sighted no one, Dorinda inquired, "Pray tell: who has tendered such a thoughtful offer?" Groomed in courtly speech, she could talk like a princess when convenient.

Peculiarly, a blinking, well-fed amphibian hopped toward her on the rim of the well and croaked, "It was I."

At this, Dorinda let loose a spine-tingling shriek and started to run. In a moment, however, her inquisitiveness got the better of her, and she turned back to the frog.

"How is it you can talk, Mr. Frog?"

"It's a dull story, but maybe I'll tell it to you one day. For the present, would you like me to salvage your ball?"

Week 9

Affect versus *Effect*

LEARN IT

The words *affect* and *effect* are commonly misused. However, there are some tricks to tell which one is right for a sentence. Use the grammar card for future reference.

1. Decide if the word is being used as a noun or a verb. If a noun (test: the _____), it is probably *effect*, which indicates the effect of something or the result of a change.

    Years of indulgence had the obvious **effect** of spoiling Dorinda.

2. If the word is a verb, it is likely *affect*, which means to influence, act on, or produce a change in something.

    Maybe Dorinda was too self-centered for others to **affect** her deeply.

✎ **Teacher's note.** In psychology, *affect* can be a noun referring to a person's emotional state, but it is rarely used outside that field so there is no need to bring it up at this level.

✎ **Teacher's note.** *Effect* is occasionally a verb meaning to bring about or accomplish something: The king finally *effected* a change in Dorinda when he blocked her phone from the castle's wireless.

◆ **Listen.** To help you keep grammar in perspective, listen to Andrew Pudewa's talk "But, But, But … What About Grammar?" Instructions to download the mp3 can be found on the blue page in the front of this book.

Page 20, *Fix It! Grammar: Frog Prince, or Just Deserts*, **Student Book 3**

DAY 1

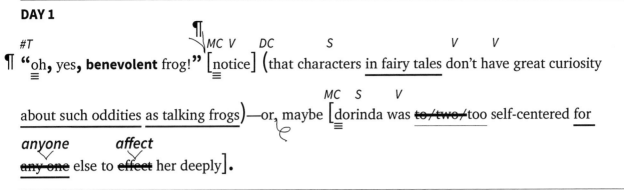

¶ "oh, yes, **benevolent** frog!" [notice] (that characters in fairy tales don't have great curiosity about such oddities as talking frogs)—or, maybe [dorinda was ~~to two~~ too self-centered for ~~any one~~ anyone else to ~~effect~~ affect her deeply].

Fixes

INDENT both ¶s: 1) new speaker; 2) change in topic.

CAPITALIZATION. Oh, Notice, Dorinda.

HOMOPHONES AND USAGE.

- Use *too* to mean excessively: Dorinda was **too** self-centered.
- **Anyone** is one word.
- Use the verb *to affect* instead of the noun *effect*: for anyone else to **affect** her deeply.

COMMAS AND OTHER PUNCTUATION. Ask questions to guide students to find for themselves the ones they miss.

- **Quotations.** Enclose speech in quotes and put the exclamation inside the quotation: "Oh … frog!"
- **Interjections and transitions** take commas. Fix: **Oh, yes,** benevolent frog. The comma after *yes* is also there to set off the NDA (*benevolent frog*).
- **Em dash.** Ask: Is this em dash used 1) to draw attention, or 2) to signal a switch in thought? Answer: 2) a switch in thought. See ✏ **1.**
- **Coordinating conjunctions** do not take commas after them. Fix: **or maybe** Dorinda was too self-centered.

Grammar Notations

PREPOSITIONAL PHRASES. in fairy tales, about such oddities, as talking frogs, for anyone. *See* ✏ **2.**

Students may be confused by *as*, which often is a subordinating conjunction (one of the www words) but can be a preposition: *as* (preposition) + *talking* (adjective) + *frogs* (noun). *Talking* is an adjective in this phrase since it describes a noun, *frogs*.

CLAUSES, PHRASES, AND OPENERS.

- #T transitional opener: Oh, yes.
- **ADVANCED.** #1 subject opener and MC: **Notice.** If students overlook this, mention that it is instruction (imperative mood) with the subject, *you* (the reader), understood.
- DC: that **characters** in fairy tales **don't have** great curiosity about such oddities as talking frogs. *See* ♡.
- MC: **Dorinda was** too self-centered for anyone else to affect her deeply.

benevolent: charitable; kindly

✏ **1. Teacher's note.** Remind students that em dashes are the longest dash mark, formed by typing two hyphens or typing option-shift-hyphen. A single hyphen is used to join compound words.

✏ **2. Teacher's note.** As needed, continue to guide students to see the pattern: preposition + noun (no verb). These phrases begin with a preposition, end with a noun, and have no verb. Other words may come between the preposition and its object (the noun), but never a verb.

♡ **Grammar lovers.** This is a noun clause following a verb (*notice*) and starting with the relative pronoun *that*.

DAY 2

¶ MCS V   V   MC   S   V   \   #1 MC   S   V   V
¶ "[i'll gladly do so]—but with one **stipulation**," [the frog responded]. "anything! [my dad will kill me],
         V
         AC S *lose*   DC S   V
(if i ~~loose~~ that ball), (which cost him a royal fortune), you know."

stipulation: condition; demand

Fixes

INDENT both ¶s because of new speakers.

CAPITALIZATION. I'll, Anything, My, I.

> Lowercase: *My dad*. Capitalize family relations when used as a substitute for a name but not otherwise. Contrast this sentence using *Dad* in place of his name: You know **Dad** will kill me if I lose that ball.

SPELLING. I **lose** that ball. To *lose* something is to misplace it or no longer have it. To *loose* something is to free it from something that binds it.

COMMAS AND OTHER PUNCTUATION.

- **Em dash.** Ask: Is this long em dash used for 1) emphasis, or 2) a switch in thought? Answer: 1) to emphasize that he has one stipulation.

- **Quotations.** Fixes: "I'll … stipulation," the frog responded. ¶ "Anything … you know." Rules: 1) Enclose speech in quotes. 2) Add a comma after *stipulation*. Rule: quotation + comma + speaking verb (*responded*). 3) Commas and periods go inside closing quotations.

- **Mid-sentence adverb clauses.** Ask: Is the comma before the *if* clause correct, and why? Answer: No, adverb clause dress-ups do not take commas. Pattern: MC AC. Fix: My dad will kill me **if I lose that ball**.

- **ADVANCED. Essential elements.** Ask: Do *who-which* clauses always take commas? Answer: No, only when they are nonessential. This *which* clause is not needed to make sense of the main clause (if we remove it, Dorinda's dad will still kill her if she loses the ball) but only adds information (the ball was expensive). Since it is nonessential, it should be set off with commas. The original is correct: that ball, **which cost him a royal fortune**. *See* ✎.

- **Interrupters** take commas. Fix: which cost him a royal fortune, **you know**.

✎ **Teacher's note.** Remember not to push advanced concepts unless students are ready. This essential and nonessential concept usually takes repeated thinking through the logic before students catch on, even older students. This book introduces it to them in the second half.

Grammar Notations

PREPOSITIONAL PHRASES. with one stipulation.

CLAUSES, PHRASES, AND OPENERS.

- #1 subject opener and MC: **I'll** gladly **do** so. Ask: What is the helping verb? Answer: *will*, which helps out *do*.

- MC: the **frog responded**.

- **ADVANCED.** Anything!

  This is not a vss because it is not a sentence. Her answer works because it does not leave us hanging but should not be labeled because it is a sentence fragment.

- #1 subject opener and MC: My **dad will kill** me.

- AC (adverb clause): if **I lose** that ball.

- DC (*who-which* clause): **which cost** him a royal fortune.

  If students have trouble identifying the subject, tell them that the subject of a *who-which* clause is usually *who* or *which*. No need to label the interrupter *you know*.

DAY 3

#T MCS V   V   MC S V   V DCS V   V
¶ "<u>well</u>, [i don't know anything <u>of the sort</u>], but [i do think] (i can retrieve it <u>with tolerable **dexterity**</u>).

#1 MC   V   S MC S V   V   AC   S   V   V   V
[here are my terms]: [i'll bring you the ball], (if you'll treat me <u>at your table</u> <u>in the castle</u>, let me dine

                                          V
from <u>your own plate</u>, and allow me to dwell one night <u>in the palace</u>)."

Fixes

dexterity: skill, especially with one's hands

INDENT ¶ because of a new speaker.

CAPITALIZATION. Well, I, I, I, Here, I'll.

COMMAS AND OTHER PUNCTUATION. *See* ✎.

- **Quotations.** Enclose speech with quotations; the period goes inside closing quotes: "Well … palace."
- **Introductory transitions** take commas. Fix: **Well,** I don't know.
- **MC, cc MC.** Compound sentence needs a comma before the coordinating conjunction: Ask students to find the cc; ask them what the two MCs are; ask them where the comma goes. Fix, with MCs italicized: *I don't know anything of the sort,* **but** *I do think I can retrieve it.*
- **ADVANCED. Colon.** The original is correct: **Here are my terms:** I'll bring you the ball. Colons introduce a list or explanation but only when they follow a main clause.
- **Mid-sentence adverb clauses** do not take commas. Rule: MC AC. Fix: I'll bring you the ball **if you'll treat me.**

  If students miss this, ask them to locate the www word. Ask them how the www dress-up should be punctuated. Remind them of the rule if needed.
- **Items in a series.** Use commas with three or more items in a series: a, b, and c. Remind students: The items must be the same part of speech or construction. Ask: What part of speech are the items in this series? Answer: verb phrases, all using the same subject (*you*) and helping verb (*will*).

  Fix: if you'll **treat** me at your table in the castle, **let** me dine from your own plate, **and allow** me to dwell one night in the palace.

✎ **Teacher's note.** Always ask questions to guide students to figure out solutions. If they do not know a rule, you can tell them the rule and then challenge them to find an example in the passage.

Grammar Notations

PREPOSITIONAL PHRASES. of the sort; with tolerable dexterity; at your table; in the castle; from your own plate; in the palace. If needed, guide students to see the pattern in each: preposition + noun (no verb).

CLAUSES, PHRASES, AND OPENERS.

- #T: Well.
- MC: I **don't know** anything of the sort. The *n't* part of *don't* means *not* and is an adverb.
- MC: I **do think.**
- **ADVANCED.** DC: I **can retrieve** it with tolerable dexterity. This is a noun clause with an invisible *that*, not a main clause: I do think *that* I can retrieve it.

- #1 subject opener and MC: Here **are** my **terms**. Check that students do not mark *here* as the subject. To find the subject and verb, it may help them to hear the sentence revised: *My terms are here.*
- MC: **I'll bring** you the ball. Ask: What is the helping verb? Answer: *will*, which helps out *bring*. Do not mark this as a #1 opener because it does not begin a sentence.
- AC (adverb clause): if **you'll treat** me at your table in the castle, **let** me dine from your own plate, and **allow** me to dwell one night in the palace. Check that students marked all three verbs. Show them the subject and helping verb that helps out all three: you will treat, *you will* let, *you will* allow.

DAY 4

$$V$$
#T   MC   S   *responded*   ¶ #2

¶ "well, like, sure," [dorinda ~~responds~~ hastily], perhaps a little ~~to / two /~~ too **curtly**. with that,

MC   S   *hopped*   *disappeared*

[the frog ~~hops~~ back into the water, ~~disappears~~ for a few moments, and then ~~returns~~], panting

AC   S   V   V   V

(as only frogs can pant). ~~with the ball~~   *returned with the ball*

Fixes

INDENT both ¶s because of a new speaker and a new topic.

CAPITALIZATION. Well, Dorinda, With.

VERB TENSE. Keep using past tense. Dorinda **responded**; the frog **hopped** … **disappeared** … **returned**.

HOMOPHONES. Use *too*, meaning excessively: **too** curtly.

    ADVANCED. This is a case where an adverb (*too*) modifies another adverb (*curtly*).

MISPLACED PREPOSITIONAL PHRASE. Prepositional phrases should come immediately after what they describe. When they are misplaced, they convey something different from what is intended. In this case, *with the ball* should follow *returned*, not *pant*. He is not panting with the ball but returning with it! Fix: the frog … **returned with the ball.**

COMMAS AND OTHER PUNCTUATION.

- **Quotations.** Fix: "Well, like, sure," Dorinda responded. Rules: 1) Enclose speech in quotations. 2) Add a comma after *sure* inside closing quotes because a speaking verb sets up the quote.
- **Interjections** and interrupters (even meaningless ones like *like*) take commas. Fix: **Well, like, sure.**
- **ADVANCED. Nonessential elements** take commas. The original is correct: Dorinda responded hastily, **perhaps a little too curtly.** This phrase is nonessential because it does not change the fact that she responded hastily; it just adds information.
- **Items in a series.** Three or more items take commas: a, b, and c. Fix: the frog **hopped** back into the water, **disappeared** for a few moments, and then **returned**. *See ✏ 1.*
- **ADVANCED. Nonessential elements** take commas. If we remove the phrase *panting as only frogs can pant* from the sentence, it does not alter the meaning of the rest of the sentence (the frog still hops, disappears, and returns), so it is nonessential. *See ♡.*

curtly: briefly, to the point of rudeness

✏ 1. Teacher's note. The last comma before *and* is known as the Oxford comma. It is never wrong to include it and often wrong to omit it, so include it always.

♡ Grammar lovers. Calling this a phrase may confuse some sharp students because there is a subject and verb in it, but these belong to the adverb clause that starts with *as* (*as only frogs can pant*) and that is inside the phrase.

Grammar Notations

PREPOSITIONAL PHRASES. With that; into the water; for a few moments; with the ball. Guide students to see the pattern: preposition + noun (no verb).

CLAUSES, PHRASES, AND OPENERS.

- #T: Well, like, sure.
- MC: **Dorinda responded** hastily.
- #2 prepositional phrase opener: With that.
- MC: the **frog hopped** back into the water, **disappeared** for a few moments, and then **returned** with the ball. Check that students marked all three verbs, which go with the same subject, *frog*.
- AC (adverb clause): as only **frogs can pant**. Ask: Why is this an adverb clause and not a prepositional phrase since *as* can start either? Answer: There is a S-V pair, so it can only be a clause, not a phrase.

Style

If desired, have students identify the strongest of the vocabulary dress-ups this week. Discuss their answers. Suggestions:

- **Strong verbs.** No particularly strong verbs this week.
- **Quality adjectives.** benevolent, self-centered (*see* ✎ **2**), tolerable.
- **-ly adverbs.** deeply, hastily, curtly.

✎ **2. Teacher's note.** If students do not realize that *self-centered* is an adjective (*Dorinda was too self-centered*), you could explain that sometimes adjectives come after linking verbs instead of before the noun.

STUDENT REWRITE

"Oh, yes, benevolent frog!"

Notice that characters in fairy tales don't have great curiosity about such oddities as talking frogs—or maybe Dorinda was too self-centered for anyone else to affect her deeply.

"I'll gladly do so—but with one stipulation," the frog responded.

"Anything! My dad will kill me if I lose that ball, which cost him a royal fortune, you know."

"Well, I don't know anything of the sort, but I do think I can retrieve it with tolerable dexterity. Here are my terms: I'll bring you the ball if you'll treat me at your table in the castle, let me dine from your own plate, and allow me to dwell one night in the palace."

"Well, like, sure," Dorinda responded hastily, perhaps a little too curtly.

With that, the frog hopped back into the water, disappeared for a few moments, and then returned with the ball, panting as only frogs can pant.

Week 10

Remember, you do not need to cover all these notations with your student. Limit the teaching to fifteen minutes, knowing that you will review the concepts many times. Keep these lessons light and fun.

Different Ways to Fix Run-On Sentences

LEARN IT

You have had some practice finding and correcting run-on sentences. They can come in the form of a comma splice (MC, MC) or a fused sentence (MC MC). Both patterns are wrong and need something stronger than a comma to fix them.

There are four common ways to fix run-on sentences, which are listed on the back of the Stop Run-on Sentences! grammar card. Although simply adding a period between the sentences is usually the easiest fix, it is not always the best.

Think about how we can fix this fused sentence:

Dorinda glumly peered into the well the ball was nowhere in sight.

- **Insert a period.** This is the simplest way to fix a run-on.

  Dorinda glumly peered into the well. **T**he ball was nowhere in sight.

- **Use a semicolon.** If the two clauses are close in construction and meaning, you can use a semicolon (;). Think of a semicolon as a soft period, but use it sparingly.

  Dorinda glumly peered into the well**;** the ball was nowhere in sight.

- **MC, cc MC.** Combine the sentences with a comma plus a coordinating conjunction. Remember that the comma without a cc is a comma splice; the cc without a comma is a comma error.

  Dorinda glumly peered into the well**, but** the ball was nowhere in sight.

- **Use a www word.** Make one of the clauses dependent by starting it with a www.asia.b word. Remember to punctuate properly: AC, MC but MC AC.

  Although Dorinda glumly peered into the well, the ball was nowhere in sight.

  Dorinda glumly peered into the well **because** the ball was nowhere in sight.

  (The second sentence does not make sense in the context, so it is not an effective option.)

From now on when encountering run-on sentences, explore the various methods to correct them and choose the one you like best.

Page 22, *Fix It! Grammar: Frog Prince, or Just Deserts*, Student Book 3

DAY 1

¶ " [you didn't tell me] (it was solid gold)," [he **wheezed**]. [princess dorinda didn't hear him], [she

had ~~all ready~~ **already** skipped back to the palace], tickled with the return of her treasure.

Fixes

INDENT ¶s: 1) new speaker; 2) new topic, pulling out of his speech.

CAPITALIZATION. You, Princess Dorinda, She.

USAGE. Use *already*, meaning by that time, not *all ready*, meaning completely prepared. Fix: she had **already** skipped back.

COMMAS AND OTHER PUNCTUATION.

- **Quotations.** Fix: "You didn't tell me it was solid gold," he wheezed. Rules: 1) Enclose speech in quotes. 2) Add a comma after *gold* and inside the closing quotes: quotation + comma + speaking verb.

- **Run-on sentence** (comma splice MC, MC). A comma is not strong enough to hold two main clauses together. Using the questions below, guide students to consider different ways to fix comma splices.

  Ask: What do we call it when two MCs are joined with only a comma? Answer: Comma splice, a type of run-on. Ask: Where is a comma splice? Answer: *Princess Dorinda didn't hear him, she had already skipped back to the palace.*

  Teach the four most common solutions and ask your students which they like best and why. All four are decent solutions. Let your students go with the one they like best.

  - **Period:** Princess Dorinda didn't hear him. She had already skipped back to the palace.
  - **Semicolon:** Princess Dorinda didn't hear him; she had already skipped back to the palace.
  - **Use a www word** in front of one of the clauses (make it dependent): Princess Dorinda didn't hear him **because** she had already skipped back to the palace.
  - **Comma plus cc:** Princess Dorinda didn't hear him, **for** she had already skipped back to the palace.

- **ADVANCED. Nonessential elements** take commas. The comma setting off *tickled with the return of her treasure* is correct because this is a nonessential participial phrase. Inside the phrase are two prepositional phrases, which are correctly not set off with commas.

Grammar Notations

PREPOSITIONAL PHRASES. to the palace; with the return; of her treasure. *See* ✎ **1.**

CLAUSES, PHRASES, AND OPENERS.

- #1 subject opener and MC: **You didn't tell** me.
- **ADVANCED.** DC: **it was** solid gold. *See* ✎ **2.**
- MC: **he wheezed.**
- #6 vss and MC: **Princess Dorinda didn't hear** him.
- #1 subject opener and MC: **She had** already **skipped** back to the palace.

wheezed: breathed with difficulty and a whistling sound

✎ **1. Teacher's note.** Guide students to see the pattern in each: preposition + noun (no verb). These phrases begin with a preposition, end with a noun, and have no verb. Other words may come between the preposition and its object (the noun), but never a verb.

✎ **2. Teacher's note.** This is a noun clause beginning with an invisible *that*, but you do not have to teach this concept now.

DAY 2

```
#2                    AC                    S      V              MC  S      V
¶ during the evening (while the royal family dined sumptuously), [they heard a faint tapping at the

                         MC    S         V
castle door], moments later [a footman appeared, with a message for princess dorinda].
```

Fixes

INDENT ¶ because time has passed.

CAPITALIZATION. During, Moments, Princess Dorinda.

COMMAS AND OTHER PUNCTUATION.

- **Multiple openers.** Ask: Did you put a comma in the first sentence? Where? Answer: Not after *evening* but after *sumptuously* at the end of both openers (prepositional phrase and adverb clause). *See* ✎.

  Fix: **During the evening while the royal family dined sumptuously,** they heard a faint tapping.

- **Run-on sentence.** Ask students to locate a comma splice, reminding them that they are looking for two MCs with only a comma joining them.

  The comma splice with MCs italicized: *they heard a faint tapping at the castle door,* moments later, *a footman appeared. Moments later* goes with the MC after it, not before, so the comma after *door* needs to be changed into a period. That is the best solution this time.

- **Short #2 prepositional openers** (under five words): commas are optional unless there should be a pause. *Moments later* is correct with or without a comma.

- **Mid-sentence prepositional phrases** do not take commas. Fix: footman appeared **with a message for Princess Dorinda.**

sumptuously: magnificently; luxuriously

✎ **Teacher's note.**
While can count as a www word dress-up since it does not begin the sentence. Like an adverb clause dress-up, it does not have a comma before it, but like a #5 sentence opener, it is followed by a comma. It is a little of both since it does not start the sentence but comes before the MC.

Grammar Notations

PREPOSITIONAL PHRASES. During the evening; at the castle door; with a message; for Princess Dorinda. Guide students to see the pattern in each prepositional phrase: preposition + noun (no verb).

CLAUSES, PHRASES, AND OPENERS.

- #2 prepositional phrase opener: During the evening.

  If students mark this as a #4 -ing opener, explain that *during* is not something one can do because it is a preposition. The family does not *dure*!

- AC (adverb clause): while the royal **family dined** sumptuously.

- MC: **they heard** a faint tapping at the castle door.

- **ADVANCED.** Invisible #2 prepositional phrase: Moments later. *Moments later* is not a prepositional phrase but can be counted as a #2 opener with a preposition like *in* or *during* implied.

- MC: a **footman appeared** with a message for Princess Dorinda.

DAY 3

¶ "princess," [he began], "[you have a visitor at the door]." excusing herself from the table, [dorinda hastened away]. (when she opened the door), however, [blood drained from her face], .

[there /their/they're squatted the **forbearing** frog].

forbearing: patient and self-controlled when provoked

Fixes

INDENT ¶s 1) new speaker; 2) new topic, Dorinda's response.

CAPITALIZATION. Princess, Excusing, Dorinda, When, There.

HOMOPHONE. Use the adverb *there* meaning in that place: **There** squatted the forbearing frog.

COMMAS AND OTHER PUNCTUATION.

- **NDAs** take commas. Ask: Would you need a comma after *Princess* if *he began* were removed? Answer: Yes, because it is a NDA (noun of direct address), which always takes commas: **Princess,** you have a visitor.

- **Quotations.** Fix: "Princess," he began, "you have a visitor at the door." Rules: 1) Enclose speech in quotes. 2) Set off an interruption to a quoted sentence with commas. 3) Commas and periods go inside closing quotes.

- **#4 -ing openers** take commas. Fix: **Excusing herself from the table,** Dorinda hastened away. Check: Is the person after the comma the one doing the -inging? Answer: Yes, Dorinda is excusing herself, so this is a legal #4.

- **#5 clausal openers** take commas: AC, MC. Fix: **When she opened the door,** blood drained from her face.

- **Transitions** take commas when they interrupt the flow of the sentence. Fix: When she opened the door, **however,** blood drained.

- **Run-on sentence** (comma splice MC, MC). Ask: Where are two MCs with only a comma joining them? Answer: after *face*. Some decent solutions:
  - **Period:** When she opened the door, however, blood drained from her face. There squatted the forbearing frog. This works well because it makes the last clause a vss, drawing attention to the frog's presence.
  - **Subordinating one clause:** When she opened the door, however, blood drained from her face **because** there squatted the forbearing frog.
  - **comma + cc:** When she opened the door, however, blood drained from her face, **for** there squatted the forbearing frog.

Grammar Notations

PREPOSITIONAL PHRASES. at the door; from the table; from her face.

CLAUSES, PHRASES, AND OPENERS.
- MC: "Princess," **he began.**
- MC: **you have** a visitor at the door.
- #4 -ing participial phrase opener: Excusing herself from the table.
- MC: **Dorinda hastened** away.
- #5 clausal opener and AC: When **she opened** the door.
- MC: **blood drained** from her face.
- #6 vss and MC: There **squatted** the forbearing **frog.** *There* is not the subject, which instead comes after the verb.

DAY 4

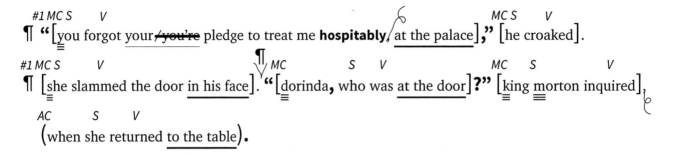

Fixes

INDENT ¶s: 1) new speaker; 2) new topic: 3) new speaker.

CAPITALIZATION. You, She, Dorinda, King Morton.

HOMOPHONES. Use *your* for the possessive: **your** pledge.

COMMAS AND OTHER PUNCTUATION. Ask students to explain commas they added and to find the incorrect commas. Guide them to figure out the why's by asking questions like, "How should we punctuate mid-sentence adverb clauses?"

- **Quotations.** Fix: "You ... palace," he croaked. "Dorinda ... door?" King Morton inquired. Rules: 1) Enclose speech in quotes. 2) Use commas with speaking verbs that set up quotations (*croaked* and *inquired*). 3) Exception: Use a question mark instead of the comma when the quote asks a question.
- **Mid-sentence prepositional phrases** do not take commas. Fix: to treat me hospitably **at the palace.**
- **NDAs** take commas. Fix: **Dorinda,** who was at the door?
- **Mid-sentence adverb clauses** do not take commas. Rule: MC AC. Fix: King Morton inquired **when she returned to the table.**

hospitably: treating guests warmly and generously

Grammar Notations

PREPOSITIONAL PHRASES. at the palace; in his face; at the door; to the table. Guide students to see the pattern: preposition + noun (no verb).

CLAUSES, PHRASES, AND OPENERS.

- #1 subject opener and MC: **You forgot** your pledge to treat me hospitably at the palace.
- MC: **he croaked.**
- #1 subject opener and MC: **She slammed** the door in his face.
- **ADVANCED.** #Q (question) and MC: Dorinda, **who was** at the door?

  If students mark *Dorinda* as the subject, ask them: Is it saying Dorinda was at the door? That would be silly! Guide them to see that *Dorinda* is an NDA. King Morton is calling her by name to get her attention. The true subject is *who*.

  By now students should know the *be* verbs. If they miss *was*, have them find a *be* verb using the verb card list. Also have them memorize these verbs.

- MC: **King Morton inquired.**
- AC (adverb clause): when **she returned** to the table.

Style

If desired, have students identify the strongest of the vocabulary dress-ups from this week. Discuss their answers. Suggestions:

- **Strong verbs.** wheezed, skipped, hastened, drained, squatted, croaked, slammed, inquired.
- **Quality adjectives.** tickled (verbal), faint, forbearing.
  - ✏ **Teacher's note.** If students mark *tickled* as a verb (*tickled with the return of her treasure*), you can decide whether to mention that it is actually an adjective taken from the past participle. Verbals usually do not function as verbs but are derived from them, which makes them tricky to label. This concept is too hard for most students at this level and not necessary to teach now.

✏ **-ly adverbs.** sumptuously, hospitably.

STUDENT REWRITE

"You didn't tell me it was solid gold," he wheezed.

Princess Dorinda didn't hear him. She had already skipped back to the palace, tickled with the return of her treasure.

During the evening while the royal family dined sumptuously, they heard a faint tapping at the castle door. Moments later a footman appeared with a message for Princess Dorinda.

"Princess," he began, "you have a visitor at the door."

Excusing herself from the table, Dorinda hastened away. When she opened the door, however, blood drained from her face. There squatted the forbearing frog.

"You forgot your pledge to treat me hospitably at the palace," he croaked.

She slammed the door in his face.

"Dorinda, who was at the door?" King Morton inquired when she returned to the table.

Week 11

#Q Opener

LEARN IT

When a sentence asks a question, it may be marked with a #Q.

Questions beginning with a *who* or *which* do not count as a *who-which* dress-up. Similarly, sentences that begin with a *when* or *where* and ask a question are not #5 openers; they should be marked with a #Q instead.

> #Q Where are you going in such haste?
>
> #Q Who will rescue my ball?
>
> #Q Which story ends happily?
>
> #Q What would have happened to me had I drunk the poisoned water?
>
> #Q Can you forgive me, nephew?

There is no grammar card for this concept. If you think you might forget, add *#Q* to the Sentence Opener grammar card to remember it.

Page 24, *Fix It! Grammar: Frog Prince, or Just Deserts,* **Student Book 3**

DAY 1

#1 MC S V V V   MC S V V   AC   V
¶ [dorinda, may have had her **deficiencies**], but, [she did tell the truth], (when asked directly).

¶ #Q
MC   V S V
"a frog." "[what did he want]?"

Fixes

deficiencies: inadequacies; faults

INDENT ¶s: 1) new topic, turning to Dorinda's response; 2) new speaker.

CAPITALIZATION. Dorinda, A, What.

COMMAS AND OTHER PUNCTUATION. Guide students to figure out what they missed by asking questions.

- **Subject-verb.** Put commas around names only when used as NDAs, not the situation here. No comma should be used between a subject-name and its verb. Fix: **Dorinda** may have had her deficiencies.

- **MC, cc MC.** Ask: What does *but* join and is it punctuated correctly? Answer: The comma before it is correct (comma + cc to join two main clauses) but no comma after coordinating conjunctions.

  Fix: Dorinda may have had her deficiencies, **but** she did tell the truth.

- **Mid-sentence adverb clauses** do not take commas. Fix: she did tell the truth **when asked directly.**

- **Quotations.** Fix: "A frog." ¶ "What did he want?"

  Rules: 1) Enclose speech in quotations. 2) Periods and commas go inside the closing quotes. 3) Close the king's question with a question mark inside quotes.

  ✎ **Teacher's note.** If students put a comma after *directly*, explain that *tell* does not set up the quotation but sets up its object, *the truth*, instead, so a period should precede the quotation. Contrast this: She answered, "A frog."

Grammar Notations

CLAUSES, PHRASES, AND OPENERS.

- #1 subject and MC: **Dorinda may have had** her deficiencies.

  Ask: What are the helping verbs? Use the Verb grammar card to help. Answer: *may* and *have*, which help out *had*. Some of the helping verbs can be action verbs as well but never both at the same time.

- MC: **she did tell** the truth.

- AC (adverb clause): when **asked** directly. The subject and helping verb are understood: when *she was* asked directly.

- No label: A frog.

  This is a sentence fragment, acceptable as Dorinda's casual answer to the question. It is not a vss because it is not a sentence (no subject-verb). Do not label sentence fragments.

- #Q and MC: What **did he want**?

DAY 2

¶ now, [you and ~~me~~ might have trouble with king mortons **rejoinder**]—[isn't it unusual, for a frog to knock at a castle door]?—but [remember], [this is a fairy tale], (which is allowed to be bizarre).

Fixes

INDENT ¶ because of a new topic.

CAPITALIZATION. Now, I (in revision), King Morton's.

PRONOUN USAGE. Fix: you and I might have trouble. Trick to tell which pronoun: Drop the first pronoun and ask if the second alone sounds correct. Would we say, "Now, me might have trouble"? No, we would say, "Now, I might have trouble." Therefore, use *I* with two pronouns also. *See* ♡.

COMMAS AND OTHER PUNCTUATION. *See* ✎ **1.**

- **Introductory transitions** take commas: **Now,** you and I might have trouble.
- **Apostrophes** for possession. Fix: King **Morton's** rejoinder.
- **ADVANCED.** Ask if these em dashes are used to 1) indicate a break in thought, or 2) draw attention to what they enclose. Answer: 1) a break in thought. Notice that em dashes come in pairs unless what they enclose ends the sentence. A question or exclamation mark may be used with a dash.
- **Mid-sentence prepositional phrases** do not take commas. Fix: isn't it unusual **for a frog** to knock.
- **ADVANCED. Nonessential** *who-which* **clauses** take commas. Ask: Why is this *which* clause nonessential? Answer: If removed, it does not change the rest of the sentence—this is still a fairy tale—or specifically identify the noun before it. The original is correct: this is a fairy tale, **which is allowed to be bizarre.**

Grammar Notations

PREPOSITIONAL PHRASES. with King Morton's rejoinder; for a frog; at a castle door. *See* ✎ **2.**

CLAUSES, PHRASES, AND OPENERS.

- #T: Now.
- MC: **you and I might have** trouble with King Morton's rejoinder. If students mark *trouble* as a verb, explain that it is a noun here, the direct object of *have*. No one is troubling someone else.
- MC: **isn't it** unusual for a frog to knock at a castle door? If students cannot find the *be* verbs, have them check the *be* verbs on the Verb grammar card to find three *is*'s.
- **ADVANCED.** MC: **remember.** This is in the imperative (advice or command) mood, where the subject, *you*, is understood.

  If students ask why two MCs are back to back with only a comma, explain that *remember* sets up what the reader is to remember in the same way that a speaking verb sets up a quotation with a comma—that is, it is an exception to the usual rule. A colon could be used instead, but a colon draws more attention to what follows than fits this context.
- MC: **this is** a fairy tale.
- DC (*who-which* clause): **which is allowed** to be bizarre.

rejoinder: response; answer to a reply

♡ **Grammar lovers.** Since *you and I* functions as the subject of the clause, it takes the subjective pronoun *I* instead of the objective pronoun *me*.

✎ **1. Teacher's note.** Remember, the points marked *advanced* are for your information and can be discussed if your students ask or if you wish to cover that point of grammar for an older or stronger student.

✎ **2. Teacher's note.** Guide students to see the pattern: preposition + noun (no verb). These phrases begin with a preposition, end with a noun, and have no verb. Other words may come between the preposition and its object (the noun), but never a verb.

DAY 3

#4   DC   S V   V   MC S V

¶ gushing tears yet again, (which dorinda could **expediently** turn on and off like a faucet), [she sobbed

the story of the frogs rescue of her ball/ and the promises], (that she had foolishly made).

                   DC S V   V

Fixes

INDENT ¶ because of a new topic: back to the story after the narrator's interruption.

CAPITALIZATION. Gushing, Dorinda.

SIMILE. like a faucet. A simile compares unlike items using a comparison word. In IEW writing, it is a decoration. Students do not need to mark these, but point them out and ask what is being compared. Answer: she can control her tears like a faucet.

COMMAS AND OTHER PUNCTUATION.

- **#4 -ing openers** take commas. The original is correct: **Gushing tears yet again,** which Dorinda could expediently turn on and off like a faucet, she sobbed the story.

  - 🖉 **Teacher's note.** Normally, the subject doing the -inging comes right after the comma, but this one (*she*) comes after the *which* clause. Since *who-which* clauses have their own subject-verb, they do not interfere with the #4 pattern: -ing word or phrase + comma + subject/-inger + main clause.

- **Apostrophes** for possession. Fix: the **frog's** rescue.

- **ADVANCED. Nonessential *who-which* clauses** take commas. The *which* clause adds important information but does not affect the meaning of the rest of the sentence (she still sobbed the story), so it is nonessential and takes commas on both sides of the clause. The original is correct: Gushing tears yet again, **which Dorinda could expediently turn on and off like a faucet,** she sobbed the story.

- **Items in a series.** Ask students what the second *and* joins. Answer: rescue and promises. Ask: What is the punctuation before a cc that joins two items? Answer: No comma: a and b.

  Students may hear this better if you add the preposition again after *and*: of the frog's rescue and *of* the promises. Fix: of the frog's rescue of her ball **and** the promises that she had foolishly made.

- ***That* clauses** do not take commas. Fix: the promises **that she had foolishly made.**

Grammar Notations

PREPOSITIONAL PHRASES. like a faucet; of the frog's rescue … and the promises; of her ball. Guide students to see the pattern in each prepositional phrase: preposition + noun (no verb). *See* 🖉 **1.**

CLAUSES, PHRASES, AND OPENERS.

- #4 -ing participial phrase opener: Gushing tears yet again.
- DC (*who-which* clause): which **Dorinda could** expediently **turn** on and off like a faucet.
- MC: **she sobbed** the story of the frog's rescue of her ball and the promises.
- DC (*that* adjective clause): that **she had** foolishly **made.** *See* 🖉 **2.**

expediently: to her advantage; out of self-interest

🖉 **1. Teacher's note.** If students are confused about the second prepositional phrase, you might point out that there is one (*of her ball*) inside another (*of the frog's rescue and the promises*). *Promises* is a second object of the preposition *of*.

🖉 **2. Teacher's note.** This is an essential *which* clause that uses *that* in place of *which*. In IEW writing, do not mark *that* clauses as dress-ups, however, only *who, whom, whose, which*.

DAY 4

#3   *MC S*   *V*   *V*   *MC S*   *V*

¶ "surely, [you wouldn't make me, like, touch that nasty, old thing]?" [she pleaded **piteously**].

#1 MC   *S*   *V*

¶ [the king was ~~to/two/~~too ~~use/~~used to ~~two/too~~ her **histrionics** to be affected ~~effected~~ by tears].

    MC   *S V*   *#1 MC*   *S*   *V*   *V*

"[daughter, you are a royal princess], . [your word—of all people's—must be trustworthy]."

Fixes

INDENT ¶s because of new speakers. The second paragraph begins with a sentence that directly relates to the king's words so may go in the same paragraph. If students prefer to have the actual speech in its own paragraph, that is fine, too.

CAPITALIZATION. Surely, The, Daughter, Your.

Ask: Why is *she* lowercase after the quote? Answer: It is part of the same sentence since the subject and speaking verb set up the quotation. If the quoted words did not ask a question, there would be a comma after *thing*, so the lowercase *she* would be more obvious.

HOMOPHONES, USAGE, AND SPELLING. The king was **too used to** her histrionics to be **affected** by tears.

- The first *too* means excessively (so use the one with too many *o's*!); the second is the preposition *to*.
- Sometimes students do not hear the *d* in *used to*, so check their spelling.
- *Affected* is the verb meaning influenced.

COMMAS AND OTHER PUNCTUATION.

- **Quotations.** Fix: "Surely … thing?" ¶ "Daughter … trustworthy." Rules: 1) Enclose speech in quotations. 2) Add a question mark after Dorinda's question. 3) Check that punctuation is inside closing quotes.
- **#3 -ly adverb openers.** Keep the comma after *Surely* since it requires a pause. *See* ✏ **1.**
- **Adjectives before a noun.** Guide students through the two tests to determine if *nasty old thing* needs the comma: 1) *that old nasty thing* sounds awkward; 2) *that nasty and old thing* sounds awkward. Since both tests fail, the adjectives are cumulative, so no comma. *See* ✏ **2.**
- **NDAs** take commas. Ask: How is *Daughter* being used? Answer: noun of direct address, so add a comma. Fix: **Daughter,** you are a royal princess.
- **Run-on sentence** (comma splice MC, MC). Ask: Find two main clauses joined with only a comma. Answer: comma after *royal princess*. Ask how they fixed this. Three effective solutions:
  - ◆ Period (MCs italicized): Daughter, *you are a royal princess.* *Your word*—of all people's—*must be trustworthy.*
  - ◆ Convert one MC to adverb clause. Fix: Daughter, **since** you are a royal princess, **your** word—of all people's—must be trustworthy.
  - ◆ Convert to MC, cc MC. Fix: Daughter, you are a royal princess, **so** your word—of all people's—must be trustworthy.
- **ADVANCED. Apostrophes** for possession: The original is correct: **people's.** The king means *of all people's word*, with *word* implied.

---

piteously: sorrowfully; in a way that encourages pity

histrionics: exaggerated behavior or speech for effect

✏ **1. Teacher's note.** *Surely* modifies the sentence, so the comma is needed. Dorinda is not saying, "You would not *surely make* me touch the frog" but "it is surely true that you would not."

✏ **2. Teacher's note.** The tests are subjective, not foolproof. They work best if students go with their first reaction. Tip: When the last adjective deals with age or time (as with *old*), the adjectives are cumulative.

Grammar Notations

PREPOSITIONAL PHRASES. by tears; of all people's.

Like is a meaningless filler word, not a preposition or verb here. (It fits Dorinda's character.) If students label *to her histrionics*, explain that this phrase does not make sense because *to* belongs with the idiom *used to*. Prepositional phrases should make sense by themselves.

Of all people's interrupts the flow of the sentence so is clearer set off with dashes or commas.

CLAUSES, PHRASES, AND OPENERS.

- #3 -ly adverb opener: Surely.
- MC: **you wouldn**'t **make** me, like, touch that nasty old thing.
- MC: **she pleaded** piteously.
- #1 subject opener and MC: The **king was** too used to her histrionics to be affected by tears. *See* ✎ **3**.

  If students miss *was* or *are* in the next clause, have them find *be* verbs using the verb card list.

- MC: **you are** a royal princess.
- #1 subject opener and MC: Your **word**—of all people's—**must be** trustworthy. *See* ✎ **4**.

✎ **3. Teacher's note.**
It does not matter whether or not students underline *used to* as a verb. It is an idiom meaning *accustomed to*. Do not worry about labeling parts of speech in idioms.

✎ **4. Teacher's note.**
Trustworthy is not a verb but an adjective following a linking verb.

Style

If desired, have students identify the strongest of the vocabulary dress-ups from this week. Discuss their answers. Suggestions:

- **Strong verbs.** sobbed, pleaded.
- **Quality adjectives.** bizarre, trustworthy.
- **-ly adverbs.** directly, expediently, foolishly, piteously.

STUDENT REWRITE

Dorinda may have had her deficiencies, but she did tell the truth when asked directly. "A frog."

"What did he want?"

Now, you and I might have trouble with King Morton's rejoinder—isn't it unusual for a frog to knock at a castle door?—but remember, this is a fairy tale, which is allowed to be bizarre.

Gushing tears yet again, which Dorinda could expediently turn on and off like a faucet, she sobbed the story of the frog's rescue of her ball and the promises that she had foolishly made.

"Surely, you wouldn't make me, like, touch that nasty old thing?" she pleaded piteously.

The king was too used to her histrionics to be affected by tears. "Daughter, you are a royal princess. Your word—of all people's—must be trustworthy."

Week 12

Illegal #4 -ing Openers

LEARN IT

Illegal #4s look like #4s, only the subject after the comma is not the one doing the -inging. This is known as a **dangling modifier**—an often humorous but still grammatically faulty sentence pattern.

> Example: *Gushing with tears, **the king** listened to Dorinda's pathetic story.*

This is an illegal #4 because it is not the king but the princess who is supposed to be gushing tears.

Whenever you see an -ing word at the beginning of a sentence, ask, "Is the thing after the comma the thing doing the -inging?" If not, fix the sentence to make it legal.

More examples:

*Sobbing as if her heart would break, **Dorinda** slyly opened one eye to check the effect of her tears.*

The subject after the comma, Dorinda, is the one doing the -inging, sobbing, so this is a legal #4.

*Sobbing as if her heart would break, **Dorinda's** eye slyly opened to check the effect of her tears.*

The subject after the comma is no longer Dorinda but her eye. Since it is not her eye but Dorinda herself who is sobbing as if her heart would break, this is an illegal #4.

> ✏ **Teacher's note.**
> Remember to keep the exercise light and fun. It should be like a game.

Page 26, *Fix It! Grammar: Frog Prince, or Just Deserts,* **Student Book 3**

DAY 1

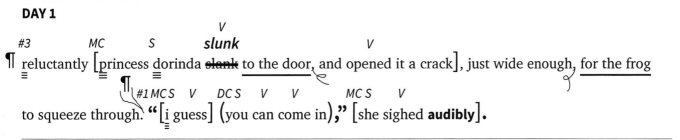

V
#3   MC   S   *slunk*   V

¶ reluctantly [princess dorinda ~~slunk~~ to the door, and opened it a crack], just wide enough, for the frog

                   ¶ #1 MC S   V   DC S   V   V   MC S   V

to squeeze through. "[i guess] (you can come in)," [she sighed **audibly**].

Fixes

INDENT ¶s because of a new topic and new speaker.

CAPITALIZATION. Reluctantly, Princess Dorinda, I.

SPELLING. *slunk* is the past tense of the verb *to slink*.

COMMAS AND OTHER PUNCTUATION.

- **#3 -ly adverb openers.** *Reluctantly* modifies the verb (she *reluctantly slunk*), so the comma after it is optional.
- **Items in a series.** Ask: What specific words does the cc *and* join? Reminder: they must be the same part of speech. Answer: *slunk* and *opened*, two verbs. Ask: Do you punctuate cc's when they join two verbs? Answer: No: MC cc 2nd verb. Fix: Princess Dorinda reluctantly **slunk** to the door **and opened** it a crack. *See ✐ 1.*
- **ADVANCED. Nonessential elements** take commas. Explain that nonessential phrases are set off with commas because the rest of the sentence makes sense if you remove them. Ask: Can you locate the nonessential phrase? The original is correct: opened it a crack, **just wide enough for the frog to squeeze through.**
- **Mid-sentence prepositional phrases.** Ask: What punctuation do we use with mid-sentence prepositional phrases? Answer: None. Ask: Can you find one that incorrectly has a comma? Fix: just wide enough **for the frog to squeeze through.**
- **Quotations.** Enclose spoken words in quotation marks. Use a comma with a verb of speaking (*sighed*) that sets up a direct quotation. Check that the comma goes inside closing quotation marks. Fix: "I … in," she sighed.

Grammar Notations

PREPOSITIONAL PHRASES. to the door; for the frog. *See ✐ 2.*

CLAUSES, PHRASES, AND OPENERS.

- #3 -ly adverb opener: Reluctantly.
- MC: **Princess Dorinda slunk** to the door and **opened** it a crack. Guide students to find both verbs and check that they understand both have the same subject. *See ✐ 3.*
- #1 subject opener and MC: **I guess.**
- **ADVANCED.** DC (noun clause): **you can come** in. This clause is dependent because an implied *that* starts it. Dependent clauses always have a word at the start (given or implied) that makes them dependent, usually a www word or *who, which,* or *that.*
- MC: **she sighed** audibly.

audibly: loudly enough to be heard

✐ **1. Teacher's note.** The trick is to look for another subject right after the *and*. If there is no noun but only a verb, you likely have a compound verb.

✐ **2. Teacher's note.** As needed, guide students to see the pattern in each prepositional phrase: preposition + noun (no verb). *Through* and *in* are adverbs here and part of the verb phrases: *squeeze through; come in.*

✐ **3. Teacher's note.** When a subject has more than one verb, we call it a compound verb.

DAY 2

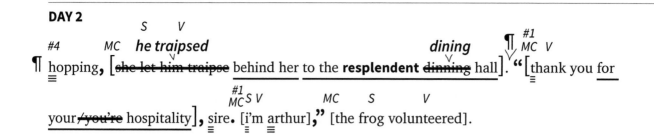

Fixes

INDENT ¶s because of a new topic and new speaker.

CAPITALIZATION. Hopping, Thank, Sire, I'm, Arthur. Capitalize titles used by themselves as NDAs: *Sire.*

SPELLING. *dining,* not *dinning.* Two consonants make the vowel short; one consonant makes it long. *Dinning* rhymes with *winning, dining* with *whining.*

HOMOPHONE. your hospitality (possessive).

COMMAS AND OTHER PUNCTUATION.

- **#4 -ing openers** are always followed by a comma and then the subject doing the -inging. Fix: **Hopping,** she let him traipse behind her.

  Ask: Is the thing after the comma the one doing the -inging? Answer: *She* follows the comma, but Dorinda is not the one doing the hopping. This is an illegal (ungrammatical) #4. See ✐.

  Fix: Change the subject to the one actually doing the -inging: **Hopping, he** [the frog] **traipsed** behind her.

- **Quotations.** "Thank … Arthur," the frog volunteered. Use quotations around spoken words and a comma with a speaking verb (*volunteered*). Check that students placed the comma inside the closing quotations.

- **NDAs** (nouns of direct address) take commas. Fix: for your hospitality, **Sire.**

- **Run-on sentence.** Ask students to tell you what a fused sentence is (two MCs joined with no cc or punctuation, which is always wrong), where one is, and how to correct it. Fix, with MCs italicized: *Thank you for your hospitality,* Sire. *I'm Arthur.*

resplendent:
splendid; magnificent; dazzling

✐ **Teacher's note.**
In grammar this error is called a dangling modifier. Do not feel you need to teach this concept if your students are not ready. They will see it again in all the later books.

Grammar Notations

PREPOSITIONAL PHRASES. behind her; to the resplendent dining hall; for your hospitality.

If students miss *behind her,* remind them that pronouns like *her* can function the same way nouns function, in this case, as the object of the preposition.

ADVANCED. Students may also be confused by *dining,* which looks like a verb but is not. Explain: -ing words are not verbs unless there is a subject and helping verb in front of them. Contrast "they were dining." Here, *dining* describes the noun *hall* so is an adjective.

CLAUSES, PHRASES, AND OPENERS.

- #4 -ing participial phrase opener: Hopping.
- MC: **he traipsed** behind her to the resplendent dining hall.
- **ADVANCED.** #1 subject opener and MC: **Thank** you for your hospitality. The subject, *I,* is understood.
- #1 subject opener and MC: **I'm** Arthur. The subject and verb are both in the contraction *I'm*: I am.
- MC: the **frog volunteered.**

DAY 3

¶ "*dorinda*, [pick arthur up]," [her father commanded], "and [let him feast **unstintingly** from your golden plate]." "yuck! [i won't touch another bite]," [she whined again]. "despite your feelings, [a promise is a promise]," [king morton reminded her].

Fixes

INDENT ¶s because of new speakers.

CAPITALIZATION. Dorinda, Arthur, Yuck, I, Despite, King Morton.

COMMAS AND OTHER PUNCTUATION.

- **NDAs** take commas. Fix: **Dorinda,** pick Arthur up.
- **Quotations.** "Dorinda … up," her father commanded, "and let … plate." "Yuck … bite," she whined again. "Despite … promise," King Morton reminded her.
  Rules:
  - Enclose spoken words in quotes.
  - Use commas around interruptions and with speaking verbs (*commanded, whined, reminded*) that set up quotations.
  - Commas and periods go inside closing quotes.
  - The sentence continues after the interruption, so use lowercase: "**and** let him feast." Use capital letters only at the start of a quoted sentence.
- **Interjections** take exclamation marks when expressing strong emotions. Fix: **Yuck!**
- **Short #2 prepositional openers** (under five words): commas are optional unless a pause is needed, as here. Fix: **Despite your feelings,** a promise is a promise.

Grammar Notations

PREPOSITIONAL PHRASES. from your golden plate, Despite your feelings. If students overlook *despite*, have them pull out their Prepositions grammar card and ask them to find a word from the middle column in this passage.

CLAUSES, PHRASES, AND OPENERS.

- MC: **pick** Arthur up. The subject, *you*, is understood.
- MC: her **father commanded.**
- MC: **let** him feast unstintingly from your golden plate. The subject, *you*, is understood.
- #1 subject opener and MC: **I** won't **touch** another bite. *Won't* is the contraction for *will not. Will* is a helping verb; *touch* is the action verb. *Not* is an adverb.
- MC: **she whined** again.
- #2 prepositional phrase opener: Despite your feelings.
- MC: a **promise is** a promise.
- MC: **King Morton reminded** her.

DAY 4

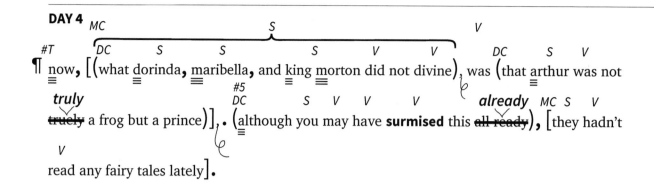

Fixes

INDENT ¶ because of a new topic.

CAPITALIZATION. Now, Dorinda, Maribella, King Morton, Arthur, Although.

USAGE AND SPELLING. 1) No *e* in **truly**. 2) Use *already*, meaning by this time: you may have surmised this **already**. *All ready* means completely prepared.

COMMAS AND OTHER PUNCTUATION. *See* ✎ **1.**

- **Introductory transitions** take commas: **Now,** what Dorinda … did not divine.

- **Items in a series** take commas when three or more but no comma when only two (except MCs).

  Fix: **Dorinda, Maribella, and King Morton** did not divine. Ask: What do we call the comma before *and*? Answer: the Oxford comma. *See* ✎ **2.**

  The second cc is already correct: not a **frog but** a **prince**. *But* joins only two nouns.

- **Subject-verb.** No comma after *divine* because that would separate the subject (the *what* clause) from its verb (*was*).

- **Run-on sentence** (comma splice MC, MC, which is always wrong). Ask students to locate and explain the comma splice. Answer: the comma after *but a prince* is not strong enough to hold together two MCs.

  Fix: period after **but a prince.** Some students may want to connect the *although* clause with the main clause before it instead of after, but it makes more sense with the one after.

- **#5 clausal openers** take commas: AC, MC. Fix: **Although you may have surmised this already,** they hadn't read any fairy tales.

Grammar Notations

CLAUSES, PHRASES, AND OPENERS.

- **#T** (transitional) opener: Now.
- **ADVANCED.** MC: **(what Dorinda, Maribella, and King Morton did not divine) was** (that Arthur was not truly a frog but a prince). This main clause has two dependent clauses inside it (see below).

  Challenge students to name the subject of *was*. Make a game of it: If they mention any of the names, for example, you could say, "King Morton *was that Arthur was not a frog*? Does that even make sense?" With guidance, advanced students can see that the *what* clause functions as the subject of *was*.

- **ADVANCED.** DC: What **Dorinda, Maribella,** and **King Morton did** not **divine.** This grammar is even more complicated: the dependent clause functioning as the subject of the MC has its own compound subject and verb inside it.

- **ADVANCED.** DC: that **Arthur was** not truly a frog but a prince. *See* ♡.

---

surmised: guessed

✎ **1. Teacher's note.** Remember to cover the Grammar Notations first, as needed. Understanding sentence structure is critical to punctuating correctly.

✎ **2. Teacher's note.** The Oxford comma (the one before a cc with three or more items in a series) goes in and out of favor but is currently in favor. It is never wrong to include it but may be wrong to leave it out, so it is best to teach keeping it always.

♡ **Grammar lovers.** This is a noun clause starting with *that* and following the verb *was*. The noun clause functions as the subject complement (a.k.a. predicate nominative): one dependent clause as subject and another dependent clause as complement with the linking verb *was* connecting them!

- #5 clausal opener and AC: Although **you may have surmised** this already.
- MC: **they had**n't **read** any fairy tales lately.

Style

If desired, have students identify the strongest of the vocabulary dress-ups from this week. Discuss their answers. Suggestions:

- **Strong verbs.** slunk, squeeze, sighed, traipsed, commanded, whined, divine, surmised.
- **Quality adjectives.** resplendent.
- **-ly adverbs.** audibly, unstintingly, truly, lately.

STUDENT REWRITE

Reluctantly Princess Dorinda slunk to the door and opened it a crack, just wide enough for the frog to squeeze through.

"I guess you can come in," she sighed audibly.

Hopping, he traipsed behind her to the resplendent dining hall.

"Thank you for your hospitality, Sire. I'm Arthur," the frog volunteered.

"Dorinda, pick Arthur up," her father commanded, "and let him feast unstintingly from your golden plate."

"Yuck! I won't touch another bite," she whined again.

"Despite your feelings, a promise is a promise," King Morton reminded her.

Now, what Dorinda, Maribella, and King Morton did not divine was that Arthur was not truly a frog but a prince. Although you may have surmised this already, they hadn't read any fairy tales lately.

Week 13

That Clauses and Alliteration

LEARN IT

That Clauses

You have learned that the words *who, which,* and *that* start dependent clauses. The *who-which* clauses take commas or not depending on how the clause is used. You will be glad to know that the rule for the *that* clause is much more consistent: *that* clauses never take commas.

Alliteration

Advanced. If you have been doing IEW writing, you may have been introduced to the decorations. One of the decorations is alliteration: the repetition of the same initial consonant sounds in two or more words in close proximity. It adds flavor to writing when used judiciously.

Example: Dorinda *ravaged* the *royal red roses* that used to adorn the garden.

She could not as easily crush the *chestnut* and *cherry* trees.

Crush is not part of the alliteration in the second example because it does not have the same initial sound as the other *c* words. It is not the letter that matters but the sound. Thus, *chestnut* and *cherry* are alliterative, but *crush* and *chestnut* are not. In the same way, *crush* and *kick* could count for alliteration because of the *k* sound.

In academic writing, alliteration usually sounds awkward unless found in a title or the first or last sentence of a paper. It can appropriately dramatize those parts.

✏ **Teacher's note:** *That* clauses are always essential so they never take commas. This will come up on day 3 of this week.

Page 28, *Fix It! Grammar: Frog Prince, or Just Deserts*, **Student Book 3**

DAY 1

#2   MC   S   *used* (V)

¶ as a teenager, [prince arthur ~~use~~ to be a bit swollen-headed, and **pretentious**]. one humid afternoon

    MC   S   V   V

in july, [young arthur was riding through a forest in his fathers kingdom], seeking some shady relief

from the sweltering sun.

Fixes

INDENT ¶ because of a flashback (a switch to an earlier time) to the story of how Arthur became a frog.

CAPITALIZATION. A*s*, Prince Arthur (capitalize titles when used with a name), One, July (capitalize names of months), Arthur.

SPELLING. Arthur **used** to be. Students often do not hear the *d* in *used* and misspell the word.

ALLITERATION. seeking some … sweltering sun. *Shady* is not part of the alliteration because its initial sound, *sh*, is different from the *s* sounds that start the other words. Encourage your students to keep an eye out for alliteration just for fun. *See* ✎ **1**.

COMMAS AND OTHER PUNCTUATION. *See* ✎ **2**.

- **ADVANCED.** The comma after **short #2 prepositional openers** is usually optional, but a comma is needed here for clarity: it is not "as a teenager prince," but "As a teenager, Prince Arthur."
- **Items in a series.** Ask: Is the comma before the cc *and* correct or not, and why? Answer: Incorrect because the cc joins only two adjectives, not three or more: a and b. Fix: swollen-headed **and** pretentious.
- **ADVANCED. Long #2 prepositional openers** (five or more words) take commas. The original is correct: **One humid afternoon in July,** young Arthur was riding.
- **Apostrophes** for possession. Fix: **father's** kingdom.
- **ADVANCED. Nonessential participial phrases.** Teach: -ing openers take commas even when they are enders and not openers! The original is correct: Arthur was riding … in his father's kingdom, **seeking some shady relief from the sweltering sun.**

Grammar Notations

PREPOSITIONAL PHRASES. As a teenager; in July; through a forest; in his father's kingdom; from the sweltering sun. *See* ✎ **3**.

CLAUSES, PHRASES, AND OPENERS.

- #2 prepositional phrase opener: As a teenager. *As* can be either a preposition or a www word (subordinating conjunction). To test, ask if this opener has a verb. It does not, so it cannot be a clause and has to be a phrase. All clauses have a subject-verb pair.
- MC: **Prince Arthur used** to be a bit swollen-headed and pretentious.
- **ADVANCED.** Invisible #2 prepositional phrase opener: One humid afternoon in July. This is not technically a prepositional phrase, but it functions like one with an implied preposition like *on* in front.
- MC: young **Arthur was riding** through a forest in his father's kingdom.

Sidebar notes:

pretentious: showy; pompous; self-important

✎ **1. Teacher's note.** Alliteration, the repetition of initial consonant sounds, is another IEW decoration.

✎ **2. Teacher's note.** Reminder: Understanding sentence structure using the Grammar Notations will help students to punctuate correctly. Also, discuss advanced concepts only with students who are ready.

✎ **3. Teacher's note.** Guide students to see the pattern in each prepositional phrase: preposition + noun (no verb). For *as a teenager*, see Clauses, phrases and sentence openers. Note that *father's* is possessive; it is not the object of the preposition.

DAY 2

#1

#2   MC   S   V   MC   S   V

about halfway through the forest, [his horse reared up], startled, . [a young boy stood in the path].

      MC S V   V   MC   S   V   #Q MC V   S   V

¶ "please, sir, [i've lost my way]," [the boy explained]. "[would you kindly give me a ride out of

this **desolate** forest]?"

Fixes

INDENT second part because of a new speaker.

CAPITALIZATION. About, A, Please, I've, Would.

> ✒ **Teacher's note.** The words *sir* and *madam* are not capitalized when used as NDAs, the one exception to the rule that titles used as NDAs are capitalized.

COMMAS AND OTHER PUNCTUATION.

- **Quotations.** Fix: "Please ... way," the boy explained. "Would ... forest?" Rules: 1) Enclose speech in quotes. 2) Use commas when speaking verbs (*explained*) set up quotes. 3) Add a question mark inside the last quotations. See Run-on, below, for the period after *explained*.
- **Long #2 prepositional openers** (five or more words) take commas. When there are two or more prepositional phrases, place the comma after all of them. Fix: **About halfway through the forest,** his horse reared up.
- **Run-on sentences.** Ask your students to find and correct one of each kind of run-on in this passage.

  Comma splice (MC, MC): The comma after *startled* should be a period to hold the two main clauses together: *His horse reared up, startled. **A** young boy stood in the path.* The context makes it clear that *startled* describes the horse and not the boy.

  Fused sentence (MC MC): The two MCs that the boy speaks need a period somewhere between them. Place it after the interrupter: *"I've lost my way," the boy explained. "Would you kindly give me a ride ... ?"*
- **NDAs** take commas. Fix: Please, **sir,** I've lost my way.

Grammar Notations

PREPOSITIONAL PHRASES. About halfway; through the forest; in the path; of this desolate forest.

> ✒ **Teacher's note.** If students mark *out* as part of the phrase, let it go. *Out* is an adverb.

CLAUSES, PHRASES, AND OPENERS.

- #2 prepositional phrase opener: About halfway through the forest.
- MC: his **horse reared** up.
- #1 subject opener and MC: A young **boy stood** in the path.
- MC: **I've lost** my way. Note: *Please* is an adverb.
- MC: the **boy explained**.
- #Q (question) and MC: **Would you** kindly **give** me a ride out of this desolate forest? Check that students marked both the helping verb (*would*) and the action verb (*give*).

desolate: uninhabited; dreary; gloomy; lonely

DAY 3

¶ "out of my way, peasant," [the prince retorted], **oblivious** (that the boy was a magician in disguise).

¶ instantly [the boy's voice thundered], "for your lack of compassion and decency, [you must spend your days as a frog]."

(Annotations above the sentence: MC, S, V over "the prince retorted"; DC, S, V over "that the boy was a magician in disguise"; #3 ly, MC, comma, S, V over "instantly the boy's voice thundered"; #2 over "for your lack"; MC, S, V, V over "you must spend your")

Fixes

oblivious: unaware

INDENT ¶s because of new speakers.

CAPITALIZATION. Out, Instantly, For (capitalize the first word of a quoted sentence). Ask: Why are *peasant* and *prince* lowercase? Answer: Both are common nouns. *Prince* is capitalized when coupled with a name.

COMMAS AND OTHER PUNCTUATION.

- **Quotations.** Fix: "Out ... peasant," the prince retorted. ... the boy's voice thundered, "For ... frog." Rules: 1) Enclose quotes in quotations. 2) Use commas when speaking verbs (*retorted, thundered*) set up direct quotations. 3) Commas and periods go inside closing quotation marks.
- **NDAs** take commas. Fix: Out of my way, **peasant**.
- **Apostrophes** for possession. Fix: **boy's** voice.
- **ADVANCED. Nonessential elements** take commas. The original is correct: the prince retorted, **oblivious that the boy was a magician.** This is an adjective phrase since it starts with an adjective, *oblivious*. It is nonessential because it does not affect the meaning of the rest of the sentence. The prince still retorted, regardless whether he was oblivious.
- ***That* clauses** never take commas. Remind students of the new rule this week and then ask if they caught the incorrect comma before *that*. Fix: oblivious **that the boy was a magician.** *See* ✎ **1.**
- **#3 -ly adverb opener.** Since *instantly* describes the verb *thundered*, the comma after it is optional. No pause is needed, so no comma is needed either.
- **Long #2 prepositional openers** (five or more words) take a comma. Save it for the end of both phrases. Fix: **For your lack of compassion and decency,** you must spend your days as a frog.

Grammar Notations

PREPOSITIONAL PHRASES. of my way; in disguise; For your lack; of compassion and decency (two objects to this preposition); as a frog. *See* ✎ **2.**

As is a preposition here, not a www word (subordinating conjunction). *As a frog* begins with a word that can be a preposition, ends with a noun, and has no verb, so it cannot be a clause.

CLAUSES, PHRASES, AND OPENERS.
- Out of my way, peasant. *See* ✎ **3.**
- MC: the **prince retorted**.
- DC: that the **boy was** a magician in disguise.
- #3 -ly adverb opener: Instantly.
- MC: the boy's **voice thundered**.
- #2 prepositional phrase opener: For your lack of compassion and decency.
- MC: **you must spend** your days as a frog.

✎ **1. Teacher's note.**
That clauses can function as nouns or adjectives, but the handy thing about them is they never take commas because they are always essential, so you do not need to teach students how they function.

✎ **2. Teacher's note.**
Guide students to see the pattern in each: preposition + noun (no verb).

✎ **3. Teacher's note.**
This could be one of several openers. *Out* is an adverb, *of my way* a prepositional phrase, and *peasant* a noun of direct address. The prince implies a command by this: Get out of my way! We could count it as a #1, a #2, or a mystery opener.

The main goal is sentence variety, so it is not critical to mark every sentence, especially ones like this that might involve a long debate.

DAY 4

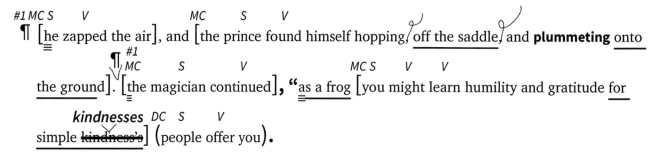

#1 MC S V   MC   S   V

¶ [he zapped the air], and [the prince found himself hopping off the saddle, and **plummeting** onto

the ground]. [the magician continued], "as a frog [you might learn humility and gratitude for

kindnesses DC S   V

simple ~~kindness's~~] (people offer you).

Fixes

INDENT ¶s because of a new topic (the magician's actions) and then a new speaker (his speech).

CAPITALIZATION. He, The, As.

COMMAS AND OTHER PUNCTUATION.

- **Items in a series.** Ask: Find two *and's* in the first sentence and explain whether the commas are needed. What is each cc joining?

  The first is correct because the comma + cc joins two main clauses: *He zapped the air,* **and** *the prince found himself hopping off the saddle.* Rule: MC, cc MC.

  The second comma should not be there because the cc *and* joins only two -ing participles, not three or more. Fix: **hopping** ... and **plummeting**.

- **Mid-sentence prepositional phrases** do not take commas. Fix: hopping **off the saddle**.

- **Quotations.** Fix: The magician continued, **"As** ... offer you. Rules: 1) Enclose speech in quotes but no close quotes because he is still speaking. 2) Use a comma with a verb of speaking (*continued*) that sets up a quote. 3) Capitalize the first word of a quoted sentence (*As*).

- **#2 prepositional openers.** Ask: Do we need a comma after *As a frog*? Answer: No, it is not required after short #2s. *See* ✏ **1.**

- **Apostrophes.** *Kindnesses* should be plural, not possessive.

Grammar Notations

PREPOSITIONAL PHRASES. off the saddle; onto the ground; As a frog (no verb, so prepositional phrase); for simple kindnesses.

CLAUSES, PHRASES, AND OPENERS.

- #1 subject opener and MC: **He zapped** the air.
- MC: the **prince found** himself hopping off the saddle and plummeting onto the ground.

  ADVANCED. *Hopping* and *plummeting* are not verbs here because they do not have a subject and helping verb directly in front of them. Contrast "The prince was hopping and plummeting."

- #1 subject opener and MC: The **magician continued**.
- MC: **you might learn** humility and gratitude for simple kindnesses.
- **Advanced.** DC: **people offer** you. This is a dependent clause with an implied *that*. *See* ✏ **2.**

---

plummeting: falling straight down; plunging

✏ **1. Teacher's note.**
As a frog works like an opener because it is the start of the quoted sentence.

✏ **2. Teacher's note.**
That clauses can start adjective or noun clauses. When they start adjective clauses, as here, you can substitute *which* for them and it makes sense. This is because *that* usually substitutes for *which* in essential *which* clauses.

In IEW's system, we do not count *that* clauses as the *who-which* dress-up, however, because it means teaching students this difficult grammar. The nice thing about *that* clauses is that they never take commas, so students do not have to learn to distinguish *that* adjective clauses from *that* noun clauses.

Style

If desired, have students identify the strongest of the vocabulary dress-ups from this week. Discuss their answers. Suggestions:

- **Strong verbs.** reared up, retorted, thundered, zapped, plummeting (verbal).
- **Quality adjectives.** swollen-headed, pretentious, humid, shady, sweltering, startled, desolate, oblivious.

  ✎ **Teacher's note.** Re "Prince Arthur used to be a bit swollen-headed and pretentious": sometimes adjectives follow a linking verb (*be*) and point back to the subject (*Arthur*).

  If students mark the verbal *startled* as a verb, that is OK. You might explain that it describes the noun *horse* so functions as an adjective.

- **-ly adverbs.** kindly.

STUDENT REWRITE

As a teenager, Prince Arthur used to be a bit swollen-headed and pretentious. One humid afternoon in July, young Arthur was riding through a forest in his father's kingdom, seeking some shady relief from the sweltering sun. About halfway through the forest, his horse reared up, startled. A young boy stood in the path.

"Please, sir, I've lost my way," the boy explained. "Would you kindly give me a ride out of this desolate forest?"

"Out of my way, peasant," the prince retorted, oblivious that the boy was a magician in disguise.

Instantly the boy's voice thundered, "For your lack of compassion and decency, you must spend your days as a frog."

He zapped the air, and the prince found himself hopping off the saddle and plummeting onto the ground.

The magician continued, "As a frog you might learn humility and gratitude for simple kindnesses people offer you.

Week 14

Additional Clausal Starters

LEARN IT

Additional Clausal Starters

You have learned the basic list of words that usually begin adverb clauses, the www.asia.b or www words: *when, while, where, as, since, if, although, because.*

Other words can also fall into the www word category. Some commonly used ones are listed on the back of the www.asia.b grammar card for easy reference: *until, unless, whereas, wherever, whenever, before, after, as if, though.*

To count as a clausal opener or dress-up, the www word must start a clause, which must always have a subject-verb. Words like *before* and *after* are double-agents because they sometimes start phrases and sometimes start clauses. Examples:

#2 **Before breakfast,** Dorinda had destroyed three figurines, two urns, and one priceless painting. (*Before breakfast:* preposition + noun, no verb)

#5 **After Dorinda apologized for her recklessness,** she tried in vain to suppress her activity. (*After Dorinda apologized:* www word + subject-verb)

Commas with www words

Remember the comma rules with these clause starters:

- #5 clausal openers take commas after the clause: AC, MC.

- Mid-sentence adverb clauses usually do not take commas: MC AC. The exceptions will be discussed as they come up in the passages.

✏ **Teacher's note.** Always discuss punctuation that is affected by the larger sentence structure after identifying phrases and clauses. Ask students to share where they put commas and the reason for each. If they do not know the reason, guide them to figure it out. If there are commas that do not belong, ask them to identify those and give the reason they should not be there.

Page 30, *Fix It! Grammar: Frog Prince, or Just Deserts,* **Student Book 3**

Institute for Excellence in Writing

DAY 1

#1 MC S   V   V   AC   S   V   *kindheartedness*
[you will remain in this form], (until a princess **bestows** on you a kiss, in true ~~kind-heartedness~~).

#5 AC S   V *anyone* DC   S   V   MC S   V   V   V
(if you ever tell ~~any one~~) (who you actually are), however, [you will be fated to frog-hood forever]."

Fixes

CAPITALIZATION. You, If.

USAGE AND SPELLING. 1) *Kindheartedness* is one word, no hyphen. 2) *Anyone* is one word. 3) *Who* versus *whom: see* ♡.

ALLITERATION. Ask students to find the alliteration in the passage. Answer: fated to frog-hood forever.

COMMAS AND OTHER PUNCTUATION.

- **Quotations.** Continue quote where the last sentence left off (no opening quotations), but close the speech with quotations (period inside): You … forever."

- **Mid-sentence adverb clauses.** The www words are not the only clausal starters (subordinating conjunctions). Three more common ones are *until, whereas, unless*. Ask students to find one of them in this passage. Answer: *until*.

  Ask: Can the *until* clause stand alone as a sentence? Answer: No, it needs an MC before or after. Ask: Should it be set off with a comma, and why? Answer: No, adverb dress-ups do not take commas. Rule: MC AC (no comma).

  Fix: You will remain in this form **until a princess bestows on you a kiss.**

- **Mid-sentence prepositional phrases** do not take commas. Fix: … a kiss **in true kindheartedness.**

- **#5 clausal opener and transitions.** Ask: Should there be any commas in the second sentence? Answer: Yes, after the #5 opener and around the transition *however*.

  Fix: **If you ever tell anyone who you actually are, however,** you will be fated to frog-hood forever.

Grammar Notations

PREPOSITIONAL PHRASES. in this form; on you; in true kindheartedness; to frog-hood. *See* ✎.

CLAUSES, PHRASES, AND OPENERS.

- #1 subject opener and MC: **You will remain** in this form.
- AC (adverb clause): until a **princess bestows** on you a kiss in true kindheartedness.
- #5 clausal opener and AC: If **you** ever **tell** anyone.
- DC (*who-which* clause): who **you** actually **are.**
- MC: **you will be fated** to frog-hood forever.

---

bestows: presents as a gift or honor

♡ **Grammar lovers.** *Who* is correct, but the reason is advanced and does not need to be taught at this level. Simply put, it functions as a subject complement: you are *he,* so *who* you are. We determine the case of *who* within its own *who* clause, not in relation to words outside the clause.

✎ **Teacher's note.** If your students still need the practice, continue to guide them to see the pattern in each prepositional phrase: preposition + noun (no verb). Ask: What does a prepositional phrase begin with? (a preposition) End with? (a noun). What is missing? (a verb). If they know this cold, just look for the underlines and guide as needed.

DAY 2

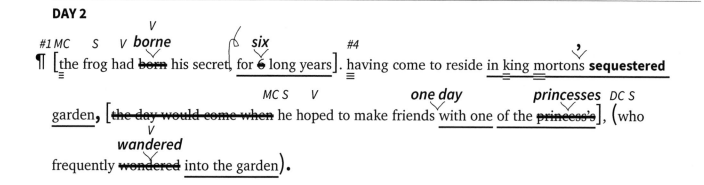

Fixes

INDENT ¶ because time has passed.

CAPITALIZATION. The, Having, King Morton's.

USAGE AND SPELLING. 1) **Borne** is the preferred spelling of the past participle of the verb *to bear*. *Born* is a different verb meaning to give birth to. 2) Not *wondered* but **wandered**.

NUMBERS. Spell out numbers written as one or two words: **six** long years.

COMMAS AND OTHER PUNCTUATION.

- **Mid-sentence prepositional phrases** do not take commas. Fix: The frog had borne his secret **for six long years**.

- **Apostrophes** for possession, not for plurals. Fixes: King **Morton's** garden; **princesses**, not *princess's*.

- **#4 -ing openers** take commas. **Having come to reside in King Morton's sequestered garden,** the day would come when he hoped to make friends.

  Ask: Is the subject after the comma (*day*) the one doing the -inging? Answer: No, it is not the day that resides in the garden but Arthur! This is an illegal #4 (a dangling modifier). Fix by making the subject after the comma the one doing the -inging.

  Fix: Having come to reside in King Morton's sequestered garden, **he hoped to make friends one day** with one of the princesses. *See ✐*.

- **ADVANCED. Nonessential elements** take commas. The *who* clause is nonessential because the two princesses are already sufficiently identified. It tells us more about them but does not specify any further which princesses are meant. The original is correct: with one of the princesses, **who frequently wandered into the garden.**

Grammar Notations

PREPOSITIONAL PHRASES. for six long years; in King Morton's sequestered garden; with one; of the princesses; into the garden.

CLAUSES, PHRASES, AND OPENERS.

- #1 subject opener and MC: The **frog had borne** his secret for six long years.

- #4 -ing participial phrase opener: Having come to reside in King Morton's sequestered garden.

- MC: **he hoped** to make friends one day with one of the princesses.

- DC (*who-which* clause): **who** frequently **wandered** into the garden. Ask students to identify the subject of *wandered*. Answer: *who*. The subject of *who-which* clauses is usually the *who* or *which*.

sequestered:
providing privacy

✐ **Teacher's note.**
Students might fix the dangling modifier by keeping more of the original wording: Having come to reside in King Morton's sequestered garden, he hoped *the day would come when he would* make friends with one of the princesses. Since this is wordy, suggest the simpler alternative of *one day*.

DAY 3

#3   MC   S *DC S first* V   V   •¶   MC S   V   DC

unluckily, [the one (he ~~1st~~ met) was dorinda], not maribella, at the table now, [he **conjectured**] (how

S   V   V

he might charm the princess).

conjectured: formed a theory; guessed

Fixes

INDENTS. Do not indent the first sentence because it is still telling his story, but indent second sentence because we return to the present time.

CAPITALIZATION. Unluckily, Dorinda, Maribella, At. Use lowercase for titles without a name: the **princess**.

NUMBERS. Spell out ordinal numbers: **first**.

COMMAS AND OTHER PUNCTUATION.

- **#3 -ly adverb openers.** Ask: Did you put a comma after *Unluckily*? Answer: Yes. We pause there so we need a comma.

  ADVANCED. We pause because the -ly adverb modifies the whole sentence, not the verb only. What is unlucky is the fact that Arthur met Dorinda first.

- **ADVANCED. Contrasting elements** take commas. The original is correct: Dorinda, **not Maribella**.

- **Short #2 openers** take commas when a pause is needed. The comma makes it clear that *now* goes with *At the table*, not *he conjectured*. The original is correct: **At the table now,** he conjectured.

- **Run-on sentence** (comma splice MC, MC). Ask students to show where the comma splice is. Answer: after *Maribella*. Fix, with MCs italicized: Unluckily, *the one he first met was Dorinda*, not Maribella. ¶ **At the table now,** *he conjectured how he might charm the princess*. See ✐.

Grammar Notations

PREPOSITIONAL PHRASES. at the table.

CLAUSES, PHRASES, AND OPENERS.

- #3 -ly adverb opener: Unluckily.
- MC: the **one** he first met **was** Dorinda.

  > ✐ **Teacher's note.** If students have trouble recognizing the subject and verb of the MC, ask them to find the verb first. Then ask who or what is doing that verb action. If students answer *he*, ask if "*he* was Dorinda"! If they answer *Dorinda* or *Maribella*, explain that the subject will come before the verb here. If they are wildly guessing, remind them that pronouns can function as subjects.
  >
  > It may help to remove the dependent clause in the middle of it so they can see the main clause better: *the **one was** Dorinda*.

- DC (invisible *who* clause): **he** first **met. ADVANCED.** *Whom* is implied: whom he first met.
- #2 prepositional phrase: At the table.
- MC: **he conjectured**.
- DC: how **he might charm** the princess.

> ✐ **Teacher's note.** If the issue comes up, explain that MCs need something as strong as a period *somewhere between them*. Often, phrases or dependent clauses will come in between the main clauses, but it is still a run-on if nothing as strong as a period comes between them.

DAY 4

S   V

#4   MC *Dorinda held her napkin*

¶ unwilling to touch the frog‚ with her own precious fingers, [~~dorinda's napkin was held~~ between her

V   ,

thumb and first finger‚ and then **uneremoniously** grabbed one of arthurs hind legs]‚ depositing him

on the table‚ beside her plate.

Fixes

INDENT ¶ because of a new topic, turning attention away from Arthur's story and to Dorinda's actions.

CAPITALIZATION. Unwilling, Dorinda, Arthur's.

COMMAS AND OTHER PUNCTUATION.

- **Mid-sentence prepositional phrases.** Ask: Are the commas after *frog* and *table* correct, and why? Answer: Incorrect because prepositional phrases do not take commas. Fixes: Unwilling to touch the frog **with her own precious fingers**; the table **beside her plate.**

- **#4 -ing openers.** Legal #4s end with a comma plus the subject doing the -inging. This one correcly has a comma, but is it legal? Answer: No, Dorinda's napkin does not care whether or not it touches the frog! This is an illegal #4 (a.k.a. dangling modifier). To fix, change the subject after the comma to *Dorinda*.

  Fix: Unwilling to touch the frog with her own precious fingers, **Dorinda held her napkin.** Now, *Dorinda* is the subject after the comma and the one doing the -inging. The sentence is now legal!

- **Items in a series.** Explain why there should or should not be a comma before each of the *and*'s.

  The first *and* correctly has no comma because it joins only two nouns, not three or more: **thumb** and first **finger.**

  The second *and* joins two verbs to the same subject (a compound verb) so should not have the comma: MC cc 2nd verb. Fix: Dorinda **held** … and then … **grabbed.**

- **Apostrophes** for possession. Fix: **Arthur's** hind legs.

- **ADVANCED. Nonessential participial phrases** take commas. Ask: Why is the participial phrase *depositing* … nonessential? Answer: If you remove it, it does not affect the meaning of the rest of the sentence: she still grabbed Arthur's leg. The original is correct with a comma before *depositing*.

unceremoniously: abruptly, without ceremony

Grammar Notations

PREPOSITIONAL PHRASES. with her own precious fingers; between her thumb and first finger; of Arthur's hind legs; on the table; beside her plate.

CLAUSES, PHRASES, AND OPENERS.

- #4 -ing participial phrase opener: Unwilling to touch the frog with her own precious fingers.

- MC: **Dorinda held** her napkin between her thumb and first finger and then unceremoniously **grabbed** one of Arthur's hind legs.

  ✐ **Teacher's note.** Check that students marked the compound verb: *held* and *grabbed*.

Style

If desired, have students identify the strongest of the vocabulary dress-ups from this week. Discuss their answers. Suggestions:

- **Strong verbs.** bestows, borne, reside, wandered, conjectured, charm, grabbed. If students choose the verbal *depositing* as a verb, that is OK. *See* ♡.
- **Quality adjectives.** sequestered, precious.
- **-ly adverbs.** actually, frequently, unceremoniously.

♡ **Grammar lovers.** *Depositing* is a participle (a type of verbal) that functions as an adjective modifying *Dorinda*.

STUDENT REWRITE

You will remain in this form until a princess bestows on you a kiss in true kindheartedness. If you ever tell anyone who you actually are, however, you will be fated to frog-hood forever."

The frog had borne his secret for six long years. Having come to reside in King Morton's sequestered garden, he hoped to make friends one day with one of the princesses, who frequently wandered into the garden. Unluckily, the one he first met was Dorinda, not Maribella.

At the table now, he conjectured how he might charm the princess.

Unwilling to touch the frog with her own precious fingers, Dorinda held her napkin between her thumb and first finger and then unceremoniously grabbed one of Arthur's hind legs, depositing him on the table beside her plate.

Week 15

Invisible #2

LEARN IT

Sometimes it is tricky to identify some of the sentence openers because they do not follow established patterns.

Students often ask how to mark sentences like these: Saturday, Dorinda was unusually bored. The night before at a lively masquerade, she had waltzed and tangoed.

These are invisible #2 openers because the preposition *on* or *during* is implied.

Invisible #2s are sentences that start with some time frame. They occur when the sentence sounds better without the preposition. Mark and punctuate invisible #2s just like regular #2s.

You have already seen a few in previous passages:

#2 **One crisp spring morning** when the cherry blossoms were just beginning to appear, Princess Dorinda was distracted.

#2 **Moments later** a footman appeared.

#2 **One humid afternoon** in July, young Arthur was riding through a forest.

Notice that only the long #2 openers take a comma. When there are multiple openers, save the comma for the end of them all.

These exercises should be a game that is fun to play. The detailed discussion notes are mainly for the teacher's benefit. You do not need to discuss them all for your student to succeed.

◆ **Listen.** If your student is struggling, reduce the number of things to look for. If you have not listened to Andrew Pudewa's Mastery Learning talk, now would be a good time. See the blue page at the front of this book for download instructions.

Page 32, *Fix It! Grammar: Frog Prince, or Just Deserts,* **Student Book 3**

DAY 1

#2 *minute*   MC S   V   AC S   V ¶ #5 / AC   S *used* V

a ~~minuet~~ later [she scrunched back into her chair] as far (as she could). (since he ~~use~~ to have a taste

                                 MC S   V

for princely but **savory fare**), [arthur politely declined the main course], sturgeon roe fricassee.

Fixes

CAPITALIZATION. A, Since, Arthur. Students should not capitalize *sturgeon roe fricassee* since dishes are usually common nouns.

INDENT ¶ second sentence because of a new topic, turning attention to Arthur.

SPELLING AND USAGE. 1) Not *minuet*, a slow and elegant type of dance, but **minute**, sixty seconds. 2) He **used** to have a taste, not *use*.

COMMAS AND OTHER PUNCTUATION. *See* ✐ **1**.

- **Run-on sentence** (fused sentence MC MC). Ask first: Does the *since* clause go with the MC before it or after it? Answer: After. Ask: Where is the fused sentence and how did you fix it? Answer: Just before the *since* clause. A period is the best fix since the MCs are about different ideas.

  Fix, with MCs italicized: *she scrunched back into her chair* as far as she could. Since he used to have a taste for princely but savory fare, *Arthur politely declined the main course.*

- **Comma questions.**

  Ask: Should there be a comma after *chair*, and why? Answer: No comma needed to set off an adverb clause dress-up: MC AC. The original is correct: she scrunched back into her chair **as far as she could**.

  Ask: Should there be a comma before the cc *but*, and why? Answer: No comma is correct: it joins only two adjectives in a series, not three or more. Note: *princely* is an adjective because it modifies a noun, *fare*.

  Ask: Did you add any commas in the second sentence, and why? Answer: Comma at the end of the #5 clausal opener. Rule: AC, MC. Fix: **Since he used to have a taste for princely but savory fare,** Arthur politely declined the main course.

  ADVANCED. The comma after *course* correctly sets off the nonessential phrase *sturgeon roe fricassee. See* ✐ **2**.

Grammar Notations

PREPOSITIONAL PHRASES. into her chair; for princely but savory fare.

CLAUSES, PHRASES, AND OPENERS.

- Invisible #2 opener: A minute later. Explain that invisible #2s begin with some time frame where a preposition like *during, on,* or *in* is implied, but the opener is more stylish without it.

- #1 subject opener and MC: **She scrunched** back into her chair.

- **ADVANCED.** AC (adverb clause): as **she could**. *As far as* is an idiom leading into the clause.

- #5 clausal opener and AC: Since **he used** to have a taste for princely but savory fare.

- MC: **Arthur** politely **declined** the main course.

---

savory: pleasant or agreeable in taste or smell

fare: food; diet

Fricassee is a meat served with a sauce. Since fish eggs only marginally count as meat, this sounds pseudo-gourmet and not tasty.

✐ **1. Teacher's note.** Always ask students why punctuation should or should not be there. Also, remember that the points marked *advanced* should be discussed only if your students ask or if you wish to cover that point of grammar for an older or stronger student. These concepts will reappear in later books!

✐ **2. Teacher's note.** This is also an invisible *who-which*: the main course, [*which was*] sturgeon roe fricassee. Invisible *who-which*'s are usually appositives with *who* or *which* plus a *be* verb implied.

DAY 2

#1 MC S V   V   *MC S   V*

¶ " [I'll take just desserts] ," [he requested], eying <u>with glee</u> the side cart piled high, <u>with **delectable**</u>

<u>tarts, scones, pies, cobblers, and cheesecakes.</u>

Pun. *I'll take just desserts* points to the pun in the story's subtitle (*Frog Prince, or Just Deserts*), as well as a common spelling confusion: *just deserts = deserved reward; just desserts = only dessert*. Arthur wants only the sweet foods. He is not asking for his just deserts.

delectable: delicious

Fixes

INDENT ¶ because of a new speaker.

SPELLING. Both *eying* and *eyeing* are correct.

COMMAS AND OTHER PUNCTUATION.

- **Quotations.** Fix: "I'll take just desserts," he requested. Rules: 1) Enclose speech in quotes. 2) When speaking verbs (*requested*) set up quotations, add a comma inside the closing quotes.

- **ADVANCED. Nonessential phrases** take commas. The comma before *eying* is correct: he requested, **eying with glee the side cart piled high**. That Arthur is eying these desserts with glee does not change the meaning of the rest of the sentence.

- **Mid-sentence prepositional phrases** do not take commas. Fix: the side cart piled high **with delectable tarts**.

- **Commas with items in a series.** Use commas with three or more items in a series, in this case, nouns. Fix: the side cart piled high with delectable **tarts, scones, pies, cobblers,** and cheesecakes.

  Students may put a colon in front of this list. If they do, explain that colons have to come after complete thoughts. They often do set up lists, but only after a main clause. You could also explain it this way: there should not be punctuation between a preposition (*with*) and its objects (the items in the list).

Grammar Notations

PREPOSITIONAL PHRASES. with glee; with delectable tarts, scones, pies, cobblers, and cheesecakes. The last phrase has five objects of the preposition *with*.

CLAUSES, PHRASES, AND OPENERS.

- #1 subject opener and MC: **I'll take** just desserts.
- MC: **he requested**.
- **ADVANCED.** -ing participial phrase (not required to mark): eying with glee the side cart.
- **ADVANCED.** -ed participial phrase (not required to mark): piled high with delectable tarts ... .

DAY 3

```
#2            )MC  S                              V                                    #1 MC  S
¶ after supper, [king morton peremptorily ordered dorinda to set up arthur in the gold room]. [velvet
                                              #1 MCS
      V                   ^ MC S    V          Arthur  V   V  DC S  V    V
carpeted the floor] /; [silk blanketed the bed]. [he could tell] (he was going to relish his palace stay).
```

Fixes

peremptorily: without room for refusal; imperiously

INDENT ¶ because time has passed and a new scene.

CAPITALIZATION. After, King Morton, Dorinda, Arthur, Gold Room, Velvet, Arthur (in revised version).

Gold Room is the name of that particular room in the palace, so it is a proper noun.

UNCLEAR ANTECEDENT. King Morton ordered Dorinda to set up Arthur … . **He** could tell he was going to relish his palace stay. Is *he* Arthur or the king? Fix: King Morton ordered Dorinda to set up Arthur … . **Arthur** could tell he was going to relish his palace stay.

COMMAS AND OTHER PUNCTUATION.

- **#2 prepositional openers.** Ask students the rule for commas with #2 openers. Answer: Required if the opener is five or more words, optional if shorter. Recommended fix: **After supper** King Morton peremptorily ordered. We do not need a strong pause here, so the comma can easily be left out. *See* ✐ **1.**

- **Run-on sentence** (comma splice MC, MC). Ask students to find the comma splice (comma after *floor*) and explain what they did to correct it. Discuss these most likely solutions and ask students which they like best:
  - ◆ **Period:** Velvet carpeted the floor. Silk blanketed the bed. Works.
  - ◆ **Semicolon:** Velvet carpeted the floor; silk blanketed the bed. Works best: these MCs both show the luxury of the room. Since they are also parallel in construction, the semicolon connecting them is perfect.
  - ◆ **Comma + cc:** Velvet carpeted the floor, and silk blanketed the bed. Weaker: *and* dilutes the impact of the second main clause.
  - ◆ **Subordinating one clause** (making it an adverb clause): Whereas velvet carpeted the floor, silk blanketed the bed. Not the best solution because it sounds a little odd; none of the other www words works, either.

✐ **1. Teacher's note.** If students want to keep it, that is also fine, but the trend is to do away with unneeded commas.

Grammar Notations

PREPOSITIONAL PHRASES. After supper; in the Gold Room. *See* ✐ **2.**

CLAUSES, PHRASES, AND OPENERS.

- #2 prepositional phrase opener: After supper.
- MC: **King Morton** peremptorily **ordered** Dorinda to set up Arthur in the Gold Room.
- #1 subject opener and MC: **Velvet carpeted** the floor.
- MC: **silk blanketed** the bed.
- #1 subject opener and MC: **Arthur could tell.**
- **ADVANCED.** DC: **he was going** to relish his palace stay. This is an invisible noun clause with *that* understood: Arthur could tell *that* he was going to relish.

✐ **2. Teacher's note.** *Up* is not a preposition here but an adverb. If students mark it as a preposition, explain that prepositional phrases will make sense alone. *Up Arthur* does not make sense, but *to set up* does.

DAY 4

#2   *morning*   MC   S   V
¶ the next ~~a.m.~~, during a **substantial** breakfast, of sturgeon roe omelet, [king morton graciously insisted],
DC   S   V
(that arthur stay, at least a week).

Fixes

INDENT ¶ because time has passed.

CAPITALIZATION. The, King Morton, Arthur.

USAGE. Use words instead of casual abbreviations. Not *a.m.* but *morning*.

COMMAS AND OTHER PUNCTUATION. Ask students which commas belong, which do not, and why!

- **Invisible #2 prepositional openers** are punctuated like any regular #2.

  Ask: What is the rule for commas with #2 openers? Answer: Required if the opener is five or more words, including openers with multiple phrases. This one has three in a row, so place only one comma at the end of all of them.

  Fix by removing the first two commas: **The next morning during a substantial breakfast of sturgeon roe omelet,** King Morton graciously insisted.

- ***That* clauses** never take commas. Fix: King Morton graciously insisted **that Arthur stay.**

- **Mid-sentence prepositional phrases** do not take commas. Fix: that Arthur stay **at least a week.**

  This also explains why there is no comma on either side of *during a substantial breakfast* near the beginning of the sentence.

Grammar Notations

PREPOSITIONAL PHRASES. during a substantial breakfast; of sturgeon roe omelet; at least. *See* ✏ **1.**

CLAUSES, PHRASES, AND OPENERS.

- Invisible #2 prepositional opener: The next morning during a substantial breakfast of sturgeon roe omelet.

  This begins with a time frame. A preposition (*During, On*) is implied, but the sentence is stronger without it.
- MC: **King Morton** graciously **insisted.**
- DC: that **Arthur stay** at least a week. *See* ♡.

Style

If desired, have students identify the strongest of the vocabulary dress-ups from this week. Discuss their answers. Suggestions:

- **Strong verbs.** scrunched, declined, carpeted, blanketed, relish (a verbal).
- **Quality adjectives.** princely, savory, delectable, substantial. *See* ✏ **2.**
- **-ly adverbs.** politely, peremptorily, graciously.

---

substantial: of ample or considerable quantity

✏ **1. Teacher's note.** *Least* can be a noun but is not a typical one. *At least* is also an idiom, so do not worry about it if students do not underline it.

♡ **Grammar lovers.** This is a noun clause, not an adjective clause, because it follows a verb (*insisted*) and functions as its direct object, answering the question *what*. Adjective clauses usually follow a noun.

✏ **2. Teacher's note.** If students think *princely* is an adverb, ask them what it describes. Answer: a noun, *fare*, so it has to be an adjective. This is an imposter -ly adverb—that is, an adjective instead.

Eying also functions as an adjective, modifying *he*, and could count as a quality adjective, but do not teach this unless it comes up.

STUDENT REWRITE

A minute later she scrunched back into her chair as far as she could.

Since he used to have a taste for princely but savory fare, Arthur politely declined the main course, sturgeon roe fricassee.

"I'll take just desserts," he requested, eying with glee the side cart piled high with delectable tarts, scones, pies, cobblers, and cheesecakes.

After supper King Morton peremptorily ordered Dorinda to set up Arthur in the Gold Room. Velvet carpeted the floor; silk blanketed the bed. Arthur could tell he was going to relish his palace stay.

The next morning during a substantial breakfast of sturgeon roe omelet, King Morton graciously insisted that Arthur stay at least a week.

Week 16

Imperative Mood

LEARN IT

At the beginning of this book, you reviewed how to identify the subject-verb of clauses. The subject is the noun or pronoun that performs a verb action.

When a sentence is issuing a command or giving advice such as "Slow down," the subject *you* is implied, so the only thing to mark is the verb. This kind of sentence is written in the imperative mood. Watch for it this week.

Examples:

Don't tip over that vase! **You** *do not do this* is implied.

Stop texting your sister in the same room! **You** *stop* is implied.

Feed Arthur from your plate. **You** *feed* is implied.

Entertain him while he's convalescing. **You** *entertain* is implied.

Page 34, *Fix It! Grammar: Frog Prince, or Just Deserts,* **Student Book 3**

DAY 1

#6 MC S   V   #4   MC S   V   ,
¶ [dorinda groaned], . ~~and~~ glancing down, [she noticed arthurs hind leg **inadvertently** touching

                    ¶   MC S   V
her omelet]. "ew," [she cried], sweeping him from her plate, and accidentally hurling him

against the wall.

Fixes

inadvertently: not intentionally

INDENT ¶s for new topic (turning attention to her response) and new speaker.

CAPITALIZATION. Dorinda. Glancing, Arthur's, Ew.

COMMAS AND OTHER PUNCTUATION. Use the following discussion to guide students how to edit these sentences.

- **Misuse of coordinating conjunction.** Ask: Does the first cc *and* help the sentence, or is there a better construction? Answer: Better as two sentences. Her groaning is in response to her father's insistence that Arthur stay a week. Her glancing down is a separate idea. Also, a vss can make a more powerful statement than two MCs joined together.

  Fix: Dorinda **groaned. Glancing** down, she noticed Arthur's hind leg inadvertently touching her omelet.

- **#4 openers.** Ask: What opener is *Glancing down*? Answer: #4. What punctuation do #4s take? Answer: Always a comma. Fix: **Glancing down,** she noticed Arthur's hind leg.

  Ask: Is the subject after the comma the one doing the -inging? Answer: Yes, she is glancing down while noticing his hind leg, so this is a legal #4.

- **Apostrophes.** Use apostrophes to show possession: **Arthur's** hind leg.

- **Quotations.** Fix: "Ew," she cried. Rules: 1) Enclose speech in quotes. 2) Include a comma inside the closing quotes since a speaking verb (*cried*) sets up the quotation.

- **ADVANCED.** Ask: Why is there a comma before *sweeping*? Answer: it starts a nonessential participial phrase.

- **Items in a series.** Ask: What does the last cc *and* join, and is the comma correct? Answer: two -ing words, *sweeping* and *hurling*. No comma with two items.

  Fix: **sweeping** him from her plate **and** accidentally **hurling** him against the wall.

Grammar Notations

PREPOSITIONAL PHRASES. from her plate; against the wall.

CLAUSES, PHRASES, AND OPENERS.

- #6 vss and MC: **Dorinda groaned.**
- #4 -ing participial phrase opener: Glancing down.
- MC: **she noticed** Arthur's hind leg inadvertently touching her omelet.
- MC: **she cried.** See ✏.
- **ADVANCED.** -ing participial phrase (not required to mark): **sweeping** him from her plate and accidentally **hurling** him against the wall.

✏ **Teacher's note.**
Narration setting up a quotation (known as the attribution) has its own subject-verb and is a main clause, but it does not make sense as a complete thought without the quote. However, we determine punctuation of quoted speech apart from its attribution, so label attributions independently from the speech they set up.

If students label this a #1 opener and include the speech (*ew*), that is also fine since that is all Dorinda says.

DAY 2

$$\P\ \text{``}\underset{=}{\text{ow}}\text{!''}\ \overset{MC}{[}\underset{=}{\text{grunted}}\ \underset{S}{\text{arthur}}]\text{.}\ \overset{\P}{}\text{``}\underset{=}{\text{oops}}\text{!}\ \overset{\#1}{[}\underset{i}{\overset{MC\ S}{}}\ \underset{V}{\text{do}}\ \underset{V}{\text{believe}}]\ \overset{DC\ S\ V}{(}\underset{i\text{'ve}}{}\ \text{broken}\ \underset{V}{\text{your leg}})\ \text{.}\ \overset{\#1}{[}\underset{i}{\overset{MC\ S\ V}{\text{'m so sorry}}}]\text{,''}\ \overset{MC\ S}{[}\underset{=}{\text{dorinda}}$$

MC V · · · S ¶ · #1 MC S V · V · DC S V · V · #1 MC S V · MC S

¶ **"ow!"** [grunted arthur]. **"oops!** [i do believe] (i've broken your leg) . [i'm so sorry]," [dorinda

V · #1 MC V · DC S V · V · MC S · V

feigned. **"**[wish] (i had broken more than just your leg)," [she muttered].

Fixes

feigned: pretended

INDENT ¶s twice because of new speakers.

CAPITALIZATION. Ow, Arthur, Oops, I, I've, I'm, Dorinda, Wish, I.

COMMAS AND OTHER PUNCTUATION.

- **Interjections.** An interjection is a word that expresses emotion. Ask: Where are two interjections, and how are they punctuated? Answer: **Ow!** and **Oops!** Since they express strong emotion, use exclamations.

- **Quotations.** Fix: "Ow!" grunted Arthur. ¶ "Oops … sorry," Dorinda feigned. "Wish … leg," she muttered.

   Rules: 1) Enclose speech in quotes. 2) Add commas inside closing quotes when speaking verbs (*muttered, feigned*) set up the quotes. Exception: not after exclamations. 3) Keep *grunted* lowercase since it sets up "Ow!" and is therefore part of the same sentence.

- **Run-on sentence** (comma splice MC, MC). Ask student to locate the comma splice and explain their solution. Answer: Use a period to hold together these two MCs. *I do believe I've broken your leg. I'm so sorry.*

Grammar Notations

PREPOSITIONAL PHRASES.

- ✎ **Teacher's note.** The word *than* is usually a conjunction (which starts a clause), sometimes a preposition (which takes a noun). Complete the construction to figure out which: "I wish I had broken more than I had broken just your leg"? No, that does not make sense. "I wish I had broken more parts than just your leg"? Yes, comparing nouns makes sense, which would make *than* a preposition here. However, this is difficult and not important to understand, so no need to teach it to your students.

CLAUSES, PHRASES, AND OPENERS.

- MC: **grunted Arthur**.

   If students label this a #6 and include "Ow!" that is fine, but it is better to treat the attribution apart from the speech it *sets up*.

- #1 subject opener and MC: **I do believe.**

- **ADVANCED.** DC: **I've broken** your leg. *That* is understood, so this is a dependent clause. *See* ♡ **1.**

- #1 subject opener and MC: **I'm so sorry.**

- MC: **Dorinda feigned.**

- #1 subject opener and MC: **Wish. ADVANCED.** The subject, *I*, is implied: **I wish.**

- **ADVANCED.** DC: **I had broken** more than just your leg. *See* ♡ **2.**

- MC: **she muttered.**

♡ **1. Grammar lovers.** This is an invisible noun clause with *that* understood. It follows a verb (*believe*) and functions as its direct object.

♡ **2. Grammar lovers.** This is another invisible noun clause with *that* understood. It follows a verb (*wish*) and functions as its direct object.

DAY 3

#3   *MC*   *S*   *V*   *#5 AC*   *S*   *V*

¶ fortunately for arthur, [the palace vet knew how to set broken frog legs]. "(because frogs are slow

                AC

       MC S   *V*   ***as if*** *S*   *V*   *V*   *MC S*   *V*

healers), however, [it looks] (~~like~~ it will be a lengthy **convalescence**)," [he informed king morton and

        #1

        MC S   *V*   *V*

his daughter]. "[he will have to stay in the infirmary for a month at least]."

Fixes

INDENT ¶s because of a new topic and a new speaker.

CAPITALIZATION. Fortunately, Arthur, Because, King Morton, He. Do not capitalize *palace vet*, which is not an honorific title.

USAGE. Use *like* when comparing two nouns; use *as* or *as if* when comparing a noun to an idea, which has a subject-verb. Fix: it looks **as if** it will be a lengthy convalescence. See ♡.

COMMAS AND OTHER PUNCTUATION.

- **#3 opener with prepositional phrase.** Add a comma before the MC because the opener needs a pause. Fix: **Fortunately for Arthur,** the palace vet knew.

  ADVANCED. *Fortunately* modifies the whole sentence, not just the verb, so it requires a comma, but save the comma for the end of all the openers.

- **Quotations.** "Because … convalescence," and "He … least." Rules: 1) Enclose speech in quotes. 2) Use a comma with a speaking verb to set up a quote. 3) Check that the comma and period are inside the closing quotes.

- **#5 clausal openers and transitions** take commas. Fix: **Because frogs are slow healers, however,** it looks … .

- **Run-on sentence** (fused sentence MC MC). Looking only at the vet's words, ask students to locate the fused sentence and explain its correction. Answer: A period is needed before the second quote. It may help to remove the interrupter: It looks as if it will be a lengthy convalescence. **He** will have to stay.

  When we add back in the interrupter, there still must be a period. Fix: "It looks as if it will be a lengthy convalescence," he informed King Morton and his daughter. "He will have to stay."

Grammar Notations

PREPOSITIONAL PHRASES. for Arthur; in the infirmary; for a month; at least.

CLAUSES, PHRASES, AND OPENERS.

- #3 -ly adverb opener: Fortunately for Arthur. This has an -ly adverb and a prepositional phrase before the MC, but we label the sentence by the first opener.
- MC: the palace **vet knew** how to set broken frog legs.
- #5 clausal opener and AC: Because **frogs are** slow healers.
- MC: **it looks**.
- AC (adverb clause): as if **it will be** a lengthy convalescence.
- MC: **he informed** King Morton and his daughter.
- #1 subject opener and MC: **He will have** to stay in the infirmary for a month at least.

convalescence: the time of gradual return to health

♡ **Grammar lovers.** As a preposition, *as* means in the role of; when *as* is comparing something, it starts an adverb clause. *Like* can also compare, but only to a noun since it is a preposition and cannot have a verb in its phrase.

DAY 4

MC S V MC V S V
¶ "what rotten luck!" [dorinda thought to ~~two/too~~ herself]. [not only was he going to stick around],

MC S V DC S V ¶ #1 MC V
but [her father insisted] (she bring to ~~two/too~~ him all his meals). "[do whatever you can to ~~two/too~~

AC S V MC S V
make him comfortable], (while he's **recumbent**)," [king morton ordered].

Fixes

INDENT both ¶s because of new speakers. Treat unspoken thoughts like spoken words.

CAPITALIZATION. What, Dorinda, Not, Do, King Morton.

HOMOPHONES. All need the preposition *to*: thought **to** herself; bring **to** him; **to** make.

COMMAS AND OTHER PUNCTUATION.

- **Punctuating thoughts.** Fix: "What rotten luck!" Dorinda thought to herself.

  Rules: Usually use italics for characters' thoughts. However, handwriting italics is difficult, so students may use quotes instead. *What rotten luck* is exclamatory, so follow it with an exclamation inside the closing quotes.

  Ask: Is the second sentence (*Not only …*) her direct thoughts or indirect (as in, *she thought that*)? Answer: Indirect, so do not use quotation marks. Ask: How do we know this is indirect? Answer: It says *her father* and refers to Dorinda as *she*. If she were thinking this, she would say *my dad* and *I*.

- **MC, cc MC.** Comma before the cc *but*. Fix: Not only was he going to stick around, **but** her father insisted she bring to him all his meals. *See* ✏ **1.**

- **Quotations.** Fix: "Do … recumbent," King Morton ordered. Rules: 1) Use quotation marks with direct quotations. 2) Use a comma with speaking verb + direct quotation. 3) Check that students put the comma inside the closing quotation marks.

- **Mid-sentence adverb clauses** do not take commas: MC AC. Fix: Do whatever you can to make him comfortable **while he's recumbent.**

Grammar Notations

PREPOSITIONAL PHRASES. to herself; to him.

CLAUSES, PHRASES, AND OPENERS.

- MC: **Dorinda thought** to herself.
- MC: Not only **was he going** to stick around.

  ✏ **Teacher's note.** *To stick*, an infinitive, is not part of the verb. Infinitives never function as verbs.

  ADVANCED. The sentence is a #1 but the "not only" MC requires another MC ("but…") to complete the thought. "Not only" and "but also" are correlative conjunctions.

- MC: her **father insisted**.
- **ADVANCED.** DC: **she bring** to him all his meals. *That* is implied.
- #1 subject opener and MC: **Do** whatever you can to make him comfortable. Ask: What is the subject of *do*? Answer: An implied *you*. This is in the imperative (command) mood. *See* ✏ **2.**
- AC (adverb clause): while **he's** recumbent. *See* ✏ **3.**
- MC: **King Morton ordered.**

recumbent: lying down; inactive

✏ **1. Teacher's note.** *Not only … but (also)* is known as a correlative conjunction. Each part must be followed by the same grammatical construction (MCs, here). What may confuse students is that the first part does not sound like a MC because it needs the second part to complete it, but grammatically we treat this like any MC, cc MC.

✏ **2. Teacher's note.** *Whatever* starts a dependent clause with *you can* its subject-verb. This does not affect grammar or punctuation and is too hard for this level, so do not worry about marking it as a clause.

✏ **3. Teacher's note.** If students have trouble finding the subject and verb, ask them what *he's* means. Remind them that pronouns (*he*) can function as subjects. By now they should know that *is* is a *be* verb.

Style

If desired, have students identify the strongest of the vocabulary dress-ups from this week. Discuss their answers. Suggestions:

- **Strong verbs.** groaned, grunted, feigned, muttered.
  - ✏ **Teacher's note.** If students mark *sweeping* and *hurling* as verbs, let it go. They are formed from verbs but function as adjectives in the Day 1 passage.
- **Quality adjectives.** lengthy, recumbent.
  - ✏ **Teacher's note.** Sometimes adjectives come after a linking verb (*was*) and point back to the subject (*he*): while he is recumbent.
- **-ly adverbs.** inadvertently, accidentally.

STUDENT REWRITE

Dorinda groaned. Glancing down, she noticed Arthur's hind leg inadvertently touching her omelet.

"Ew," she cried, sweeping him from her plate and accidentally hurling him against the wall.

"Ow!" grunted Arthur.

"Oops! I do believe I've broken your leg. I'm so sorry," Dorinda feigned. "Wish I had broken more than just your leg," she muttered.

Fortunately for Arthur, the palace vet knew how to set broken frog legs.

"Because frogs are slow healers, however, it looks as if it will be a lengthy convalescence," he informed King Morton and his daughter. "He will have to stay in the infirmary for a month at least."

"What rotten luck!" Dorinda thought to herself. Not only was he going to stick around, but her father insisted she bring to him all his meals.

"Do whatever you can to make him comfortable while he's recumbent," King Morton ordered.

Week 17

Transitional #2 Openers

LEARN IT

You have learned that #2 prepositional openers take commas when they are five or more words long but that the comma is optional with shorter #2 openers. Until now, you have used the pause test to decide whether a short #2 takes a comma.

When short #2s need a pause, they usually function as transitional expressions, which do require commas. Therefore, an advanced version of the #2 rule is this: when short prepositional openers work transitionally, they will need a comma, just as any transitional opener should take a comma. Usually the pause test is sufficient to determine this.

These are some common transitional #2 openers:

For example, no one dared discipline Dorinda.

In addition, she had unlimited credit at all the village stores.

Of course, that boosted the local economy.

In response, palace employees soon wearied of her self-indulgence.

On the other hand, the regional merchants catered to her.

After all, Dorinda was their leading customer.

Be verbs

Have you learned the *be* verbs? Recite them to your teacher. If you cannot remember, review the back of the Verb grammar card.

✎ **Teacher's note.** Remember to keep the exercise light and fun. It should be like a game. If your student groans when you say, "Time for Fix It!" something is wrong.

DAY 1

¶ "cool," [she cooed], (while secretly wondering how to escape **infirmary** duty), [she may have to

treat this slime-ball royally], but [she knew how to make herself a royal pain].

Fixes

infirmary: a place that cares for the sick or injured

INDENT ¶ because of a new speaker. The second sentence continues her private thoughts so is in the same paragraph.

CAPITALIZATION. Cool, She.

COMMAS AND OTHER PUNCTUATION.

- **Quotations.** Fix: "Cool," she cooed. Rules: 1) Enclose speech in quotes. 2) Add a comma inside the closing quotes when a speaking verb sets up the quote.

- **MC, cc MC.** Ask students to identify two MCs joined with only a cc. Answer: *She may have to treat this slime-ball royally* **but** *she knew how to make herself a royal pain.* What is missing? Answer: a comma before the cc *but.* Rule: MC, cc MC.

- **ADVANCED. Commas with contrasts.** Normally *while* clauses are not set off with a comma, but when they present a contrast to the clause before them (*she cooed* contrasts with what she is privately thinking), they take a comma. The original is correct.

- **Run-on sentence** (comma splice MC, MC). Ask students to find and correct the comma splice. Answer: The comma after *duty* is not strong enough to hold the two main clauses together. A period is the best solution.

  Fix, with MCs italicized: "Cool," *she cooed*, while secretly wondering how to escape infirmary duty. *She may have to treat this slime-ball royally.*

  Students may be confused because the MCs are not side by side, separated by a dependent clause instead. It is still a comma splice. Somewhere between the two MCs we need something stronger than a comma. Since the *while* clause goes with *she cooed*, the period should follow that dependent clause.

Grammar Notations

CLAUSES, PHRASES, AND OPENERS.

- MC: **she cooed.** *See* ✏.

- DC (www clause): while secretly **wondering** how to escape infirmary duty. If students label this an adverb clause (AC), let it go.

  ADVANCED. The subject and helping verb are understood: while **she was** wondering.

- #1 subject opener and MC: **She may have** to treat this slime-ball royally.

- MC: **she knew** how to make herself a royal pain.

✏ **Teacher's note.** The attribution has its own subject-verb and is a MC even though it does not make sense as a complete thought without the quote. Since we determine punctuation of speech apart from its attribution, we can label attributions independently from the speech they set up.

DAY 2

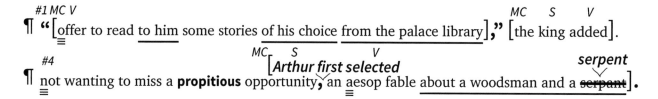

¶ <del>was the first selection arthur made</del>

Fixes

propitious: favorable

INDENT both ¶s because of a new speaker and a new topic.

CAPITALIZATION. Offer, Not, Arthur, Aesop. Use lowercase for titles without a name: the king.

SPELLING. *Serpent* has two *e*'s and no *a*'s.

COMMAS AND OTHER PUNCTUATION.

- **Quotations.** Fix: "Offer … library," the king added. Rules: 1) Enclose speech in quotes. 2) Add a comma inside the closing quotes when a speaking verb sets up the quote.

- **#4 -ing openers** take commas: **Not wanting to miss a propitious opportunity,** an Aesop fable … .

  Ask: Is the subject after the comma the one doing the -inging? Answer: No, the Aesop fable is not the one wanting, so this is an illegal #4 (a.k.a. dangling modifier). Fix by making the subject after the comma the true -inger, Arthur.

  Fix: Not wanting to miss a propitious opportunity, **Arthur first selected an Aesop fable about a woodsman and a serpent.**

  If students write, "Arthur's first selection was," explain that *Arthur's* is possessive and that *selection* is the subject after the comma, which is still illegal since it is not his selection that does not want to miss this opportunity.

  If they write, "Arthur first made the selection of an Aesop fable," ask if there is a less wordy way to say "made the selection of" and guide them to substitute the simple verb, *selected*.

Grammar Notations

PREPOSITIONAL PHRASES. to him; of his choice; from the palace library; about a woodsman and a serpent.

CLAUSES, PHRASES, AND OPENERS.

- #1 subject opener and MC: **Offer** to read to him some stories of his choice from the palace library. This is in the imperative (command) mood where the subject, *you*, is understood.

- MC: the **king added.**

- #4 -ing participial phrase opener: Not wanting to miss a propitious opportunity.

- MC: **Arthur** first **selected** an Aesop fable about a woodsman and a serpent. For change in wording, see #4 -ing openers, above.

DAY 3

#3   MC S   V   DC S   V   V

secretly [arthur hoped] (dorinda would gain something from this **apropos** story about ingratitude).

#6 MC S   V   •¶ #2   ,   AC   V   MC *woodsman*   V

¶ [dorinda then began the tale], "one winters day (while traipsing home), [a ~~woods man~~ stumbled

across a black serpent lying on the snow], seemingly dead.

Fixes

CAPITALIZATION. Secretly, Arthur, Dorinda, Dorinda, One.

INDENT ¶s: new topic, Dorinda's reading of the story; the start of the story.

APOSTROPHE. Use apostrophes to show possession: one **winter's** day.

SPELLING. *Woodsman* is one word, not two. *See* ✐ **1.**

COMMAS AND OTHER PUNCTUATION.

- **#3 -ly adverb openers** do not need commas when they modify the verb. Since it is correct to say *Arthur secretly hoped*, *secretly* modifies the verb. The original is correct.
- **Run-on sentence** (comma splice MC, MC). Ask students to identify and correct the comma splice. Remind them that other constructions (#2 opener; adverb clause) can come between the two main clauses. It is still a comma splice if nothing stronger than a comma is anywhere between them.

  Fix, with MCs italicized: *Dorinda then began the tale*. "One winter's day while traipsing home, *a woodsman stumbled across a black serpent lying on the snow*. *See* ✐ **2.**
- **Quotations.** "One winter's day … . Only open quotes because Dorinda is not finished.
- **Invisible #2 prepositional openers.** Ask: What opener do you think this is? Answer: An invisible #2 because a preposition like *on* is implied before a time frame. Ask: Does it need a comma? Answer: Yes, but after both openers. Fix: **One winter's day while traipsing home,** a woodsman stumbled. *See* ✐ **3.**
- **ADVANCED. Nonessential elements** take commas. *Seemingly dead* adds important information, but if removed, it does not change the meaning of the rest of the sentence (the woodsman still stumbled across a serpent), which is the test for nonessential phrases. The original is correct.

Grammar Notations

PREPOSITIONAL PHRASES. from this apropos story; about ingratitude; across a black serpent; on the snow.

CLAUSES, PHRASES, AND OPENERS.

- #3 -ly adverb opener: Secretly.
- MC: **Arthur hoped.**
- **ADVANCED.** DC with *that* understood: **Dorinda would gain** something from this apropos story about ingratitude.
- #6 vss and MC: **Dorinda** then **began** the tale.
- Invisible #2 opener: [*On*] one winter's day.
- AC (adverb clause): while **traipsing** home. **ADVANCED.** The subject and helping verb are understood: While *he was* traipsing home.
- MC: a **woodsman stumbled** across a black serpent lying on the snow.

apropos: fitting the circumstances well; pertinent

✐ **1. Teacher's note.** Unfortunately, rules do not help with compound words, which can be written as one word, two words, or one hyphenated word. When in doubt, consult a dictionary.

✐ **2. Teacher's note.** If students argue that *began* is a speaking verb setting up the quotation and therefore needing the comma, explain that *began* sets up a direct object, *the tale*. It cannot set up both *tale* and the quotation. Therefore, *Dorinda then began the tale* is a complete thought, which requires a period after it.

✐ **3. Teacher's note.** Check that students do not add a comma after *One winter's day*. Too many pauses are too choppy! No comma before *while* is also correct since it starts a mid-sentence adverb clause.

DAY 4

#4 MC S V   AC S V

picking it up, [he clasped the serpent <u>inside his coat to warm it</u>], (while he hastened home).

#T MC S V   #5 AC S   V MC S V

there, [he placed it <u>near the fire</u>]. (as the creature slowly revived), [his son stooped to stroke it].

#2   MC S   V

in response, [the serpent **nefariously** extended it's fangs].

Fixes

nefariously:
wickedly; villainously

CAPITALIZATION. Picking, There, As, In

USAGE. Not the contraction *it's* but the possessive pronoun, which has no apostrophe: **its** fangs.

COMMAS AND OTHER PUNCTUATION. For commas students miss, ask questions to lead them to figure out the correction for themselves.

- **#4 -ing openers** take commas. Fix: **Picking it up,** he clasped the serpent. Ask: Is the subject after the comma the one doing the -inging? Answer: Yes, so this is a legal #4.

- **Mid-sentence adverb clauses** do not take commas. Fix: he clasped the serpent inside his coat to warm it **while he hastened home.**

- **Run-on sentences.** Ask students to find and correct the two run-ons. A comma splice (MC, MC) is after *home* and a fused sentence (MC MC) after *fire.* Both places need a period to hold the two main clauses together.

  Fixes, with MCs italicized: *he clasped the serpent inside his coat to warm it* while he hastened home. **There,** *he placed it near the fire.* **As** the creature slowly revived, *his son stooped to stroke it.*

  The comma after *home* is not strong enough to hold together two MCs. Since the *while* clause goes with the first MC, add a period after *home.* Fix, with MCs italicized: *he clasped the serpent inside his coat to warm it* while he hastened home. There, *he placed it near the fire.*

  The comma after *fire* is not strong enough to hold together two MCs. Since the *as* clause best goes with the second MC, the period belongs after *fire.* Fix: … *he placed it near the fire.* As the creature slowly revived, *his son stooped to stroke it.*

- **Introductory transitional words and phrases** take commas. Fix: **There,** he placed it near the fire.

- **#5 clausal openers** take commas. Fix: **As the creature slowly revived,** his son stooped.

- **#2 prepositional openers** take commas if they are transitional, even when they are short. Fix: **In response,** the serpent nefariously extended its fangs.

Grammar Notations

PREPOSITIONAL PHRASES. inside his coat; near the fire; In response.

CLAUSES, PHRASES, AND OPENERS.

- #4 -ing participial phrase opener: Picking it up.
- MC: **he clasped** the serpent inside his coat to warm it.
- AC: while **he hastened** home.
- #T: There.
- MC: **he placed** it near the fire.

- #5 and AC: As the **creature** slowly **revived**.
- MC: his **son stooped** to stroke it.
- #2 prepositional phrase opener: In response.
- MC: the **serpent** nefariously **extended** its fangs.

Style

If desired, have students identify the strongest of the vocabulary dress-ups from this week. Discuss their answers. Suggestions:

- **Strong verbs.** cooed, traipsing, stumbled, clasped, hastened, revived, stooped, extended.
- **Quality adjectives.** propitious, apropos.
- **-ly adverbs.** seemingly, nefariously.

STUDENT REWRITE

"Cool," she cooed, while secretly wondering how to escape infirmary duty. She may have to treat this slime-ball royally, but she knew how to make herself a royal pain.

"Offer to read to him some stories of his choice from the palace library," the king added.

Not wanting to miss a propitious opportunity, Arthur first selected an Aesop fable about a woodsman and a serpent. Secretly Arthur hoped Dorinda would gain something from this apropos story about ingratitude.

Dorinda then began the tale.

"One winter's day while traipsing home, a woodsman stumbled across a black serpent lying on the snow, seemingly dead. Picking it up, he clasped the serpent inside his coat to warm it while he hastened home. There, he placed it near the fire. As the creature slowly revived, his son stooped to stroke it. In response, the serpent nefariously extended its fangs.

Week 18

Essential and Nonessential

LEARN IT

Some *who-which* clauses take commas and others do not. The way to tell is to determine if the clause is essential or nonessential to the sentence. This is an advanced concept; you do not need to figure this out on your own just yet.

If the clause is necessary to the meaning of the rest of the sentence or if it specifies which one of something is being discussed, it is essential and should not be enclosed in commas.

If it does not alter the meaning of the rest of the sentence or if the person or thing is adequately identified, it is nonessential and needs commas, even though it may be adding important information. **Nonessential does not mean unimportant.**

Tricks to test:

1. Mentally remove the clause from the sentence to see if it alters the information in the rest of the sentence or specifies who or what is meant. If it does not, the element is nonessential and should be set off with commas.

2. Put parentheses around the clause. If the sentence still seems to work, the clause or phrase is probably nonessential.

3. *That* clauses are always essential, so do not use commas with them.

Examples:

- "My dad will kill me if I lose that ball, *which cost him a royal fortune*." (nonessential *which* clause so use a comma)

    If we remove the *which* clause from the sentence, the main clause meaning does not change: the ball in question is already clear (*that ball*), and her dad will still kill her if she loses it. The *which* clause is therefore nonessential. Even though it adds important information, it should be set off with a comma.

- She broke the vase *that her mother held most dear*. (essential *that* clause so no comma)

    This clause is essential because it specifies which particular vase. She did not break just any vase but one that had been special to her mother.

- They agreed that the maid *who dressed Dorinda* should guard the knick-knacks when Dorinda headed into the hall. (essential *who* clause so no comma)

    The *who* clause specifies which maid—the one who dressed the princess—so is needed in the sentence and therefore not set off with commas. It restricts the information to that particular maid, which is why these are sometimes called restrictive clauses.

- All the palace footmen, *who were privately irked by Dorinda's antics*, decided to form a union to demand higher pay. (nonessential *who* clause so commas on both sides of the clause)

    The *who* clause is nonessential because it does not specify which footmen. *All the palace footmen* already indicates that all are involved.

Teacher's note. If this concept is too difficult or too much for your students now, you can skip it in this book because it will be covered in all the later *Fix It! Grammar* books.

Because most *who-which* clauses take commas, you could simply require that younger students put commas around them all and only later teach essential and nonessential *who-which* clauses.

Guide students to put the comma before the *who* or *which* and after the entire clause (unless it ends the sentence), not after the word *who* or *which*.

This week, the Day 1 passage has a nonessential participial phrase, which students will not need to correct.

On Day 4, help your students see how to apply this concept to a nonessential *which* clause.

Page 38, *Fix It! Grammar: Frog Prince, or Just Deserts,* **Student Book 3**

DAY 1

#2

with the serpent **poised** to strike, [the alarmed woodsman seized his ax, and cut it in twain],

thus saving his childs life. 'alas,' [he lamented], '[there is no gratitude from the wicked].'"

Fixes

CAPITALIZATION. With, Alas.

COMMAS AND OTHER PUNCTUATION. Ask students to explain their corrections. Guide them to figure out the answers for those they missed.

- **Long #2 prepositional openers** (five or more words) take commas. Fix: **With the serpent poised to strike,** the alarmed woodsman seized his ax.
- **Commas with cc's.** No comma before *and* because it joins only two verbs to one subject: MC cc 2nd verb. Fix: the alarmed woodsman **seized** his ax **and cut** it in twain.
- **ADVANCED. Nonessential elements** take commas. It is not only *who* and *which* clauses that can be nonessential. Most participial phrases are also nonessential. The original is correct (*thus* does not affect the pattern or punctuation): cut it in twain, **thus saving his child's life.**
- **Apostrophe for possession.** his child's life.
- **Quotations.** Fix: **With** the serpent … saving his child's life. 'Alas,' he lamented, 'there … wicked.'"

Rules:

- ◆ No open quotes for continued speech, but close quotes at the end because Dorinda is finished speaking.
- ◆ Use single quotations for quotes within quotes. This means both single and double quotes after *wicked.*
- ◆ Put commas on both sides of interruptions to speech (*he lamented*).

Grammar Notations

PREPOSITIONAL PHRASES. With the serpent; in twain; from the wicked.

CLAUSES, PHRASES, AND OPENERS.

- #2 prepositional phrase opener: With the serpent poised to strike. *See* ✎.
- MC: the alarmed **woodsman seized** his ax and **cut** it in twain.
- **ADVANCED.** If students mark *saving his child's life* as a clause, explain that -ing participles do not function as verbs unless coupled with a subject and helping verb, as in *he was saving his child's life,* which is why they start phrases (no verb) and not clauses (subject-verb).
- #T transitional opener: Alas.
- MC: **he lamented.**
- MC: there **is** no **gratitude** from the wicked. If students mark the subject-verb as *there is,* explain that *there* is not the subject. When a sentence starts with *there* and a *be* verb, the true subject comes after the verb.

poised: teetering; wavering

Twain means two.

✎ **Teacher's note.** *Poised* is not a verb here because there is no helping verb with it. Contrast this: The *serpent was poised to strike.* Instead, it is a past participle describing *serpent* so functions as an adjective, but this is too advanced for this level.

DAY 2

#1 MC   S   V   AC   S   V   DC S   V   #1
                                                                                          MC S   V
¶ [dorinda squirmed], (as she read the story), (that was so **germane**, to her situation). "[i was, like,

V
wanting something lighter to read], you know," [she hinted hopefully]. "sure enough," [arthur

    #1
    MC V   S V
complied]. "[read the next one]—[its more upbeat]."

Fixes

germane: related to the issue at hand

INDENT ¶ first sentence because of a new topic, Dorinda's reaction to the story, and the second part for a new speaker.

CAPITALIZATION. Dorinda, I, Sure, Arthur, Read.

USAGE. Not the possessive *its* but the contraction *it's* for *it is*: **it's** more upbeat.

COMMAS AND OTHER PUNCTUATION.

- **Mid-sentence adverb clauses** do not take commas: MC AC. Fix: Dorinda squirmed **as she read the story**.

- *That* **clauses** do not take commas. Fix: the story **that was so germane to her situation**. See ✎.

- **Mid-sentence prepositional phrases** do not take commas. Fix: germane **to her situation**.

- **Interrupters** take commas. Fix: " … wanting something lighter to read, **you know,**" she hinted. The interrupter *like* has commas around it for the same reason.

- **Quotations.** Fix: "I … know," she hinted hopefully. ¶ "Sure enough," Arthur complied. "Read … upbeat."

  Rules: 1) Enclose speeches in quotes. 2) Add commas inside closing quotes with speaking verbs. 3) Keep the period after *complied* because *sure enough* forms a complete thought.

✐ **Teacher's note.**
This is an adjective clause because it follows a noun, *story*, which it also describes. It is essential because it specifies which story—not just any story but the one that was germane to her situation.

That substitutes for *which* in essential adjective clauses and is usually the subject of its own clause.

Grammar Notations

PREPOSITIONAL PHRASES. to her situation. *Like* is a meaningless filler word here, not a preposition.

CLAUSES, PHRASES, AND OPENERS.

- #1 subject opener and MC: **Dorinda squirmed**.
- AC (adverb clause): as **she read** the story.
- DC (adjective clause): **that was** so germane to her situation.
- #1 subject opener and MC: **I was**, like, **wanting** something lighter to read.
- MC: **she hinted** hopefully.
- Idiom: Sure enough. Students do not need to label idioms that start sentences.
- MC: **Arthur complied**.
- #1 subject opener and MC: **Read** the next one. Ask: What mood is this verb? Answer: The imperative mood, used for commands or requests. The subject is an understood *you*.
- MC: **it's** more upbeat.

DAY 3

      MC S   V   #1   S V   V   ¶ #3

¶ "phew!" [dorinda exclaimed]. ["OK, its titled 'the dove and the ant.]' "early one morning,"

MC S   V   MC   S   #4
                       ant

[she read], "[a tiny ~~aunt~~ strove to **allay** its thirst in a stream]. dislodged by the rush of the stream,

MC S   V

[it struggled to stay above water].

Fixes

INDENT ¶s first part, new speaker; second part, new topic (start of the story).

CAPITALIZATION. Phew, Dorinda, The Dove and the Ant, Early, Dislodged.

Capitalize key words in titles, including the first and last words. Do not capitalize cc's (*and*) or articles (*the*) when they fall in the middle of a title: **The Dove and the Ant.**

SPELLING. Not *aunt*, one's relative, but **ant**, the insect.

USAGE. The first *its* is the contraction *it's* for *it is*: **it's** titled. The second *its* correctly uses the possessive: **its** thirst. *See* ✒.

COMMAS AND OTHER PUNCTUATION.

- **Interjections** take commas or exclamations. 1) Since Dorinda exclaims *Phew*, it is exclamatory. She is relieved she does not have to read another serious tale. 2) Add a comma after *OK*. Fix: **OK,** it's titled.

- **Titles** of short works go in quotes, in this case, single quotations for a quote within a quote: 'The Dove and the Ant.' *See* ♡.

  ADVANCED. Commas with titles. Titles are not always set off with commas. This title is the direct object of the verb *titled* so does not take commas. It is correct in the original: it's **titled 'The** Dove and the Ant.'

- **Quotations.** Fix: "Phew!" Dorinda exclaimed. "OK, it's titled 'The Dove and the Ant.' ¶ "Early one morning," she read, "a … water.

  Rules: 1) Enclose speech in quotes, but do not end either paragraph with double quotations because Dorinda is not finished speaking. 2) Add a period after *exclaimed* because Dorinda's exclamation stands alone. 3) Set off with commas interruptions to a sentence (*she read*).

- **#4 openers** take commas. Fix: **Dislodged by the rush of the stream,** it struggled.

Grammar Notations

PREPOSITIONAL PHRASES. in a stream; by the rush; of the stream; above water.

CLAUSES, PHRASES, AND OPENERS.

- MC: **Dorinda exclaimed.**
- #1 subject opener and MC: OK, **it's titled** 'The Dove and the Ant.' Ignore the interjection in labeling the opener. The verb includes the helping verb *is*.
- #3 -ly adverb opener: Early one morning.
- MC: **she read**.
- MC: a tiny **ant strove** to allay its thirst in a stream.
- #4 invisible -ing opener with *being* implied: Dislodged by the rush of the stream.
- MC: **it struggled** to stay above water.

allay: lessen or relieve

✏ **Teacher's note.**
We use the pronouns *it* and *which* instead of *he*, *she*, and *who* when referring to animals in the wild. Animals in stories that speak and act like humans take *who*, but the ant and dove in this story neither speak nor act like humans, so *it* and *which* work. However, they are motivated like humans, so if your students prefer using *he*, *she*, and *who*, that is fine. Just check for consistency. Teach this only if students are curious.

♡ **Grammar lovers.**
Single quotation marks are only for quotes within quotes, not for single words or phrases used in unusual ways. What confuses the matter is that the British commonly do the reverse, using single quotation marks for quotations and double for quotes within quotes!

DAY 4

#4   MC   S   V   V
noticing the struggle, [a dove plucked a leaf from a **proximate** tree, and let it fall near the ant],

DC S   V   V   ¶/#T   MC   S   V
(which was able to climb aboard and float to shore). "soon after, [a **fowler** noticed the dove,

                          V
and stealthily sought to grab it in his net].

Fixes

CAPITALIZATION. Noticing, Soon.

INDENT second sentence because of a new time.

COMMAS AND OTHER PUNCTUATION.

- **Quotations.** No quotes for continued speech. When a speaker changes topic, end the first paragraph without quotes to indicate the speaker is not finished, but start the next paragraph with quotes to signal that someone is still speaking. Fix: "Soon after.

- **#4 -ing openers** take commas. Fix: **Noticing the struggle**, a dove plucked a leaf. Ask: Is the subject after the comma the -inger? Answer: Yes, the dove is noticing, so this is a legal #4. *See* 🖉 **1.**

- **Items in a series.** Ask what words each *and* joins, what punctuation is needed before it, and why.

    - Two verbs, *plucked* and *let,* so no comma. Pattern: MC cc 2nd verb. Fix: a dove **plucked** a leaf from a proximate tree **and let** it fall near the ant. *See* 🖉 **2.**

    - Two verbals, *to climb* and *float,* so no comma. The original is correct: **to climb** aboard and **float** to shore.

    - Two verbs, *noticed* and *sought,* so no comma. Pattern: MC cc 2nd verb. Fix: a fowler **noticed** the dove **and** stealthily **sought** to grab it.

- **Nonessential elements** take commas. Fix: let it fall near the ant, **which was able to climb aboard and float to shore.**

    This *which* clause is nonessential because it does not affect the meaning of the rest of the sentence even though it adds important information. If we remove it, the dove still let the leaf fall near the ant. *See* 🖉 **3.**

- **#T transitional openers** take commas. Fix: **Soon after**, a fowler noticed the dove. Without the comma, the opener could be misread as a #5 clausal opener: soon after the fowler did this, something else happened.

Grammar Notations

PREPOSITIONAL PHRASES. from a proximate tree; near the ant; to shore; in his net.

🖉 **Teacher's note.** No need to mark the infinitive *to climb* since the preposition *to* in infinitives works differently from regular prepositions.

CLAUSES, PHRASES, AND OPENERS.

- #4 -ing participial phrase opener: Noticing the struggle.
- MC: a **dove plucked** a leaf from a proximate tree and **let** it fall near the ant.

proximate: close or very near

fowler: a hunter of birds

🖉 **1. Teacher's note.** Ask the -inger question every time to train students to check their own participial openers. If the subject after the comma is not doing the -inging, it is a dangling modifier.

🖉 **2. Teacher's note.** Coordinating conjunctions connect items that are parallel: each item will be the same part of speech and will come after the same words: *a dove plucked* and *a dove let.* If students choose another pair of words, such as *tree* and *let,* make a joke about how that sounds to guide them to find the correct words: *from a proximate* tree and *from a proximate* let? H'm, does that work?

🖉 **3. Teacher's note.** If this concept of essential elements is too difficult, you may skip it. It will continue to be taught and practiced through the rest of the *Fix It! Grammar* books.

Institute for Excellence in Writing

- DC (*who-which*): **which was able** to climb aboard and float to shore.
  - ✎ **Teacher's note.** The subject of most *who-which* clauses is *who* or *which*. If students mark *climb* or *float* as the verb, help them see that these are part of infinitives with the second *to* implied (*to climb ... to float*). Infinitives do not function as verbs.
- #T transitional opener: Soon after.
- MC: a **fowler noticed** the dove and stealthily **sought** to grab it in his net.
  - ✎ **Teacher's note.** *To grab* is another infinitive, not the true verb. Check that students marked the compound verb, two verbs with one subject.

Style

If desired, have students identify the strongest of the vocabulary dress-ups from this week. Discuss their answers. Suggestions:

- **Strong verbs.** lamented, squirmed, hinted, complied, strove, allay (a verbal), struggled, plucked.
- **Quality adjectives.** poised, alarmed, germane, upbeat, proximate.
- **-ly adverbs.** hopefully, stealthily.

STUDENT REWRITE

With the serpent poised to strike, the alarmed woodsman seized his ax and cut it in twain, thus saving his child's life. 'Alas,' he lamented, 'there is no gratitude from the wicked.'"

Dorinda squirmed as she read the story that was so germane to her situation. "I was, like, wanting something lighter to read, you know," she hinted hopefully.

"Sure enough," Arthur complied. "Read the next one—it's more upbeat."

"Phew!" Dorinda exclaimed. "OK, it's titled 'The Dove and the Ant.'

"Early one morning," she read, "a tiny ant strove to allay its thirst in a stream. Dislodged by the rush of the stream, it struggled to stay above water. Noticing the struggle, a dove plucked a leaf from a proximate tree and let it fall near the ant, which was able to climb aboard and float to shore.

"Soon after, a fowler noticed the dove and stealthily sought to grab it in his net.

Week 19

Semicolons

LEARN IT

Use semicolons instead of periods to join main clauses when the MCs are so closely linked that they belong together in one sentence: MC; MC. A sentence is an expression of one idea, so if the two MCs are separate ideas, they belong in two sentences linked with a period, not a semicolon.

A semicolon is one valid way to fix a run-on but cannot join any two main clauses, only those that express one idea. Importantly, they must join main clauses, not one main clause to a dependent clause or phrase.

Semicolons are especially useful to join main clauses that are parallel in structure:

- If Dorinda would stop and think, fewer things would break; if fewer things were broken, everyone would rejoice.

- At breakfast Dorinda terrorized the cook; at tea she pestered her maid.

- The king fumed; Dorinda just laughed.

Using semicolons well is an advanced skill, but watch for situations where they might work.

✎ Teacher's note. Semicolons are advanced for this level, so use this lesson to expose students to the concept but do not worry if they struggle to implement it consistently.

Page 40, *Fix It! Grammar: Frog Prince, or Just Deserts,* **Student Book 3**

Institute for Excellence in Writing

DAY 1

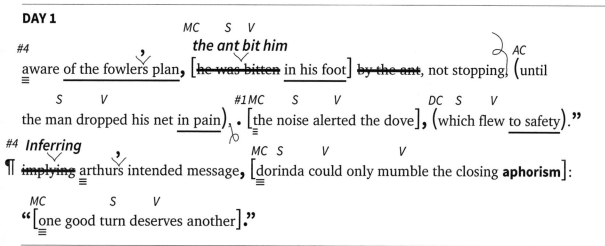

Fixes

CAPITALIZATION. Aware, The, Inferring (see Usage), Arthur's, Dorinda, One (first word of quoted sentence).

APOSTROPHE. Use apostrophes to show possession: the **fowler's** plan; **Arthur's** intended message.

USAGE. *Imply* means to suggest without stating directly. The context calls for its opposite, *to infer*, to draw a conclusion from evidence, in this case, the storyline. Fix: **Inferring** Arthur's intended message.

INDENT at *Inferring* because of a new topic, the message.

COMMAS AND OTHER PUNCTUATION. Guide students to correct what they missed by asking questions.

- **Quotations.** 1) No open quotes with continued speech, but close the story with quotes after *safety:* … to safety." 2) Quotes around the aphorism, which Dorinda is reading: "One … another." Check that students placed periods inside the closing quotes.

- **#4 -ing openers** take commas: **Aware of the fowler's plan,** he was bitten in his foot by the ant.

  Ask: Is the subject after the comma the one doing the -inging? Answer: No, it is not the fowler who is aware of his own plan! This is an illegal #4. Fix by changing the subject to *the ant:* Aware of the fowler's plan, **the ant bit him in his foot.** See ♡.

- **Mid-sentence adverb clauses** do not take commas: MC AC. Fix: the ant bit him in his foot, not stopping **until he dropped the net in pain.** See ✎ 1.

- **Run-on sentence** (comma splice MC, MC). Ask students to locate, explain, and correct the comma splice. Answer: The comma after *pain* is not strong enough to hold together the two main clauses. Fix, with MCs italicized: *the ant bit him in his foot,* not stopping until he dropped the net in pain. *The noise alerted the dove.*

- **Nonessential elements** take commas. Fix: The noise alerted the dove, **which flew to safety.** Guide students to understand why the *which* clause is nonessential. Answer: If we remove it from the sentence, it does not alter the fact that the noise alerted the dove. It does add important information, but this information is not essential to the meaning of the rest of the sentence. See ✎ 2.

- **#4 -ing openers** take commas. Fix: **Inferring Arthur's intended message,** Dorinda could only mumble. This is a legal #4 because Dorinda is doing the inferring.

aphorism: a brief saying expressing a general truth

♡ **Grammar lovers.** Fixing the dangling modifier has the added advantage of converting a wordy passive voice construction to active voice: not *he was bitten by the ant,* but *the ant bit him.*

✎ **1. Teacher's note.** If students do not recognize that *until* is a www word, ask them to check their www.asia.b grammar card from Week 2 and find one of the words from the list on the back in this passage.

✎ **2. Teacher's note.** Remember, if this concept of essential and nonessential elements is too difficult or too much, you may skip it.

Grammar Notations

PREPOSITIONAL PHRASES. of the fowler's plan; in his foot; in pain; to safety.

CLAUSES, PHRASES, AND OPENERS.

- **ADVANCED.** #4 invisible -ing opener with *being* implied: Aware of the fowler's plan.
- MC: the **ant bit** him in his foot.
- AC (adverb clause): until the **man dropped** his net in pain.
- #1 subject opener and MC: The **noise alerted** the dove.
- DC (*who-which*): **which flew** to safety.
- #4 -ing participial phrase opener: Inferring Arthur's intended message.
- MC: **Dorinda could** only **mumble** the closing aphorism.
- MC: One good **turn deserves** another.

DAY 2

#1 MC S   V   V   #4 *Wandering*

¶ [she slammed the book shut and **ignobly** fled to the palace grounds]. ~~wondering~~ through the

    MC S   V   #4   MC S   V

gardens, [she approached the fateful well]; . surprised, [she noticed there, ~~their/they're~~ an old

    DC S   V   V

woman], (who was attempting to draw water from the deep well).

Fixes

CAPITALIZATION. She, Wandering, Surprised.

INDENT twice: 1) New topic after quote. 2) New scene.

SPELLING AND HOMOPHONE. Fix: **wandering** (not *wondering*) through the gardens; she noticed **there** (in that place).

COMMAS AND OTHER PUNCTUATION.

- **Items in a series.** Ask: What does the cc *and* join, and is it punctuated correctly? Answer: Two verbs, so no comma: MC cc 2nd verb. The original is correct: She **slammed** the book shut **and** ignobly **fled**.
- **#4 -ing openers** take commas. Fix: **Wandering through the gardens,** she approached the fateful well. Ask: Is the subject after the comma the one doing the -inging? Answer: Yes, she (Dorinda) is both wandering and approaching, so this is a legal #4. See ✎ **1**.
- **Semicolons.** Ask: When do we use semicolons? Answer: To join two MCs expressing one idea so that they belong in one sentence. Ask: Does this semicolon work, and why?

  Answer: No, because the two MCs are different ideas, one about her approach and the other about what she sees when she gets to the well. Use a period instead. Fix: Wandering through the gardens, *she approached the fateful well.* Surprised, *she noticed there an old woman.*
- **Nonessential elements** take commas. Fix: an old woman, **who was attempting to draw water from the deep well.** Guide students to understand why this is nonessential. Answer: *An old woman* sufficiently identifies her. The *who* clause adds more information but does not affect the meaning of the rest of the sentence.

ignobly: shamefully; dishonorably

✎ **1. Teacher's note.** *Surprised* is an invisible #4, which is why it also takes a comma. It is legal since Dorinda (*she*) is the one who is surprised, not the old woman.

Grammar Notations

PREPOSITIONAL PHRASES. to the palace grounds; through the gardens; from the deep well.

CLAUSES, PHRASES, AND OPENERS.

- #1 subject opener and MC: **She slammed** the book shut and ignobly **fled** to the palace grounds.
- #4 -ing participial phrase opener: Wandering through the gardens. *See* ✏ **2.**
- MC: **she approached** the fateful well.
- **ADVANCED.** #4 invisible -ing opener with *being* implied: surprised.
- MC: **she noticed** there an old woman.
- DC (*who-which*): **who was attempting** to draw water from the deep well. Ask students what the subject is. Answer: *who*. Remind them that the subject of a *who-which* clause is usually the *who* or *which*.

✏ **2. Teacher's note.** Remind advanced students that -ing words are not verbs unless coupled with a subject and helping verb. At the start of a sentence, participles function as adjectives modifying the subject after the comma, which is why this is a phrase and not a clause—that is, there is no verb.

DAY 3

#1 MC   S   V   DC S   V   V   #3   MC   S
[the old woman **futilely** tried to turn the crank], (which would not budge), . clearly, [her fingers

V   MC   S   DC S   V   V   #5 AC   S   V   MC   S
ached], and [the slight strength (she had in them) gave way]. (when she heard steps), [the woman

V
turned her attention to the curious princess].

Fixes

futilely: uselessly; ineffectively

CAPITALIZATION. The, Clearly, When.

INDENT the second part because the story turns to Dorinda's arrival and interaction with the old woman.

COMMAS AND OTHER PUNCTUATION. Continue to lead your students to find and correct problems they missed.

- **Nonessential elements** take commas. Ask: Why is the *which* clause nonessential? Answer: The fact that the crank would not budge does not alter the meaning of the rest of the sentence. She still futilely tried to turn it. Fix: The old woman futilely tried to turn the crank, **which would not budge**.

Nonessential does not mean unimportant!

- **Run-on sentence** (comma splice MC, MC). Ask students to identify and correct the comma splice. Answer: The comma after *budge* is not strong enough to connect the two MCs. Fix: *The old woman futilely tried to turn the crank*, which would not budge. *Clearly her fingers ached.*
- **#3 -ly adverb openers.** The comma after *clearly* is needed because the adverb modifies the whole sentence, not the verb alone: it is clear that her fingers ached and that she had little strength. If students have trouble seeing this (after all, *her fingers clearly ached* also sounds OK), you can let it go.
- **MC, cc MC.** Guide students to find the main clauses first (see Grammar Notations on next page) and then ask them to identify the rule. Fix: Clearly *her fingers ached*, **and** *the slight strength she had in them gave way.*
- **#5 clausal openers** take commas: AC, MC. Fix: **When she heard steps,** the woman turned her attention to the curious princess.

Grammar Notations

PREPOSITIONAL PHRASES. in them; to the curious princess.

CLAUSES, PHRASES, AND OPENERS.

- #1 subject opener and MC: The old **woman** futilely **tried** to turn the crank.
- DC (*who-which* clause): **which would** not **budge**.
- #3 -ly adverb opener: Clearly.
- MC: her **fingers ached**.
- MC: the slight **strength** (she had in them) **gave** way. *See* ✎.
- **ADVANCED.** DC: **she had** in them. This is an essential *which* clause with an implied *that* used in place of *which*.
- #5 clausal opener and AC: When **she heard** steps.
- MC: the **woman turned** her attention to the curious princess.

> ✎ **Teacher's note.**
> This main clause has inside it a dependent clause. If students mark *had* as the verb, point out that it is not the *strength* that had but *she*. If they mark *she* as the subject of *gave*, ask if "she gave way" makes sense here.

DAY 4

¶ "lovely princess," [the woman began], "[i've got rheumatism in my **palsied** hands], (which makes it painful to draw up the brimming bucket)} . [would you be so kind as to fetch me a cup of water]?"

Fixes

INDENT because of a new speaker.

CAPITALIZATION. Lovely, Princess, I've, Would.

Capitalize titles used as NDAs (*Princess*) because they substitute for the person's name.

palsied: unable to control certain muscles

COMMAS AND OTHER PUNCTUATION.

- **Quotations.** Fix: "Lovely Princess," the woman began, "I've … water?"
  Rules:
    - Enclose speech in quotes.
    - Use commas on both sides of the interruption because the thought continues. A comma is also needed after *Princess* because it is an NDA.
    - Since she is asking a question, end with a question mark inside the closing quotes.
- **Nonessential elements** take commas. Correct in the original: I've got rheumatism in my palsied hands, **which makes it painful to draw up the brimming bucket**. The *which* clause modifies the entire idea before it, not just the noun *hands*. Even though it adds information, it is nonessential because it does not change the fact that she has rheumatism in her hands.
- **Semicolons.** Ask: When do we use semicolons? Answer: To join two MCs that express one idea. Ask: Does this semicolon work, and why? Answer: No. The first MC is a statement about her rheumatism; the second poses a question asking for help. These are two separate ideas so belong in separate sentences with a period instead of the semicolon after *bucket*.

Grammar Notations

PREPOSITIONAL PHRASES. in my palsied hands; of water. *See* ✎ **1.**

CLAUSES, PHRASES, AND OPENERS.

- NDA: Lovely Princess. If students mark this as a #3, ask them what *Lovely* describes. Answer: The noun *Princess*. Ask what part of speech describes nouns. Answer: Adjectives. Adverbs modify verbs and adjectives, never nouns. *See* ✎ **2.**
- MC: the **woman began.**
- MC: **I've got** rheumatism in my palsied hands.
- DC (*who-which*): **which makes** it painful to draw up the brimming bucket.
- #Q (question) and MC: **Would you be** so kind as to fetch me a cup of water?

Style

If desired, have students identify the strongest of the vocabulary dress-ups from this week. Discuss their answers. Suggestions:

- **Strong verbs.** alerted, mumble, slammed, fled, budge, ached, fetch (a verbal).
- **Quality adjectives.** fateful, slight, palsied, brimming.
    - ✎ **Teacher's note.** *Palsied* is an adjective because it describes a noun: *palsied hands. Brimming* is an easy-to-teach example of an -ing word that functions as an adjective, not a verb. It comes right before the noun it describes, which makes it an adjective: *brimming bucket.* The point is that not all -ing and -ed words are verbs.
- **-ly adverbs.** ignobly, futilely

✎ **1. Teacher's note.**
Up the brimming bucket does not make sense as a phrase and *to draw up* does, which means *up* is an adverb going with the verbal *to draw*, not a preposition going with *the brimming bucket.* This does not affect grammar or punctuation but may come up if students are confused.

✎ **2. Teacher's note.**
In IEW's writing, we call -ly adjectives imposter -ly's since the -ly openers and dress-ups are adverbs only. Do not worry about labeling this sentence since it begins with an NDA before the main clause.

STUDENT REWRITE

Aware of the fowler's plan, the ant bit him in his foot, not stopping until the man dropped his net in pain. The noise alerted the dove, which flew to safety."

Inferring Arthur's intended message, Dorinda could only mumble the closing aphorism: "One good turn deserves another."

She slammed the book shut and ignobly fled to the palace grounds.

Wandering through the gardens, she approached the fateful well. Surprised, she noticed there an old woman, who was attempting to draw water from the deep well. The old woman futilely tried to turn the crank, which would not budge. Clearly, her fingers ached, and the slight strength she had in them gave way.

When she heard steps, the woman turned her attention to the curious princess.

"Lovely Princess," the woman began, "I've got rheumatism in my palsied hands, which makes it painful to draw up the brimming bucket. Would you be so kind as to fetch me a cup of water?"

Week 20

Quotations

LEARN IT

You have been punctuating quotations quite a bit in this story. Now is a good time to review the rules.

When narrative sets up quotations with a speaking verb, add a comma. This narrative can come before, after, or in the middle of the quotation. Patterns: **speaking verb, "quote"** or **"quote," speaking verb**. Commas and periods always go inside closing quotations.

> She *answered*, "I am not sure I like this book."

> "Give it a try anyway," *suggested* Arthur.

When a spoken sentence is interrupted, close the first part and begin the second with quotation marks. Do not capitalize the first letter of the continuation.

> "May I stop reading," *responded* Dorinda, "if I find it too dismal?"

Exclamation marks and question marks go inside closing quotations when they are part of the material quoted; otherwise, they go outside. Also, if a quote ends in an end mark but is followed by narrative setting it up, keep the attribution lowercase because it is part of same sentence.

> "Dorinda, who was at the door?" inquired King Morton.

> "If only I could have my ball back," sighed Dorinda, "I would bestow a handsome reward on my benefactor!"

This one is a little tricky: in conversation, if someone is speaking and changes topic, start a new paragraph. However, close his first paragraph without a quotation mark and open his new paragraph with a quotation mark.

The missing quotation mark at the end of the first paragraph signals that he has not finished speaking. The opening quotation mark in the next paragraph reminds us that someone is still speaking. Also, notice that quotations within a quotation use single instead of double marks:

> "Phew!" Dorinda exclaimed. "OK, it's titled 'The Dove and the Ant.'

> "Early one morning," she read, "a tiny ant strove to allay its thirst in a stream. Dislodged by the rush of the stream, it struggled to stay above water.

Page 42, *Fix It! Grammar: Frog Prince, or Just Deserts,* **Student Book 3**

DAY 1

#4   MC S   V   ¶ #Q / MC   V   S   V   DC

¶ tossing her golden locks**,** [dorinda quickly turned away]**.** "[why does everyone, like, think] (that

S V   MC S   V

i ought to be, like, ~~there~~/their ~~they're~~ servant)?" [she mumbled **querulously**]**.**

Fixes

INDENT ¶s: 1) new topic; 2) new speech.

CAPITALIZATION. Tossing, Dorinda, Why, I.

USAGE. Dorinda's use of *like* is not only annoying, but also confusing. She is not asking why everyone thinks she ought to be *like* their servant—that is, to resemble their servant—but to *be* their servant. *Like* is a meaningless filler word but one appropriate to Dorinda's character. Keep it in commas to signify it is an interruption.

HOMOPHONES. Use the possessive: **their** servant.

COMMAS AND OTHER PUNCTUATION.

- **#4 -ing openers** take commas. Fix: **Tossing her golden locks,** Dorinda quickly turned away. Ask: Is the subject after the comma the one doing the -inging? Answer: Yes, Dorinda is both turning away and tossing her hair, so this is a legal #4.

- **Run-on sentence** (comma splice MC, MC). Ask students to find and correct the comma splice. Fix: *Dorinda quickly turned away. "Why does everyone, like, think that I ought to be their servant?"* The first sentence does not set up the quote since there is no speaking verb so does not use a comma.

  - ✎ **Teacher's note.** Explain that we do not correct comma splices by removing the comma but by making it stronger. If we remove it, we turn a comma splice into a fused sentence, which is worse. Both are types of run-ons and are most easily corrected with a period.

- **Quotations.** Fix: "Why … servant?" she mumbled querulously.

  Rules:

  - ◆ Enclose speech in quotes.
  - ◆ She is asking a question, so add a question mark inside the closing quotes, not after *querulously.*
  - ◆ *She mumbled* is part of the same sentence because it sets up the quote, so *she* should be lowercase.

Grammar Notations

CLAUSES, PHRASES, AND OPENERS.

- #4 -ing participial phrase opener: Tossing her golden locks.
- MC: **Dorinda** quickly **turned** away.
- #Q (question) and MC: Why **does everyone**, like, **think**.
- DC: that **I ought** to be, like, their servant. *See* ♡.
- MC: **she mumbled** querulously.

querulously: in a complaining manner

♡ **Grammar lovers.** This is a noun clause because it follows a verb (*think*) and answers the question *what.*

DAY 2

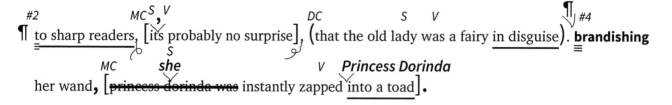

Fixes

brandishing: waving or flourishing

INDENT because of new topics: 1) the narrator's interruption; 2) the consequence to Dorinda for her rudeness.

CAPITALIZATION. To, Brandishing, Princess Dorinda.

USAGE. Not the possessive pronoun *its* but the contraction *it's*, meaning *it is*: **it's** no surprise.

COMMAS AND OTHER PUNCTUATION.

- **Short #2 prepositional openers** (under five words) take commas if they need a pause, which this one does not. No comma is preferred: **To sharp readers** it's probably no surprise.

- ***That* clauses** do not take commas. Fix: it's probably no surprise **that the old lady was a fairy in disguise**.

- **#4 -ing openers** take commas. Fix: **Brandishing her wand,** Princess Dorinda was instantly zapped into a toad.

  Ask: Is the subject after the comma the one doing the -inging? Answer: No! Dorinda is not the one brandishing the wand, but the fairy. This is an illegal #4 (a.k.a. dangling modifier).

  Correct by placing the true -inger after the comma: Brandishing her wand, **she** instantly zapped Princess Dorinda into a toad.

Grammar Notations

PREPOSITIONAL PHRASES. To sharp readers; in disguise; into a toad.

CLAUSES, PHRASES, AND OPENERS.

- #2 prepositional phrase opener: To sharp readers.
- MC: **it's** probably no surprise.
  - ✏ **Teacher's note.** If your students do not recognize this subject-verb, brush off the verb card from Week 1 and remind them about *be* verbs.
- DC: that the old **lady was** a fairy in disguise.
- #4 -ing participial phrase opener: Brandishing her wand.
- MC: **she** instantly **zapped** Princess Dorinda into a toad. See fix to this construction under #4 -ing openers, above.

DAY 3

1 MC S   DC S   V   V

[all, (that remained of the lovely lady), was her crown, conveniently miniaturized to fit her diminished

among

stature, and her beauty spot], **prominent** on her high cheekbone ~~between~~ the other toady warts.

Fixes

CAPITALIZATION. All.

USAGE. Use *between* with two, *among* with three or more: **among** the other toady warts.

COMMAS AND OTHER PUNCTUATION. Work through the Grammar Notations before addressing punctuation. This is always helpful but especially needful with this passage.

- *That* **clauses** do not take commas. Fix: All **that remained of the lovely lady** was her crown.

  - ✏ **Teacher's note.** The *that* clause is essential since it specifies what is meant by *all*. "All was her crown" does not make sense alone. Also, *that* replaces *which* in most essential *which* clauses, as here.

- **ADVANCED. Nonessential elements** take commas. The passage contains two nonessential invisible *which's*. Fix: crown, **conveniently miniaturized to fit her diminished stature,** and her beauty spot, **prominent on her high cheekbone.** *See* ✏ **1.**

Grammar Notations

PREPOSITIONAL PHRASES. of the lovely lady; on her high cheekbone; among the other toady warts. *See* ✏ **2.**

CLAUSES, PHRASES, AND OPENERS.

- #1 subject opener and MC: **All** (that remained of the lovely lady) **was** her crown ... and her beauty spot.

  Students may have trouble recognizing the subject-verb pair of this MC. It is complicated by an intervening dependent clause. Explain that **All** is a pronoun here that acts as the subject.

- DC: **that remained** of the lovely lady.

  - ✏ **Teacher's note.** This is an essential *which* clause using *that* in place of *which*.

- **ADVANCED.** Invisible *which*: 1) crown, *which was* conveniently miniaturized to fit her diminished stature; 2) her beauty spot, *which was* prominent on her high cheekbone among the other toady warts.

  Invisible *which's* are not clauses because the *which* and *be* verb are missing. However, since they function like *which* clauses, we call them invisible *who-which's*. They are actually adjective phrases or appositives describing the noun right before them.

prominent: easily visible; standing out

Real toads do not have actual warts, just bumps that appear like warts.

✏ **1. Teacher's note.** Remember that you can wait until later books to teach the concept of essential and nonessential elements if it is too difficult or too much to cover now.

✏ **2. Teacher's note.** Check that students can still explain how these fit the prepositional phrase pattern: preposition + noun, no verb. Tip: In the last phrase, *other* and *toady* are adjectives; *the* is an article.

DAY 4

#1 MC S V   V   MC   S   V   #T   MC S V   V
¶ "[that will teach you some manners], <u>miss priss</u>," [the fairy snapped]. "maybe [you'll learn a little

#5 AC S   V   DC S   V   V
humbleness in your altered state]! (if you ever find a **gallant** prince), (who will kiss you <u>in true love</u>),

MC S   V   V   V
[you might be restored to <u>humanity</u>]."

gallant: chivalrous and noble-minded

Fixes

INDENT because of a new speaker.

CAPITALIZATION. That, Miss Priss, Maybe, If.

COMMAS AND OTHER PUNCTUATION.

- **Quotations.** Fix: "That … Miss Priss," the fairy snapped. "Maybe … humanity." Rules: 1) Enclose speech along with the comma or period in quotes. 2) Use a comma after the first quotation because a speaking verb (*snapped*) sets it up. If students prefer an exclamation mark, that works too. 3) A period follows *snapped* because she starts a new sentence.
- **NDAs** take commas: " … manners, **Miss Priss**," the fairy snapped.
- **Essential elements** do not take commas. Fix: If you ever find a gallant prince **who will kiss you in true love**. We are not talking about any prince but one who will kiss her out of love, so the *who* clause is needed to define which particular kind of prince. *See* ✎ **1.**
- **#5 clausal openers** take commas: **If you ever find a gallant prince who will kiss you in true love,** you might be restored to humanity.

Grammar Notations

PREPOSITIONAL PHRASES. in your altered state; in true love; to humanity.

CLAUSES, PHRASES, AND OPENERS.

- #1 subject opener and MC: **That will teach** you some manners. *See* ✎ **2.**
- MC: the **fairy snapped**.
- #T (transition): Maybe.
- MC: **you'll learn** a little humbleness in your altered state!
- #5 clausal opener and AC: If **you** ever **find** a gallant prince.
- DC (*who-which* clause): **who will kiss** you in true love.
- MC: **you might be restored** to humanity.

Style

If desired, have students identify the strongest of the vocabulary dress-ups from this week. Discuss their answers. Suggestions:

- **Strong verbs.** mumbled, brandishing (verbal), zapped, snapped.
- **Quality adjectives.** miniaturized, diminished, prominent, altered. *See* ✎ **3.**
- **-ly adverbs.** querulously, instantly.

✎ **1. Teacher's note.** The comma after the *who* clause is there for the next reason and has nothing to do with the essential *who* clause.

Tip: If a comma and a no-comma vie for attention in the same place, the comma wins. In other words, a needed comma will supersede a need for no comma.

✎ **2. Teacher's note.** Although the word *that* usually starts a dependent clause, it does not when it is a demonstrative pronoun (as in *that will teach you*) or adjective (as in *that princess*).

✎ **3. Teacher's note.** If students do not recognize that *miniaturized* and *prominent* from Day 3 are adjectives coming after the noun they describe, point it out only if they are ready for it. If not, just mark adjectives that come before nouns.

STUDENT REWRITE

Tossing her golden locks, Dorinda quickly turned away.

"Why does everyone, like, think that I ought to be, like, their servant?" she mumbled querulously.

To sharp readers it's probably no surprise that the old lady was a fairy in disguise.

Brandishing her wand, she instantly zapped Princess Dorinda into a toad. All that remained of the lovely lady was her crown, conveniently miniaturized to fit her diminished stature, and her beauty spot, prominent on her high cheekbone among the other toady warts.

"That will teach you some manners, Miss Priss," the fairy snapped. "Maybe you'll learn a little humbleness in your altered state! If you ever find a gallant prince who will kiss you in true love, you might be restored to humanity."

Week 21

Personal Pronouns

LEARN IT

Personal pronouns such as *he, she, it,* and *they* refer back to a person or thing recently mentioned, the antecedent. It is important to be clear what the pronoun is referring back to.

- Unclear: King Morton summoned the butler. **He** called for the wine master to hurry.

    Grammatically, *he* could refer to either the butler or the king. It is not clear which. Since it is the king who is doing the calling, *he* should be changed to *the king.*

    Fix: King Morton summoned the butler. **The king** called for the wine master to hurry.

- Unclear: When ten clumsy underservants entered the dining hall loaded with wine bottles, **they** tumbled onto the carpet.

    It is not clear whether it is the servants or the bottles—or both—that tumbled. Change *they* to *who* or *what* is tumbling.

    Fix: When ten clumsy underservants entered the dining hall loaded with wine bottles, **the servants** tumbled onto the carpet.

Page 44, *Fix It! Grammar: Frog Prince, or Just Deserts*, **Student Book 3**

DAY 1

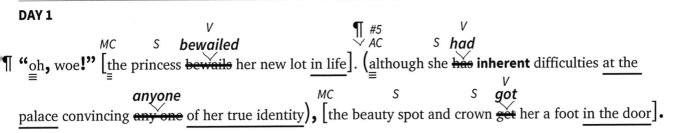

¶ "oh, woe!" [the princess ~~bewails~~ *bewailed* her new lot in life]. (although she ~~has~~ **inherent** difficulties at the palace convincing ~~any one~~ *anyone* of her true identity), [the beauty spot and crown ~~get~~ *got* her a foot in the door].

Fixes

inherent: built-in; occurring as a natural result

INDENT ¶s: 1) new speaker, with the second sentence relating directly to what she said; 2) new scene.

CAPITALIZATION. Oh, The, Although.

TENSE. Do not switch tenses from past to present: The princess **bewailed**; she **had**; beauty spot and crown **got**.

SPELLING. *anyone* is one word.

COMMAS AND OTHER PUNCTUATION.

- **Quotations and interjections.** Fix: "Oh, woe!" Rules: Use quotation marks around spoken words, a comma after the introductory interjection, and an exclamation at the end since this is exclamatory.

  - ✏ **Teacher's note.** *The princess bewailed* does not set up the quotation before it but an object after (*her lot*) so should be treated as a separate sentence with *The* capitalized. Contrast this: The princess bewailed, "Oh, woe!"

- **#5 clausal openers** take commas: AC, MC. Fix: **Although she had inherent difficulties at the palace convincing anyone of her true identity,** the beauty spot and crown got her a foot in the door.

Grammar Notations

PREPOSITIONAL PHRASES. in life; at the palace; of her true identity; in the door.

CLAUSES, PHRASES, AND OPENERS.

- **ADVANCED.** Oh, woe! Students do not need to identify fragments, but if it comes up, this is a sentence fragment, acceptable in this case because it does not leave us hanging.
- MC: The **princess bewailed** her new lot in life.
- #5 clausal opener and AC: Although **she had** inherent difficulties at the palace convincing anyone of her true identity.

  If students mark *convincing* as part of the verb, point out that the sentence is not saying "she had convincing," which does not make sense. *Convincing* describes the noun *difficulties* so functions as an adjective.

- MC: the **beauty spot** and **crown got** her a foot in the door.

  - ✏ **Teacher's note.** Check that students understand there are two subjects and one verb. It is also fine if they mark *spot* alone instead of *beauty spot*, which is a compound noun.

DAY 2

#4   DC   S   V   V   MC   S   V
¶ puzzling over the crown, (which did look familiar), [lady constance decided to put the toad to the

        ¶ #5
        AC   S   V   MC S   V   MC V   AC   S   V
test]. "(if you truly are the princess)," [she began], "[tell me] (where you have a **bona fide** wart),

not that counterfeit beauty spot."

Fixes

bona fide: genuine; real

INDENT ¶ both sentences because of a new topic and a new speaker.

CAPITALIZATION. Puzzling, Lady Constance, If.

COMMAS AND OTHER PUNCTUATION.

- **#4 -ing openers** take commas. Fix: **Puzzling over the crown,** which did look familiar, Lady Constance decided to put the toad to the test. *See* 🖊 **1.**

  Ask: Is the subject of the MC after the comma the one doing the -inging? Answer: Yes, Lady Constance is both puzzling and deciding, so this is a legal #4.

- **Nonessential elements** take commas. Fix: Puzzling over the crown, **which did look familiar,** Lady Constance decided to put the toad to the test.

  Ask: Why is this nonessential? Answer: It is not needed for the rest of the sentence to make sense. Without it, Lady Constance is still puzzling over the crown and deciding to put the toad to the test.

- **Quotations.** Fix: "If … princess," she began, "tell … spot." Rules: 1) Enclose speech in quotes with the punctuation inside the quotations. 2) Narrative that interrupts a spoken sentence (*she began*) is set off with commas. Check that *tell* is lowercase since it continues the same sentence.

- **Mid-sentence adverb clauses** do not take commas (MC AC). The original is correct: tell me **where you have a bona fide wart.**

- **ADVANCED. Contrasting phrases** take commas. The original is correct: tell me where you have a bona fide wart, **not that counterfeit beauty spot.**

🖊 **1. Teacher's note.** A *which* clause comes in between the -ing opener and the subject of the MC rather than the subject coming right after the comma, which is more common. This does not change the #4 pattern.

Grammar Notations

PREPOSITIONAL PHRASES. to the test. *See* 🖊 **2.**

CLAUSES, PHRASES, AND OPENERS.

- #4 -ing participial phrase opener: Puzzling over the crown.
- DC (*who-which* clause): **which did look** familiar. Ask students what the subject of this verb is. Answer: *which*. Remind students that the subject of a *who-which* clause is usually *who* or *which*.
- MC: **Lady Constance decided** to put the toad to the test.
- #5 clausal opener and AC: If **you** truly **are** the princess.
- MC: **she began.**
- MC: **tell** me. Ask students to identify the subject of *tell*. Answer: An implied *you*. This is in the imperative (command) mood.
- AC (adverb clause): where **you have** a bona fide wart.

🖊 **2. Teacher's note.** If students mark *over the crown,* you can let it go. However, those words as a phrase do not fit the context because *over* is an adverb that goes with *puzzled,* not a preposition. This does not affect grammar or punctuation so is not important.

DAY 3

6 MC   S   V   #1 MC   S V   MC   S   V

¶ [that one was easy] . "[~~its~~ it's on the back of my head hidden by all my hair]," [dorinda croaked].

6 MC   S   V   #1 MC   S V   DC   S   V   V   **two**

¶ [a palace maid **snickered**]. "[so that's] (why she'd never let us style her hair in ~~2~~ braids in back)."

           S

¶ *Dorinda* V

¶ [~~she~~ glared a toady glare].

Fixes

INDENT three times because of a new speakers and a new topic. The short sentences relating directly to the quotes can stay in the same paragraphs as the quotes after them.

CAPITALIZATION. That, It's, Dorinda, A, So, Dorinda.

USAGE. Use the contraction meaning *it is*: **It's** on the back of my head.

NUMBERS. Spell out numbers that can be written in one or two words: **two** braids.

UNCLEAR PRONOUN. *She* in the last sentence grammatically refers back to the last woman named, which is the palace maid, but it is actually Dorinda who glares. Change *she* to *Dorinda*: **Dorinda** glared a toady glare. *See* ♡ **1.**

COMMAS AND OTHER PUNCTUATION.

- **Run-on sentence** (comma splice MC, MC). Ask students to locate the comma splice and explain its correction. If they have trouble doing this, ask them to find two MCs that have nothing stronger than a comma joining them.

  Answer: The camma after *That one was easy* is not strong enough to hold together the two MCs. Since the first MC does not set up the second with a speaking verb, it needs a period. Fix: That one was easy. "It's on the back of my head."

- **Quotations.** Fix: "It's … hair," Dorinda croaked. ¶ A palace maid snickered. "So … back." Rules: 1) Enclose speech in quotes. 2) Add a comma inside closing quotes when a speaking verb (*croaked*) sets up the quote. *See* ✎ **1.**

- **ADVANCED. Essential or nonessential?** If students put a comma in front of *hidden*, that is fine. *Hidden by all my hair* is an adjective phrase, arguably either essential or nonessential—that is, grammarians will disagree over whether it is necessary to the meaning of the main clause.

Grammar Notations

PREPOSITIONAL PHRASES. on the back; of my head; by all my hair; in two braids; in back.

CLAUSES, PHRASES, AND OPENERS.

- #6 vss and MC: That **one was** easy. *See* ♡ **2.**
- #1 subject opener and MC: **It's** on the back of my head. Remind students that *be* verbs are sometimes buried in contractions. This is true twice in today's work: *It's* and *that's* have *is* in them.
- MC: **Dorinda croaked.**
- #6 vss and MC: A palace **maid snickered.**

snickered: uttered a partly stifled laugh

♡ **1. Grammar lovers.** This is known as an unclear antecedent. The pronoun does not clearly refer back to its proper antecedent (the noun it refers to).

✎ **1. Teacher's note.** Since *snickered* is not a speaking verb, *A palace maid snickered* works better as its own sentence. The period communicates that she snickers first and then speaks. With a comma, she snickers out these words, which is hard to do!

♡ **2. Grammar lovers.** When *that* comes before a noun or pronoun that it describes (*that one*), it is used as a kind of adjective, variously labeled in grammar books as demonstrative adjectives, determiners, or even determinative demonstratives (not helpful)! The terminology is not important to teach. If the issue comes up, the main point is this: Not all *that's* start dependent clauses.

- #1 subject opener and MC: So **that's**. *See* ✎ **2.**
  - **ADVANCED.** DC: why **she'd** never **let** us style her hair in two braids in back. The contraction includes the helping verb *would*: **would let.**
- #6 vss and MC: **Dorinda glared** a toady glare.

DAY 4

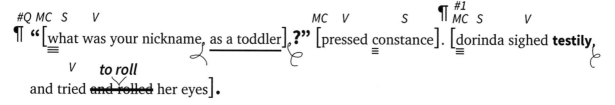

Fixes

testily: impatiently; with irritation

INDENT ¶ both sentences because of a new speaker and a new topic.

CAPITALIZATION. What, Constance, Dorinda.

USAGE. We *try to do something*, not *try and*: Dorinda sighed testily and **tried to roll** her eyes.

COMMAS AND OTHER PUNCTUATION.

- **Quotation.** Fix: "What … toddler?" pressed Constance. Rules: 1) Enclose speech in quotes with a question mark inside since she is asking a question. 2) Since the words that follow the quotation set it up with a speaking verb, they are part of the same sentence and need lowercase for *pressed*. However, do not put a comma with the question mark because that is double punctuating it.
- **Mid-sentence prepositional phrases** do not take commas. See Prepositional phrases, below. Fix: What was your nickname **as a toddler**?
- **Items in a series.** Remove the comma before the first *and* because it joins only two verbs, *sighed* and *tried*. Rule: MC cc 2nd verb (no comma when two verbs go with one subject). Fix: Dorinda **sighed** testily **and tried** to roll her eyes

Grammar Notations

PREPOSITIONAL PHRASES. as a toddler.

The word *as* can start either an adverb clause or a prepositional phrase. *As a toddler* begins with a word that can be a preposition, ends with a noun (*toddler*), and has no verb in it, so it cannot be a clause, which must have a subject-verb pair.

CLAUSES, PHRASES, AND OPENERS.

- #Q (question) and MC: **What was** your nickname as a toddler?
- MC: **pressed Constance.**
- #1 subject opener and MC: **Dorinda sighed** testily and **tried** to roll her eyes.

Check for understanding by asking, What is the subject of *tried*? Answer: *Dorinda*, the same subject for both verbs.

Style

If desired, have students identify the strongest of the vocabulary dress-ups from this week. Discuss their answers. Suggestions:

- **Strong verbs.** bewailed, croaked, snickered, glared, pressed, sighed.
- **Quality adjectives.** inherent, bona fide, counterfeit.
- **-ly adverbs.** testily.

STUDENT REWRITE

"Oh, woe!" The princess bewailed her new lot in life.

Although she had inherent difficulties at the palace convincing anyone of her true identity, the beauty spot and crown got her a foot in the door.

Puzzling over the crown, which did look familiar, Lady Constance decided to put the toad to the test.

"If you truly are the princess," she began, "tell me where you have a bona fide wart, not that counterfeit beauty spot."

That one was easy. "It's on the back of my head hidden by all my hair," Dorinda croaked.

A palace maid snickered. "So that's why she'd never let us style her hair in two braids in back."

Dorinda glared a toady glare.

"What was your nickname as a toddler?" pressed Constance.

Dorinda sighed testily and tried to roll her eyes.

Week 22

Review

LEARN IT

There are no new concepts this week. Test your grammar knowledge with these questions. Check your grammar cards if you cannot remember.

1. When are words capitalized?

2. Which kinds of adjectives before a noun requires commas: coordinate or cumulative?

3. What is a test to determine if two adjectives before a noun need a comma?

Do you remember what these vocabulary words mean? If not, look them up in your vocabulary list in the back of your notebook.

- vehemently
- obstinate
- prestigious
- mortification
- diplomatic
- lamentably
- gratify
- trepidation
- meandered
- copiously

Teacher's note. Remember to keep the exercise light and fun like a game. If your student groans when you say, "Time for *Fix It!*" something is wrong.

Teacher's answers

1. Capitalize proper nouns, the first word of a sentence, titles with a name, and titles by themselves used as NDAs.

   a. One day King Morton lacerated his finger on his royal crown.

   b. The head butler called for Dr. Stitches to attend to the king.

   c. Trembling, the king asked, "Will it hurt, Doctor?"

2. Coordinate adjectives take commas.

3. Can you reverse their order and they sound right? Can you add *and* between them? If yes, then yes to commas.

Page 46, *Fix It! Grammar: Frog Prince, or Just Deserts*, **Student Book 3**

DAY 1

#5 AC   S   V   MC   S   V   AC   S V

¶ "(when i was really little), [friends called me 'toady,'] (because i had a wart on the back of my

              MC   S   V   AC   S   V   AC   S   V   DC S V

head], but, [then they dropped it], (when we were older) (because they realized), (i wasn't a **toady** at

       MC S   V   #Q MC V S

all)," [she snapped]. "[is that, like, enough]?"

Fixes

INDENT ¶ for a new speaker. If students want this in the same paragraph as the last, let them since Dorinda's rolling her eyes sets us up for what she says.

CAPITALIZATION. When, I, Toady, I, I, Is.

WORDS AS WORDS go in quotations. If you can insert "the word/name" before the word, it is a word used as a word. Fix: " … friends called me [the name] **'Toady.'**" Since Dorinda is speaking, use single quotes around *Toady* for a quote within a quote. *See* ✏ **1.**

COMMAS AND OTHER PUNCTUATION.

- **Quotations.** Fix: "When … all," she snapped. "Is … enough?" Rules: 1) Enclose speech in quotes. 2) Add a comma inside closing quotes when a speaking verb (*snapped*) sets up the quote. 3) A question mark ends her second sentence.
- **#5 clausal openers** take commas: AC, MC. Fix: **When I was really little,** friends called me 'Toady.'
- **Mid-sentence adverb clauses** do not take commas (MC AC), so none before *because* or *when*. Fix: 1) friends called me 'Toady' **because I had a wart**; 2) they dropped it **when we were older**; 3) when we were older **because they realized**.
- **Items in a series.** Add a comma before the cc *but* because it joins two main clauses. Rule: MC, cc MC. Fix, with MCs italicized: *friends called me 'Toady'* because I had a wart on the back of my head, **but** then *they dropped it* when we were older.

  Importantly, the comma never goes after the cc, only before (sometimes), so make sure students also remove the comma after *but*. *See* ♡.
- **ADVANCED.** *That* clauses do not take commas, including understood ones. Fix: they realized **I wasn't a toady at all.**

Grammar Notations

PREPOSITIONAL PHRASES. on the back; of my head; at all.

CLAUSES, PHRASES, AND OPENERS.

- #5 clausal opener and AC: When **I was** really little.
- MC: **friends called** me 'Toady.'
- AC (adverb clause dress-up): because **I had** a wart on the back of my head.
- MC: then **they dropped** it. *See* ✏ **2.**
- AC (adverb clause dress-up): when **we were** older.
- AC (adverb clause dress-up): because **they realized.**
- **ADVANCED.** DC (*that* implied): **I wasn't** a toady at all. This is a noun clause because it answers the question *what* after the verb: They realized *what*? That I wasn't a toady.
- MC: **she snapped.**
- #Q (opener) and MC: **Is that,** like, enough? *See* ✏ **3.**

toady: a "yes" man or woman; flatterer (to excess)

Pun on *toady*: The unkind nickname her friends gave Dorinda was due to the wart; to be a toady is to flatter someone in hopes of gain. Dorinda does not flatter others but expects others to toady to her.

✏ **1. Teacher's note.** When typing, italicize words referred to as words: friends called me *Toady*. Since handwriting italics is impractical, use quotation marks.

♡ **Grammar lovers.** The only exception to no comma after a cc is when there is an intervening nonessential phrase or clause.

✏ **2. Teacher's note.** The word *then* is confusing. When we add it to a main clause, it does not change the MC status: it is still a main clause.

✏ **3. Teacher's note.** *That* is not a clausal starter if a subject-verb pair does not follow it. Here, *that* is a demonstrative pronoun. Students may also start the bracket after *then*.

DAY 2

¶ [lady constances final question, confirmed dorindas status]. (when her iPhone had mysteriously
#1 MC , *S* *V* , *#5 AC* *S* *V*

disappeared some weeks before), [dorinda had confessed the truth to her companion], (who now
V *MC* *S* *V* *V* *DC* *S*

played her **trump card**): " [what actually happened to your iPhone]?"
V *MC* *S* *V*

Fixes

INDENT because of a new topic. Students may keep the two sentences together since the first sets up the second or, if they prefer, start a new paragraph (*When her iPhone*) for a new speaker.

CAPITALIZATION. Lady Constance's, Dorinda's, When, Dorinda, What (first word of quoted sentence). Apple Inc. capitalizes just the *P* in *iPhone*, so it is correct in the original.

COMMAS AND OTHER PUNCTUATION.

- **Apostrophes.** Use apostrophes to show possession: Lady **Constance's** final question; **Dorinda's** status.

- **Subject-verb** stays together without punctuation. No comma after *question* because that would separate the subject from its verb: **question confirmed**.

- **#5 clausal openers** take commas: AC, MC. Fix: **When her iPhone had mysteriously disappeared some weeks before,** Dorinda had confessed the truth.

  This comma is especially critical to prevent misreading *before* as the start of an adverb clause (*before she had confessed*), which it is not, instead of as a simple adverb.

- **Nonessential elements** take commas. Ask: Why is the *who* clause nonessential? Answer: The *who* clause adds information but does not affect the meaning of the rest of the sentence or identify *companion*. It is clear from the story that *her companion* is Lady Constance.

  Fix: Dorinda had confessed the truth to her companion, **who now played her trump card.**

- **ADVANCED. Colons** must follow a main clause and set up an example, list, or illustration, which is exactly what this colon does. What Lady Constance says is her trump card.

Grammar Notations

PREPOSITIONAL PHRASES. to her companion; to your iPhone. *See* ✏.

CLAUSES, PHRASES, AND OPENERS.

- #1 subject opener and MC: Lady Constance's final **question confirmed** Dorinda's status. Check that students understand that *question*, not *Lady Constance*, is the subject.

- #5 clausal opener and AC: When her **iPhone had** mysteriously **disappeared** some weeks before.

- MC: **Dorinda had confessed** the truth to her companion.

- DC (*who-which* clause): **who** now **played** her trump card.

- MC: **What** actually **happened** to your iPhone?

trump card:
something giving one person an advantage over another

In some card games like bridge, *trump* is the suit that wins over other suits, hence the expression "to have, play, or hold one's trump card."

✏ **Teacher's note.**
Before is an adverb here meaning previously, not a preposition, because it does not start a phrase.

DAY 3

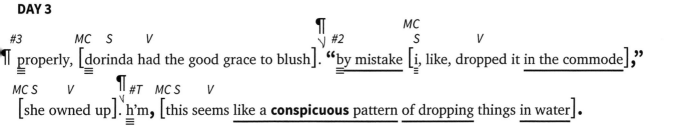

¶ properly, [dorinda had the good grace to blush]. "by mistake [i, like, dropped it in the commode],"

[she owned up]. h'm, [this seems like a **conspicuous** pattern of dropping things in water].

Fixes

conspicuous: easily observable

INDENT three times: 1) new topic, Dorinda's reaction to the question; 2) new speaker; 3) new topic, the narrator's aside.

CAPITALIZATION. Properly, Dorinda, By, I, H'm. Note that *h'm* is an interjection commonly spelled with an apostrophe; *hmm* is a less common but also correct spelling.

COMMAS AND OTHER PUNCTUATION.

- **#3 -ly adverb openers.** The comma after *Properly* is optional but may be helpful to avoid misreading the word as an adjective describing Dorinda.
- **Quotations.** Fix: "By … commode," she owned up. Rules: 1) Enclose speech in quotes. 2) Add a comma inside closing quotes when a speaking verb (*owned up*) sets up the quote.
- **Short #2 prepositional openers** (under five words) do not require commas. If students want one after *By mistake*, that is fine.
- **Interjections** take commas: **H'm,** this seems like a conspicuous pattern.

Grammar Notations

PREPOSITIONAL PHRASES. By mistake; in the commode; like a conspicuous pattern; of dropping; in water.

- The first *like* is a filler word, not a preposition: I, **like**, dropped it. The second *like* is a preposition because it fits the pattern: it begins with a word that can be a preposition (*like*), it ends with a noun (*pattern*), and there is no verb in the phrase.
- *Up* is an adverb here (*owned up*), not a preposition.

CLAUSES, PHRASES, AND OPENERS.

- #3 -ly adverb opener: Properly.
- MC: **Dorinda had** the good grace to blush.
- #2 prepositional phrase opener: By mistake.
- MC: **I, like, dropped** it in the commode.
- MC: **she owned up.** Include the adverb with its verb since *owned up* (confessed) has a different meaning from *owned*.
- #T: H'm.
- MC: **this seems** like a conspicuous pattern of dropping things in water.

DAY 4

#1 MC   S   V   MC   S   V   #2

¶ [the palace took her in], but [no one, not even faithful constance, wanted to touch her],. after all,

MC   S   V

[her skin was rough, warty, and **repulsive**].

Fixes

INDENT because of a new time.

CAPITALIZATION. The, Constance, After.

COMMAS AND OTHER PUNCTUATION.

- **MC, cc MC.** Ask: What does the cc *but* join? Answer: two main clauses. Ask: What punctuation rule? Answer: Two MCs joined by a coordinating conjunction need a comma before the cc. Fix: *The palace took her in,* **but** *no one … wanted to touch her.*

- **ADVANCED. Nonessential phrases** take commas. Fix: no one, **not even faithful Constance,** wanted to touch her. The phrase adds important information but is nonessential because taking it out does not affect the meaning of the rest of the sentence. Without the phrase, it is still true that no one wanted to touch her.

- **Run-on sentence** (comma splice MC, MC). Ask students to find and correct the comma splice. Fix: *No one … wanted to touch her.* After all, *her skin was rough, warty, and repulsive.*

- **Transitional #2 prepositional openers** take commas. *After all* takes a comma because it is a transitional expression. Without the comma, we could misread the sentence as saying *after all her skin [and then some verb].*

- **Items in a series** (adjectives) take commas. Fix: her skin was **rough, warty, and repulsive.** *See* ✎.

Grammar Notations

PREPOSITIONAL PHRASES. After all.

CLAUSES, PHRASES, AND OPENERS.

- #1 subject opener and MC: The **palace took** her in.
- MC: **no one**, not even faithful Constance, **wanted** to touch her.
- #2 prepositional phrase opener: After all.
- MC: her **skin was** rough, warty, and repulsive.

Style

If desired, have students identify the strongest of the vocabulary dress-ups from this week. Discuss their answers. Suggestions:

- **Strong verbs.** snapped, confirmed, owned up.
- **Quality adjectives.** conspicuous, repulsive.
- **-ly adverbs.** mysteriously.

repulsive: causing deep dislike or aversion

✎ **Teacher's note.** The Oxford comma, the last one before the cc, is optional but preferred. It is easier to teach students to include it always, which is never wrong, than to teach that it is optional if there is no danger of misreading. Then you step into the gray area of defining *misreading.*

STUDENT REWRITE

"When I was really little, friends called me 'Toady' because I had a wart on the back of my head, but then they dropped it when we were older because they realized I wasn't a toady at all," she snapped. "Is that, like, enough?"

Lady Constance's final question confirmed Dorinda's status. When her iPhone had mysteriously disappeared some weeks before, Dorinda had confessed the truth to her companion, who now played her trump card: "What actually happened to your iPhone?"

Properly, Dorinda had the good grace to blush.

"By mistake I, like, dropped it in the commode," she owned up.

H'm, this seems like a conspicuous pattern of dropping things in water.

The palace took her in, but no one, not even faithful Constance, wanted to touch her. After all, her skin was rough, warty, and repulsive.

Week 23

Review

LEARN IT

There are no new concepts this week. Test your grammar knowledge with these questions. Check your grammar cards if you cannot remember.

1. What is a comma splice?

2. What is a fused sentence?

3. What are three ways that run-on sentences can be fixed?

Do you remember what these vocabulary words mean? If not, look them up in your vocabulary list in the back of your notebook.

- sever
- blemished
- minuscule
- haven
- tendered
- salvage
- dexterity
- sumptuously
- histrionics
- expediently

Teacher's answers

1. Two main clauses joined with only a comma. Pattern: MC, MC.

2. Two main clauses joined with nothing. Pattern: MC MC.

3. There are four ways to fix them. Students need to list only three:

- period
- semicolon
- comma + cc
- www.asia.b word before one MC, making it a DC

Page 48, *Fix It! Grammar: Frog Prince, or Just Deserts*, **Student Book 3**

Institute for Excellence in Writing

DAY 1

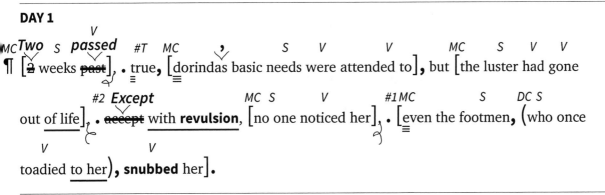

Fixes

INDENT because time has passed.

NUMBERS. Spell out numbers you can write in one or two words: **Two** weeks.

CAPITALIZATION. Two, True, Dorinda's, Except, Even.

HOMOPHONES, USAGE, AND SPELLING. 1) Use the verb *passed*, not the adjective *past*: Two weeks **passed.** 2) Not *accept* (to take or receive) but *except* (excluding; save; but): **Except** with revulsion.

COMMAS AND OTHER PUNCTUATION.

- **Run-on sentences** (comma splice MC, MC). Ask students to find, correct, and explain any comma splices. To help, ask them to find main clauses that have nothing stronger than a comma to connect them. Adverbs and prepositional phrases are add-ons to main clauses, not connectors that can link them grammatically.

  Answer: There are three. The best fixes for all three are periods. The other solutions such as comma + *and* or subordinating one of the clauses sound wordy or less effective here.

  Fix: *Two weeks passed. … the luster had gone out of life.* Except with revulsion, *no one noticed her. Even the footmen … snubbed her.*

- **Transitional words** take commas. Fix: **True,** Dorinda's basic needs were attended to.

- **Apostrophes.** Use apostrophes to show possession: **Dorinda's** basic needs.

- **MC, cc MC.** Comma needed before a cc that joins two main clauses. Fix: *Dorinda's basic needs were attended to,* **but** *the luster had gone out of life.*

- **Short #2 prepositional openers** (under five words). Because it presents a contrast to what follows, *except with revulsion* needs a pause, so keep the comma: **Except with revulsion,** no one noticed her.

- **Nonessential elements** take commas. Fix: Even the footmen, **who once toadied to her,** snubbed her. *See* ♡.

Grammar Notations

PREPOSITIONAL PHRASES. of life; with revulsion; to her.

CLAUSES, PHRASES, AND OPENERS.

- #6 vss and MC: Two **weeks passed.**
- #T: True.
- MC: Dorinda's basic **needs were attended to.**

  To is an adverb connected with the verb. *Attended to* (paid attention to) conveys something different from *attended* (was present at).

- MC: the **luster had gone** out of life.

revulsion: strong feeling of distaste or dislike

snubbed: treated with disdain or contempt

Point out the pun on *toadied* and *toad*. To toady to someone is to flatter them to excess. Far from flattering the toad Dorinda, they treat her with contempt.

♡ **Grammar lovers.** One could make a case for this *who* clause being either essential or nonessential.

With commas, it is saying that all footmen snubbed her, and, incidentally, all once toadied to her. Without commas it is saying that only those footmen who used to toady to her now snubbed her.

Since it is likely that all the footmen once toadied to Dorinda, it is treated as nonessential, taking commas.

- #2 prepositional phrase opener: Except with revulsion.

  Since *except* is short and since *with revulsion* is a prepositional phrase, you can count this opener as a #2.

- MC: **no one noticed** her.

- #1 subject opener and MC: Even the **footmen … snubbed** her.

  Since *even*, an adverb, is short, we can still count this as a #1 opener. If students prefer to leave it unmarked, that is fine.

- DC (*who-which* clause): **who** once **toadied** to her.

DAY 2

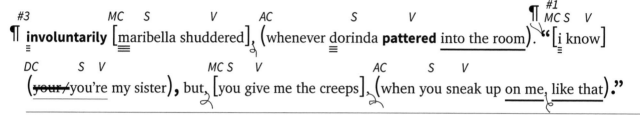

Fixes

INDENT twice because of a new topic and a new speaker.

CAPITALIZATION. Involuntarily, Maribella, Dorinda, I.

HOMOPHONE. Use the contraction for *you are*: I know **you're** my sister.

COMMAS AND OTHER PUNCTUATION.

- **#3 -ly adverb openers.** The comma after *Involuntarily* is optional since we do not need a strong pause.

  No comma because the -ly adverb modifies the verb: she involuntarily shuddered. The comma is required only when the -ly adverb modifies the whole sentence.

- **Mid-sentence adverb clauses** do not take commas: MC AC. Fixes: 1) Maribella shuddered **whenever Dorinda pattered into the room**; 2) you give me the creeps **when you sneak up on me like that**.

- **Quotations.** Fix: "I … that." Rules: 1) Enclose speech in quotes. 2) Add a period at the end of the final statement inside the closing quotations.

- **MC, cc MC.** Add a comma before, not after, the cc *but* since it joins two MCs. Fix: *I know you're my sister*, **but** *you give me the creeps*.

- **Mid-sentence prepositional phrases** do not take commas. Fix: when you sneak up on me **like that**.

Grammar Notations

PREPOSITIONAL PHRASES. into the room; on me; like that. *See ✏ 1.*

CLAUSES, PHRASES, AND OPENERS.

- #3 -ly adverb opener: Involuntarily.
- MC: **Maribella shuddered**.
- AC (adverb clause dress-up): whenever **Dorinda pattered** into the room. *See ✏ 2.*
- #1 subject opener and MC: **I know**.
- **ADVANCED.** DC (with invisible *that*): **you're** my sister.
- MC: **you give** me the creeps.
- AC (adverb clause): when **you sneak** up on me like that.

involuntarily: not by one's own choice

pattered: walked quickly or lightly

✏ **1. Teacher's note.** If students have trouble recognizing that *like that* is a prepositional phrase, show them the list of prepositions from the grammar card for Week 1. Ask them to find one of the prepositions in the third column, which would narrow the field for searching. Also remind them that pronouns (*that*) can have the same function as nouns so can be objects of prepositions.

✏ **2. Teacher's note.** Explain that *whenever* is another subordinating conjunction that is not one of the original eight www's. It is listed on the grammar card for www words from Week 2.

DAY 3

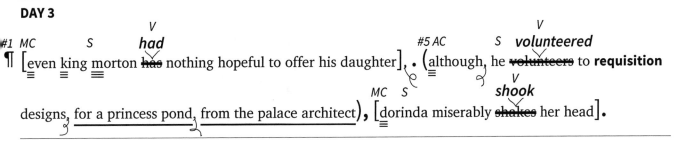

Fixes

INDENT because of a new topic, pulling out of a speech and turning attention to King Morton.

CAPITALIZATION. Even, King Morton, Although, Dorinda. Use lowercase for *princess pond* and *palace architect* because they are not titles of a particular place or job.

TENSE. Do not switch tenses: King Morton **had**; he **volunteered**; Dorinda **shook** her head.

COMMAS AND OTHER PUNCTUATION.

- **Run-on sentence** (comma splice MC, MC). Ask students to find two MCs where somewhere between them is a comma but no period. Answer: The comma after *daughter* and before *although*.

  A period is the best fix: Even *King Morton had nothing hopeful to offer his daughter.* Although he volunteered to requisition designs for a princess pond from the palace architect, *Dorinda miserably shook her head.*

  If students argue for the period after *architect* instead, it makes enough sense, so let them.

- **#5 clausal openers** take commas: AC, MC. The comma goes at the end of the clause, not after the www word although. Fix: **Although he volunteered to requisition designs for a princess pond from the palace architect,** Dorinda miserably shook her head.

- **Mid-sentence prepositional phrases** do not take commas. Fix: **to requisition designs for a princess pond from the palace architect.**

requisition: to write an order for something

Grammar Notations

PREPOSITIONAL PHRASES. for a princess pond; from the palace architect.

CLAUSES, PHRASES, AND OPENERS.

- #1 subject opener and MC: Even **King Morton had** nothing hopeful to offer his daughter.

  We can count this as a #1 opener despite the short adverb, *even,* in front of the main clause.

- #5 clausal opener and AC: Although **he volunteered** to requisition designs for a princess pond from the palace architect.

  If students think *to requisition* is a verb, point out that there is no subject directly connected to it. The sentence does not say, "He requisitioned designs." *To requisition* is an infinitive, which is formed from a verb but does not function as one.

- MC: **Dorinda** miserably **shook** her head.

DAY 4

#2   MC S   V   ¶*#4*
¶ a few days later, feeling dejected and **forlorn**, [she wandered into the infirmary]. ˅mending rapidly, ~~she~~

           MC   S   V
~~could tell that~~ [arthur was in a mood to shower a little compassion on his fellow amphibian sufferer].

Fixes

forlorn: dreary; miserable

INDENTS. 1) time has passed; 2) new topic, Arthur.

CAPITALIZATION. A, Mending, Arthur.

COMMAS AND OTHER PUNCTUATION.

- **ADVANCED. #2 opener.** A comma after *A few days later* is optional in its own right but needed to set off the nonessential participial phrase after it. Fix: A few days later, **feeling dejected and forlorn,** she wandered. Needed commas supersede unneeded ones!

- **#4 -ing openers** take commas. Fix: **Mending rapidly,** she could tell that Arthur was in a mood to shower a little compassion. Ask: Is the person after the comma also doing the -inging? Answer: No, it is not Dorinda who is mending but Arthur. This is an illegal #4 (a.k.a. dangling modifier).

  Fix by changing the subject after the comma to *Arthur*: Mending rapidly, **Arthur, she could tell, was** in a mood to shower a little compassion.

  When we convert sentences to different constructions, sometimes the end result needs tweaking. This sentence is wordy with *she could tell*, so suggest dropping it to make the sentence smoother.

  Better fix: Mending rapidly, **Arthur was** in a mood to shower a little compassion on his fellow amphibian sufferer.

- **Adjectives before a noun.** Check if *fellow amphibian sufferer* needs a comma between the two adjectives. Apply the two tests to determine if these adjectives are coordinate (commas) or cumulative (no commas):

  Both *amphibian fellow sufferer* and *fellow and amphibian sufferer* sound awkward. Since both tests fail, *fellow* and *amphibian* are cumulative adjectives and are correct without a comma.

Grammar Notations

PREPOSITIONAL PHRASES. into the infirmary; in a mood; on his fellow amphibian sufferer.

CLAUSES, PHRASES, AND OPENERS.

- Invisible #2 prepositional phrase: A few days later.

  This is an invisible #2 because a preposition like *during* or *on* is implied but more stylish without.

- MC: **she wandered** into the infirmary.

- #4 -ing participial phrase opener: Mending rapidly.

  ADVANCED. Ask advanced students how *mending* functions. Answer: not as a verb but as an adjective describing the subject (*Arthur*) after the comma.

- MC: **Arthur was** in a mood to shower a little compassion on his fellow amphibian sufferer. Check that students do not mark the infinitive *to shower* as a verb.

Style

If desired, have students identify the strongest of the vocabulary dress-ups from this week. Discuss their answers. Suggestions:

- **Strong verbs.** toadied, snubbed, shuddered, sneak, volunteered, requisition (verbal), wandered, shower (verbal).
- **Quality adjectives.** dejected, forlorn.
- **-ly adverbs.** miserably, rapidly.

STUDENT REWRITE

Two weeks passed. True, Dorinda's basic needs were attended to, but the luster had gone out of life. Except with revulsion, no one noticed her. Even the footmen, who once toadied to her, snubbed her.

Involuntarily Maribella shuddered whenever Dorinda pattered into the room.

"I know you're my sister, but you give me the creeps when you sneak up on me like that."

Even King Morton had nothing hopeful to offer his daughter. Although he volunteered to requisition designs for a princess pond from the palace architect, Dorinda miserably shook her head.

A few days later, feeling dejected and forlorn, she wandered into the infirmary.

Mending rapidly, Arthur was in a mood to shower a little compassion on his fellow amphibian sufferer.

Week 24

Rules for Punctuating Titles

LEARN IT

Titles of Works Titles of works, including titles you give your own papers, have special rules for capitalization and punctuation.

Capitalization
- Capitalize the first and last words of any title.
- Capitalize all key words in the middle.

You do not have to master this now, but words not considered key are articles (*a, an, the*), coordinating conjunctions, and prepositions.

Punctuation Applies to all titles except your own!
- Titles of long works, like books and magazines, are italicized in print. When writing by hand, underline them.
- Titles of short works, like short stories, poems, and articles, are placed in quotation marks.

Examples:

- Book: *Lord of the Rings* (typed) or <u>Lord of the Rings</u> (handwritten)

The two words in the middle are lowercase because they are a preposition (*of*) and an article (*the*).

- Short story: "The Dove and the Ant"

Capitalize the first *the* because it is the first word of the title; do not capitalize the second *the* because it is an article. *And* is a cc, so it is lowercase.

DAY 1

#1 MC   S V   MC S   V   #5 AC   S   V

¶ " [~~its /~~ it's not so dreadful being a toad]," [he assured her]. " (while people aren't always **humane**),

MC   S   V   AC   S   V   *bounties*

[~~your /~~ you're free to live (as you please), in the ~~bounty's~~ of nature]."

Fixes

humane: showing compassion for people and animals

INDENT ¶ because of a new speaker.

CAPITALIZATION. It's, While.

HOMOPHONES AND SPELLING. 1) Use the contractions: **It's** [*it is*] not so dreadful being a toad; **you're** [*you are*] free to live. 2) Not possessive but plural: the **bounties** of nature.

COMMAS AND OTHER PUNCTUATION.

- **Quotations.** Fix: "It's … toad," he assured her. "While … nature."
  Rules:
    - Enclose speech in quotes.
    - Check that commas and periods are inside closing quotations.
    - Quotation + comma + speaking verb (*assured*).
- **Run-on** (fused sentence MC MC). Look at Arthur's words alone and find two MCs joined with no punctuation. It helps to show students the sentences without the interruption (MCs italicized): *It's not so dreadful being a toad* while people aren't always humane *you're free to live as you please in the bounties of nature.*

  Problem: There is no punctuation between *toad* and *you're*, so this is a fused sentence. Since the *while* clause goes with the MC after it, correct by placing a period after *toad*.

  Fix: *It's not so dreadful being a toad.* While people aren't always humane, *you're free to live as you please in the bounties of nature.*
- **#5 clausal openers** take commas: AC, MC. Fix: **While people aren't always humane,** you're free to live as you please in the bounties of nature.
- **Mid-sentence prepositional phrases** do not take commas. Fix: to live as you please **in the bounties of nature.**

Grammar Notations

PREPOSITIONAL PHRASES. in the bounties; of nature.

CLAUSES, PHRASES, AND OPENERS.

- #1 subject opener and MC: **It's** not so dreadful being a toad.

  If students mark *being* as a verb, explain that it is a verbal that does not function as a verb here. To be a verb, *being* needs a subject and helping verb before it, as in "I am being a frog."
- MC: **he assured** her.
- #5 clausal opener and AC: While **people are**n't always humane. Remind students that *not* is an adverb, not a verb.
- MC: **you're** free to live (as you please) in the bounties of nature. This MC has inside it a dependent clause.
- AC (adverb clause dress-up): as **you please.**

DAY 2

¶ trying to cheer dorinda, [arthur offered to read to her a few stories]. [he regaled her with humorous, fairy tales, and wild, stirring adventures from the novel "the arabian nights." day after day, [arthur entertained dorinda].

Fixes

regaled: entertained agreeably

INDENT because of a new topic, pulling out of Arthur's speech.

CAPITALIZATION. Trying, Dorinda, Arthur, He, The Arabian Nights, Day, Arthur, Dorinda.

EMPHASIS. Rarely use italics, bold, or underline to show emphasis, but sometimes the sense is best communicated this way. The tables are turned: Arthur will now read stories to Dorinda, so it is correct to emphasize her.

TITLES. Capitalize and underline (or italicize when typing) titles of long works like novels: The Arabian Nights. It is also correct not to have a comma before this title: from the novel The Arabian Nights. *See* ✏ **1.**

COMMAS AND OTHER PUNCTUATION.

- **#4 -ing openers** take commas: **Trying to cheer Dorinda,** Arthur offered to read. Ask: Is the subject after the comma doing the -inging? Answer: Yes, Arthur is the one trying to cheer her, so this is a legal #4.

- **Adjectives before a noun.** Test whether they are coordinate or cumulative to determine comma usage.

  Fairy humorous tales and *humorous and fairy tales* both sound awkward, so these are cumulative adjectives and should not have the comma: **humorous fairy tales.** *See* ✏ **2.**

  Stirring, wild adventures and *wild and stirring adventures* both sound fine, so these are coordinate adjectives and need the comma: **wild, stirring adventures.**

- **Items in a series.** Pattern a and b (no comma). Fix: **fairy tales and … adventures.**

- **#2 prepositional openers** do not require commas when they are short unless they function as transitions, like *Day after day.* Keep the comma.

Grammar Notations

PREPOSITIONAL PHRASES. to her; with humorous fairy tales and wild, stirring adventures; from the novel; after day.

To keep your students on their toes, ask them to explain how each of these fits the pattern: preposition + noun, and no verb.

- *to* (prep) + *her* (pronoun). No verb.

- *with* (prep) + *humorous* (adjective) + *fairy tales* (first noun) + *and* (cc) + *wild, stirring* (adjectives) + *adventures* (second noun). The two nouns are both objects of the preposition. No verb.

- *from* (prep) + *the* (article) + *novel* (noun). No verb.

- *after* (prep) + *day* (noun). No verb.

✏ **1. Teacher's note.** *The Arabian Nights* is an essential appositive, so no comma is correct. Students may have learned that all appositives are set off with commas. This is not true; only nonessential ones are. Here, the title restricts the meaning to this particular novel; if removed, we would wonder which title.

✏ **2. Teacher's note.** These are cumulative because effectively there is only one adjective, which modifies the compound noun *fairy tales.*

CLAUSES, PHRASES, AND OPENERS.

- #4 -ing participial phrase opener: Trying to cheer Dorinda.
- MC: **Arthur offered** to read to <u>her</u> a few stories. *See* ✎ **3.**
- #1 subject opener and MC: **He regaled** her with humorous fairy tales and wild, stirring adventures from the novel <u>The Arabian Nights</u>.
- Invisible #2 prepositional phrase opener: Day after day.
    - ✎ **Teacher's note.** This is not a true prepositional phrase, but a preposition is implied (*on, during, at*), so we count it as an Invisible #2. *After day* is a prepositional phrase.
- MC: **Arthur entertained** Dorinda.

✎ **3. Teacher's note.** Check that students do not mark the infinitive *to read* as a verb. It functions as a noun, the direct object of *offered*.

DAY 3

#3   MC S   V

¶ gradually, [she grew to appreciate his sympathy toward her, and to respect his positive attitude].

#5 AC   S   V

(when the infirmary **orderly** brought him meals, with scarcely a glance in arthur's direction),

MC S   V   V

[he didn't protest].

Fixes

INDENT because of a new topic, Dorinda's notice of Arthur's kindness.

CAPITALIZATION. Gradually, When, Arthur's.

COMMAS AND OTHER PUNCTUATION.

- **#3 -ly adverb opener.** This opener does not require a strong pause, so the comma is not needed.

    ADVANCED. Ask: How do we know the comma is optional? Answer: It modifies the verb, not the whole sentence: she *gradually grew* to appreciate.

- **Items in a series.** Pattern: a and b (no comma). Fix: she grew **to appreciate** his sympathy toward her and **to respect** his positive attitude. **ADVANCED.** The two items (bolded) are infinitive phrases.

- **#5 clausal openers** take a comma, but put it after all the openers, including the two prepositional phrases. Fix: **When the infirmary orderly brought him meals with scarcely a glance in Arthur's direction,** he didn't protest.

orderly: a hospital attendant with non-medical duties

Grammar Notations

PREPOSITIONAL PHRASES. toward her; with scarcely a glance; in Arthur's direction.

CLAUSES, PHRASES, AND OPENERS.

- #3 -ly adverb opener: Gradually.
- MC: **she grew** to appreciate his sympathy toward her and to respect his positive attitude.

    If students mark *to appreciate* or *to respect*, remind them that infinitives (*to* + verb) are formed from verbs but do not function as verbs.

- #5 clausal opener and MC: When the infirmary **orderly brought** him meals with scarcely a glance in Arthur's direction.
- MC: **he didn't protest.**

DAY 4

#5 AC   S   V   DC   S   V   V

(when he nearly choked) on learning, (that the palace cook had whipped up fly soup for him),

MC S V ,   V   AC   S   V   MC S V ,   V

[he didnt grumble] ; (even when dorinda accidentally stumbled over his hurt leg), [he didnt **chastise**

V

her for being clumsy, but readily forgave her].

Fixes

chastise: criticize severely

CAPITALIZATION. When, Dorinda.

APOSTROPHES. Use apostrophes in contractions where letter(s) are missing: *didn't* for *did not* (twice).

COMMAS AND OTHER PUNCTUATION.

- *That* **clauses** do not take commas. Fix: When he nearly choked on learning **that the palace cook had whipped up fly soup for him.**
- **#5 clausal openers** take commas. Fix: **When he nearly choked on learning that the palace cook had whipped up fly soup for him,** he didn't grumble.

  Punctuate the second adverb clause like an opener. The original is correct: **even when Dorinda accidentally stumbled over his hurt leg,** he didn't chastise her. *See* ✏ **1.**

- **Run-on sentence** (comma splice MC, MC). Ask: Does the adverb clause "even when …" go with the MC before or after it? Answer: after. Ask: Find two MCs that are joined somewhere between them with only a comma. Answer: *he didn't grumble and he didn't chastise her.*

  Challenge advanced students to suggest three possible fixes; then discuss the pros and cons of each.

  - **Semicolon.** When he nearly choked on learning that the palace cook had whipped up fly soup for him, *he didn't grumble*; even when Dorinda accidentally stumbled over his hurt leg, *he didn't chastise her.*
  - **Period.** When he nearly choked on learning that the palace cook had whipped up fly soup for him, *he didn't grumble.* Even when Dorinda accidentally stumbled over his hurt leg, *he didn't chastise her.*
  - **MC, cc MC.** When he nearly choked on learning that the palace cook had whipped up fly soup for him, *he didn't grumble,* **and** even when Dorinda accidentally stumbled over his hurt leg, *he didn't chastise her.*

  All three work. The semicolon has an advantage because the constructions are parallel and the sentences are making the same point. A period means "new point, now," which does not show the connection between the points as well. *And* is smooth, but what follows it may not carry as much weight as what comes before. Let your students choose their favorite.

- **Items in a series.** Rule: MC cc 2nd verb—one subject with two verbs, so no comma. Fix: **he didn't chastise** her for being clumsy **but** readily **forgave** her.

✏ **1. Teacher's note.** In the patterns MC, cc MC and MC; MC, punctuate what follows the semicolon or comma + cc as if it started a new sentence. Therefore, this adverb clause is punctuated like an opener but labeled a dress-up since it does not begin a sentence.

Grammar Notations

PREPOSITIONAL PHRASES. on learning; for him; over his hurt leg; for being. *See* ✏ **2.**

✏ **2. Teacher's note.** The two -ing words are gerunds, which are -ing words that function as nouns, in this case, objects of the preposition.

CLAUSES, PHRASES, AND OPENERS.

- #5 clausal opener and AC: When **he** nearly **choked.** If students include *on learning* in this clause, that is fine.
- DC (*that* clause): that the palace **cook had whipped up** fly soup for him. *See* ♡.
- MC: **he didn't grumble.**
- AC (adverb clause dress-up): even when **Dorinda** accidentally **stumbled** over his hurt leg.
- MC: **he didn't chastise** her for being clumsy but readily **forgave** her.

♡ **Grammar lovers.** This clause is a noun clause because *that* follows a verbal (*learning*). You can tell it is not an adjective clause like *who-which* clauses because you cannot substitute *which* for *that* and have it make sense.

Style

If desired, have students identify the strongest of the vocabulary dress-ups from this week. Discuss their answers. Suggestions:

- **Strong verbs.** assured, regaled, choked, whipped up, grumble, stumbled, chastise.
- **Quality adjectives.** dreadful, humane, clumsy.
- **-ly adverbs.** scarcely, accidentally, readily.

STUDENT REWRITE

"It's not so dreadful being a toad," he assured her. "While people aren't always humane, you're free to live as you please in the bounties of nature."

Trying to cheer Dorinda, Arthur offered to read to her a few stories. He regaled her with humorous fairy tales and wild, stirring adventures from the novel The Arabian Nights. Day after day, Arthur entertained Dorinda.

Gradually she grew to appreciate his sympathy toward her and to respect his positive attitude. When the infirmary orderly brought him meals with scarcely a glance in Arthur's direction, he didn't protest. When he nearly choked on learning that the palace cook had whipped up fly soup for him, he didn't grumble; even when Dorinda accidentally stumbled over his hurt leg, he didn't chastise her for being clumsy but readily forgave her.

Week 25

Review

LEARN IT

There are no new concepts this week. Test your grammar knowledge with these questions. Check your grammar cards if you cannot remember.

1. List the six sentence openers by number and name.

2. Which openers always require commas?

3. Which openers sometimes require commas and when?

Do you remember what these vocabulary words mean? If not, look them up in your vocabulary list in the back of your notebook.

- deficiencies
- resplendent
- surmised
- oblivious
- conjectured
- delectable
- substantial
- recumbent
- propitious
- apropos

Teacher's answers

1. #1 subject, #2 prepositional, #3 -ly adverb, #4 -ing, #5 clausal, #6 vss

2. #4 and #5

3. #2 (5+ words) and #3 (pause test)

Page 52, *Fix It! Grammar: Frog Prince, or Just Deserts*, Student Book 3

DAY 1

#Q MC   V S   DC S   V   MC   S   V

¶ "[how is it] (you stay so **sanguine** all the time)?" [dorinda inquired of arthur one day].

#5 AC   S   V   MC S   V   #1MC S   V

"(although unpleasant things happen), [you manage to have **empathy** for others], . [you aren't

          V

affected

~~effected~~ by being a little frog]."

Fixes

INDENT because of a new speaker.

CAPITALIZATION. How, Dorinda, Arthur, Although, You.

SPELLING. *Affect* as a verb means to influence or produce a change in. *Effect* as a noun is the result of that change. Fix: You aren't **affected** [the verb meaning *influenced* or *changed*] by being a little frog.

COMMAS AND OTHER PUNCTUATION.

- **Quotations.** Enclose speech and closing punctuation in quotes. Use a question mark after the question and a period at the end of her statement, both inside the closing quotations: "How … time?" "Although … frog."

- **#5 clausal openers** take commas. Fix: **Although unpleasant things happen,** you manage to have empathy for others.

- **Run-on sentence** (comma splice MC, MC). Ask students to find, explain, and correct the comma splice.

  The comma between *others* and *you* is not strong enough to hold the two main clauses together. Fix with a period: *you manage to have empathy for others. You aren't affected by being a little frog.*

Grammar Notations

PREPOSITIONAL PHRASES. of Arthur; for others; by being. *See* ♡.

CLAUSES, PHRASES, AND OPENERS.

- **#Q** (question) and MC: How **is** it.
- **ADVANCED.** DC (*that* is implied): **you stay** so sanguine all the time.
- MC: **Dorinda inquired** of Arthur one day.

  This is not a separate sentence (so no opener) because it sets up the quotation that comes before it and is part of that sentence. The first word is capitalized only because it is a proper noun.

- #5 clausal opener and AC: Although unpleasant **things happen**.
- MC: **you manage** to have empathy for others.
- #1 subject opener and MC: **You aren't affected** by being a little frog.

---

sanguine: cheerfully optimistic; hopeful

empathy: the ability to identify with the feelings of other people

♡ **Grammar lovers.**
In *by being a little frog*, *being* is the object of the preposition, which is a noun function. We call -ing words *gerunds* when they act as nouns.

DAY 2

¶ "oh, [i learned the hard way]. (when i lose my temper), [folks just steer clear of me] ; (when i give a bit of kindness), [it comes back to me]. besides, [what is there ~~their/they're~~ to be discontented about]. ? [i have my health, water, and plenty of food]—**albeit** not always to my taste."

Annotations above the text:
#T MC S V; #5 AC S lose (V); MC S V; AC S
V; MC S V; #Q MC S V
#1 MC S V

Fixes

albeit: even though; even if

INDENT because of a new speaker.

CAPITALIZATION. Oh, I, When, I, I, Besides, I.

SPELLING AND HOMOPHONES. 1) When I **lose** my temper. *To lose* means to fail to keep; *to loose* means to release something. 2) What is **there** to be discontented about?

COMMAS AND OTHER PUNCTUATION.

- **Quotations.** Enclose speech and closing punctuation in quotes: "Oh … taste."
- **Interjections** take commas or exclamations when exclamatory. Fix: **Oh,** I learned the hard way.
- **Run-on sentence.** Ask students to find the comma splice (MC, MC) and discuss possible fixes.

  Answer: There needs to be something stronger than the comma after *me*. A period would work well but a semicolon even better. Semicolons join two MCs (especially ones that are parallel in construction) that express one idea. Since both the AC, MC patterns express the idea that our behavior affects people's treatment of us, use a semicolon.

  Fix, with MCs italicized: When I lose my temper, *folks just steer clear of me*; when I give a bit of kindness, *it comes back to me.*
- **#5 clausal openers** take commas. Fix: **When I lose my temper,** folks just steer clear of me; **when I give a bit of kindness,** it comes back to me. *See* ✎ **1.**
- **Introductory transitions** take commas. Fix: **Besides,** what is there to be discontented about?
- **End marks.** Add a question mark: What is there to be discontented about**?**
- **Items in a series.** a, b, and c. Fix: I have my health, water, **and** plenty of food.
- **ADVANCED. Em dashes** sometimes replace commas to avoid confusion. Since this dash follows the third item in a series, the sentence would be confusing with another comma. A dash draws attention to something, which also works here.

Grammar Notations

PREPOSITIONAL PHRASES. of me; of kindness; to me; of food; to my taste. *See* ✎ **2.**

CLAUSES, PHRASES, AND OPENERS.

- #T (transitional) opener: Oh.
- MC: **I learned** the hard way.
- #5 clausal opener and AC: When **I lose** my temper.
- MC: **folks** just **steer** clear of me.
- AC: when **I give** a bit of kindness.

✎ **1. Teacher's note.** Remember to punctuate what follows a semicolon like any opener.

✎ **2. Teacher's note.** *Back* is an adverb: it comes back, or returns. *About* is a preposition, but its object is *what*, which is too hard at this level. It is acceptable to end a sentence with a preposition (*discontented about*). It would be awkward to say, "about what is there to be discontented?"

- MC: **it comes** back to me.
- #Q (question) or #T (transition) and MC: Besides, **what is** there to be discontented about?
- #1 subject opener and MC: **I have** my health, water, and plenty of food.

DAY 3

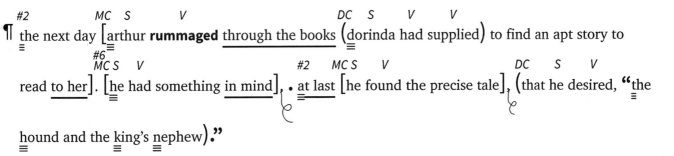

Fixes

INDENT because time has passed.

CAPITALIZATION. The, Arthur, Dorinda, He, At, The Hound and the King's Nephew (see Titles, below).

TITLES. Fix: he found the precise tale that he desired, **"The Hound and the King's Nephew."** Rules: 1) Capitalize all key words in titles, including first and last words, but not minor words in the middle of titles (*and, the*). 2) Place quotations around titles of short stories with the period inside the closing quotes. *See* ✏ **1.**

COMMAS AND OTHER PUNCTUATION.

- **Short #2 prepositional openers** do not require a comma. *The next day* is correct with or without a comma.
- **Run-on sentence.** Ask students to find and explain the comma splice (MC, MC). Answer: The comma after *in mind* is not strong enough to hold together the two MCs. Challenge advanced students to suggest three or four possible fixes and discuss each.
  - ◆ **MC, cc MC.** He had something in mind, **and** at last *he found the precise tale that he desired.* Weak to use *and* to link these ideas.
  - ◆ **Semicolon.** He had something in mind**;** at last *he found the precise tale that he desired.* A brief time of searching must occur between these two ideas. A semicolon, which implies that the two MCs express only one idea, does not connect them logically.
  - ◆ **Subordinate one clause.** As he had something in mind, at last *he found the precise tale that he desired.* *As* can mean different things when it starts a clause (*since, though, while, when*), so it can be hard to tell its meaning, especially at the start of a sentence. The other www words do not make sense either.
  - ◆ **Period.** He had something in mind. At last *he found the precise tale that he desired.* The best!
- *That* **clauses** do not take commas because they are essential. Fix: he found the precise tale **that he desired.**

  ADVANCED. Ask: Why is this clause essential? Answer: It is not just any tale but the one he desired, so this clause restricts the meaning to that particular one.

  This *that* clause is an adjective clause like *who-which* clauses because it follows the noun it describes (*tale*). Usually we use *that* in place of *which* in essential *which* clauses. To keep the concept simple, IEW asks students to mark only *who* or *which* as the *who-which* dress-up, not *that* when it substitutes for *which*.

rummaged: searched actively through

✏ **1. Teacher's note.** The rule that commas and periods go inside closing quotes applies to any quotation marks, not just those for dialogue.

The comma before the title is correct. The title is a nonessential appositive because *the precise tale that he desired* already identifies which story. The title just adds helpful information but does not alter the meaning of the rest of the sentence.

Grammar Notations

PREPOSITIONAL PHRASES. through the books; to her; in mind; At last.

CLAUSES, PHRASES, AND OPENERS.

- Invisible #2 prepositional phrase opener: The next day. *See* ✎ **2.**
- MC: **Arthur rummaged** through the books (Dorinda had supplied) to find an apt story to read to her.
- **ADVANCED.** DC (Invisible *who-which*): **Dorinda had supplied.**
- #6 vss and MC: **He had** something in mind.
- #2 prepositional phrase opener: At last.
- MC: **he found** the precise tale.
- DC (essential adjective clause): that **he desired.**

> ✎ **2. Teacher's note.**
> When openers start with a time frame before the main clause, a preposition (*on* or *during*) is implied but not stated. Treat them like any #2 prepositional opener.

DAY 4

#1 MC   S   MC S   V   V   V
¶ "[the celebrated king of the arthurian tales," [he began], "was out riding one day with his

        DC S   V   ,   *eldest*   ,
nephew robert], (who enjoyed the kings special favor as the ~~elder~~ of his sisters three boys).

#3   MC   S   V
regrettably, [the lad was **mute** from birth].

Fixes

INDENT because of a new topic, the story Arthur is reading.

CAPITALIZATION. The, Arthurian (capitalize words derived from proper nouns), Robert, Regrettably. Lowercase: king, king's (not used with a name).

USAGE. Use the superlative adjective for the most of three or more: the **eldest** of his sister's three boys.

COMMAS AND OTHER PUNCTUATION.

- **Quotation.** Fix: "The celebrated king … tales," he began, "was out riding … from birth. Arthur is reading this story aloud, so the story is all in quotes. 1) No close quotes because he is not finished speaking. 2) Set off the interruption (*he began*) with commas since the sentence continues. *See* ✎ **1.**
- **Essential and nonessential elements.** Fix: riding with his nephew Robert, **who enjoyed the king's special favor.** The *who* clause adds information but does not change the fact that they were out riding one day, so it is nonessential and set off with a comma.

  ADVANCED. *Robert* should not be set off with commas because it is an essential appositive. King Arthur has at least three nephews, as this sentence indicates, so we need Robert's name to know which nephew is intended. *See* ✎ **2.**
- **Apostrophes** for possession: the **king's** special favor; his **sister's** three boys.
- **#3 -ly adverb openers.** Add a comma after *Regrettably* because it needs a pause.

  ADVANCED. This opener modifies the whole idea that he had been mute since birth, not just the verb *was*. When -ly adverbs modify the whole sentence, they take commas.

> **mute:** incapable of speech
>
> ✎ **1. Teacher's note.**
> Since commas always hug the word that comes before them, the comma after *began* should come immediately after that word (no space), with a space after the comma and before the quotation mark. Quotations also hug the words they enclose. This is important to prevent confusion about what is being quoted.
>
> ✎ **2. Teacher's note.**
> The need for a comma supersedes the need for no comma. Even though Robert is essential (no commas), it is followed by a comma because the *who* clause demands one.

Grammar Notations

PREPOSITIONAL PHRASES. of the Arthurian tales; with his nephew; as the eldest; of his sister's three boys; from birth.

Ask: Why is *as* a preposition here and not a www word? Answer: It fits the pattern: *as* (word that can be a preposition) + *the* (article) + *eldest*—no verb. *As* cannot be a www word because it does not start a clause, which must have a verb.

If students think *eldest* is an adjective, remind them that articles (*the*) always set up a noun, and *eldest* is the only possibility.

CLAUSES, PHRASES, AND OPENERS.
- #1 subject opener and MC: The celebrated **king** of the Arthurian tales … **was** out **riding** one day with his nephew Robert.
- MC: **he began.**
- DC (*who-which* clause): **who enjoyed** the king's special favor as the eldest of his sister's three boys.
- #3 -ly adverb opener: Regrettably.
- MC: the **lad was** mute from birth.

Style

If desired, have students identify the strongest of the vocabulary dress-ups from this week. Discuss their answers. Suggestions:
- **Strong verbs.** steer, rummaged.
- **Quality adjectives.** sanguine, discontented, apt, celebrated.
- **-ly adverbs.** None to choose from. *Regrettably* is a sentence opener.

STUDENT REWRITE

"How is it you stay so sanguine all the time?" Dorinda inquired of Arthur one day. "Although unpleasant things happen, you manage to have empathy for others. You aren't affected by being a little frog."

"Oh, I learned the hard way. When I lose my temper, folks just steer clear of me; when I give a bit of kindness, it comes back to me. Besides, what is there to be discontented about? I have my health, water, and plenty of food—albeit not always to my taste."

The next day Arthur rummaged through the books Dorinda had supplied to find an apt story to read to her. He had something in mind. At last he found the precise tale that he desired, "The Hound and the King's Nephew."

"The celebrated king of the Arthurian tales," he began, "was out riding one day with his nephew Robert, who enjoyed the king's special favor as the eldest of his sister's three boys. Regrettably, the lad was mute from birth.

Week 26

Invisible #4s

LEARN IT

If you enjoy being a sentence opener detective, see if you can find another kind of invisible opener: the invisible #4. These invisibles follow the same pattern as regular #4s, but the -ing word is hidden.

Invisible #4s follow this pattern:

[Being] Adjective(s) + comma + main clause

A word like *being* or *appearing* is implied at the beginning of the sentence but not actually there.

Invisible #4s are more elegant without *being* or *appearing* but function and are punctuated just like a #4 opener.

Notice how an invisible -ing word is implied in each of these examples:

[Appearing] Carefree and cheerful, Dorinda enjoyed every moment of every day.

[Being] Ever watchful, the servants monitored her every move.

Sentences starting with a past participle ending in -ed also follow the pattern of an invisible #4 opener.

[Being] Chided by her father for her behavior, Dorinda tried to be more graceful, but her youthful vigor hindered her.

As with regular #4s, there must be a comma, and the thing after the comma must be doing the invisible -inging.

Page 54, *Fix It! Grammar: Frog Prince, or Just Deserts*, **Student Book 3**

DAY 1

#4   *MC*   *S*   *V*

quick-witted and agile, [robert **compensated** for his limitation, by an eagerness to please, and to learn].

#4   *MC S*   *V*   *V*   *aid*

ever watchful of the king, [he had sought opportunities to serve, or ~~aide~~, his uncle].

Fixes

compensated: offset; counterbalanced

CAPITALIZATION. Quick-witted, Robert, Ever.

SPELLING. Not *aide*, an assistant or helper, but *aid*, the verb meaning to help: to serve or **aid** his uncle.

COMMAS AND OTHER PUNCTUATION. As needed, remember to discuss the Grammar Notations before covering punctuation.

- **Quotations.** No quotes since this continues the story.
- **Invisible #4 -ing openers** take commas. 1) The first is correct: **Quick-witted and agile,** Robert compensated. 2) The second needs a comma: **Ever watchful of the king,** he had sought opportunities.

  With both, ask: Is the subject after the comma the -inger? Answer: Yes, Robert is the one who is quick-witted and agile as well as watchful of the king, so both are legal #4s.
- **Mid-sentence prepositional phrases** are not set off with commas. Fix: Robert compensated for his limitation **by an eagerness** to please.
- **Items in a series.** No comma before cc's that join only two items in a series that are not MCs: a and b. Fix: 1) an eagerness **to please and to learn**; 2) he had sought opportunities to **serve or aid** his uncle. Check that students also removed the comma after *or aid* since that separates *aid* from its object: *aid his uncle.*

  ADVANCED. In these examples, both cc's join two infinitives; in the second, the preposition *to* is implied before *aid*: to serve or *to* aid his uncle.

Grammar Notations

PREPOSITIONAL PHRASES. for his limitation; by an eagerness; of the king.

CLAUSES, PHRASES, AND OPENERS.

- Invisible #4 -ing participial opener: Quick-witted and agile. *Being* is implied: *Being* **quick-witted and agile.**
- MC: **Robert compensated** for his limitation by an eagerness to please and to learn.
- Invisible #4 -ing participial opener: Ever watchful of the king. *Being* is again implied.
- MC: **he had sought** opportunities to serve or aid his uncle.

DAY 2

```
 #T      MC S    V      V                                                                          ,
¶ "now, [they were riding through the royal forest with roberts beloved hound hrothgar by his side].
 #1 MC    S    V     V                           V              #5 AC S      V                        MC    S
  [the lad had raised hrothgar, and trained him well]. (as they passed through a cedar grove), [hrothgar
                       V           sight
  erratically bounded ahead and out of site].
```

Fixes

INDENT because of a new topic, the return to the action of the story.

CAPITALIZATION. Now, Robert's, Hrothgar, The, Hrothgar, As, Hrothgar.

HOMOPHONE. Students often confuse *sight* (view or seeing), *site* (a plot of ground or a website), and *cite* (to provide a source). Fix: The hound bounded out of **sight**.

COMMAS AND OTHER PUNCTUATION.

- **ADVANCED. Quotes used with new paragraphs, same speech.** The last paragraph closes with no quotes to indicate that Arthur is still speaking. This paragraph correctly opens with quotes to remind us that someone is still speaking. Since he is not finished telling the story, do not end with quotes.

- **Transitional words** take commas. Fix: **Now,** they were riding.

- **Apostrophes** show possession: **Robert's** hound.

- **ADVANCED. Essential appositives** take no commas: Robert's beloved hound **Hrothgar** by his side. Presumably Robert has more than one hound, so *Hrothgar* specifies which one is meant and is therefore essential.

- **Run-on sentence.** Ask students to find, explain, and correct the comma splice (MC, MC). See ✎.

  Answer: The comma after *by his side* is not strong enough to hold together the two MCs and should be a period instead. Fix , with MCs italicized: *They were riding through the royal forest with Robert's beloved hound Hrothgar by his side. The lad had raised Hrothgar and trained him well.*

- **Items in a series.** Unless they are main clauses, two items in a series will not have a comma before the cc.

  The first cc *and* joins only two verbs: MC cc 2nd verb. Fix: The lad had **raised** Hrothgar **and trained** him well. Tip: When a verb instead of a noun follows *and*, this is usually the pattern.

  The last cc *and* joins two adverbs, not three or more. Pattern: a and b. The original is correct: bounded **ahead and out** of sight.

- **#5 clausal openers** take commas: AC, MC. Fix: **As they passed through a cedar grove,** Hrothgar erratically bounded ahead.

Grammar Notations

PREPOSITIONAL PHRASES. through the royal forest; with Robert's beloved hound Hrothgar; by his side; through a cedar grove; of sight.

CLAUSES, PHRASES, AND OPENERS.

- #T (transitional) opener: Now.

---

erratically: not in the usual or proper course; oddly

Robert named his hound after a legendary sixth-century Danish king referenced in the Old English poem *Beowulf*. In Old English, all letters are pronounced. Good luck with *Hrothgar*!

✎ **Teacher's note.** Remind students that the two MCs will not necessarily be back to back but there will be nothing stronger than a comma between them.

- MC: **they were riding** through the royal forest with Robert's beloved hound Hrothgar by his side.
- #1 subject opener and MC: The **lad had raised** Hrothgar and **trained** him well.
- #5 clausal opener and AC: As **they passed** through a cedar grove.
- MC: **Hrothgar** erratically **bounded** ahead and out of sight.

DAY 3

#1 MC S   V   V   wildly   DC S   V   AC since   S
[robert could hear him barking ~~wild~~ in the distance], (which surprised him), (~~sense~~ his hound

V
never barked without a **creditable** reason).

Fixes

creditable: deserving credit or honor

A similar word, *credible*, means believable or trustworthy.

USAGE. Use the -ly adverb *wildly*, not the adjective *wild*, to modify a verbal: **barking wildly**. Adjectives modify nouns only.

It does not matter whether students recognize that the participle *barking* functions as an adjective or think (incorrectly) that it is a verb since adverbs modify both verbs and adjectives. The important thing to communicate is that *wild* will not work because it should modify only nouns.

CAPITALIZATION. Robert.

HOMOPHONE. Use *since* meaning *because*, not *sense* meaning one of the five senses. Fix: **since** his hound never barked.

COMMAS AND OTHER PUNCTUATION.

- **Quotation.** This continues the story in the same paragraph, so no quotes.
- **Nonessential elements** take commas. Fix: Robert could hear him barking wildly in the distance, **which surprised him since his hound never barked without a creditable reason.**

  Ask advanced students to explain why the *which* clause is nonessential. Answer: If we removed it from the sentence, it would not affect the meaning of the rest of the sentence. Robert could still hear Hrothgar barking.

- **Adverb clause dress-ups** do not take commas. Fix: which surprised him **since his hound never barked.**

Grammar Notations

PREPOSITIONAL PHRASES. in the distance; without a creditable reason.

CLAUSES, PHRASES, AND OPENERS.

- #1 subject opener and MC: **Robert could hear** him barking wildly in the distance.
- DC (*who-which* clause): **which surprised** him.
- AC (adverb clause dress-up): since his **hound** never **barked** without a creditable reason.

DAY 4

#5 AC   S   V   V   DC S   V   V   MC S   V
(even though he did not know) (what was troubling hrothgar), [he recognized the sound, as a

        #2   MC S   V
warning]. by contrast, [his uncle seemed **undaunted**, or perhaps oblivious to the noise].

Fixes

QUOTATION. This continues the story in the same paragraph, so no new quotes.

CAPITALIZATION. Even, Hrothgar, By.

COMMAS AND OTHER PUNCTUATION. *See* ✎.

- **#5 clausal openers.** Have students pull out their www.asia.b grammar card from Week 2 and read the additional words at the bottom of the back side. Challenge them to find one in this passage. Answer: *though*. Ask: How do we know it starts a clause? Answer: There is a subject-verb pair: *he did … know*.

  Ask: What is the punctuation after #5 openers? Answer: A comma after the entire clause. Fix: **Even though he did not know what was troubling Hrothgar,** he recognized the sound.

- **Mid-sentence prepositional phrases** do not take commas. Fix: he recognized the sound **as a warning**.

- **Run-on sentence.** Ask students to find and correct the comma splice (MC, MC).

  Fix:

  - **Period.** Even though he did not know what was troubling Hrothgar, he *recognized the sound as a warning.* By contrast, *his uncle seemed undaunted or perhaps oblivious to the noise.* When too many clauses are combined in one sentence, we can lose the force of each, so two sentences work best.

  ADVANCED. Discuss the pros and cons of alternatives below. If students prefer one of these and can defend their choice, let them use it!

  - **MC, cc MC.** Even though he did not know what was troubling Hrothgar, *he recognized the sound as a warning,* **but** ~~by contrast,~~ *his uncle seemed undaunted or perhaps oblivious to the noise. But* is a logical connector if we drop *by contrast,* but the sentence has too many contrasting thoughts to make it as easy to follow.

  - **Subordinate a clause** (make one dependent). Even though he did not know what was troubling Hrothgar, *he recognized the sound as a warning,* **whereas** ~~by contrast,~~ *his uncle seemed undaunted or perhaps oblivious to the noise. Whereas* (without *by contrast*) is more effective than *but* because it makes it clearer that the contrast is between the men's different responses. This is an effective fix.

  - **Semicolon.** Even though he did not know what was troubling Hrothgar, *he recognized the sound as a warning*; by contrast, *his uncle seemed undaunted or perhaps oblivious to the noise.* Weak. These are separate ideas, so there is no reason to use a semicolon.

- **Transitional #2 prepositional openers** take commas. When #2 openers work transitionally, they need a comma. Fix: **By contrast,** his uncle seemed undaunted.

- **Items in a series.** No comma before the cc or because it joins only two items in a series (adjectives), not three or more: **undaunted or** perhaps **oblivious**.

undaunted: not discouraged; undismayed

✎ **Teacher's note.** Remember to guide students as needed through the Grammar Notations before addressing punctuation.

Grammar Notations

PREPOSITIONAL PHRASES. as a warning; By contrast; to the noise.

Ask students to explain why *as a warning* is a prepositional phrase and not an adverb clause since *as* can start either. Answer: There is no verb in the phrase, so it cannot be a clause. It fits the prepositional phrase pattern of preposition (*as*) + noun (*warning*) and no verb (*a* is an article).

CLAUSES, PHRASES, AND OPENERS.

- #5 clausal opener and AC: Even though **he did** not **know**. *Even* is an adverb connected to *though*.
- **ADVANCED.** DC: **what was troubling** Hrothgar.
- MC: **he recognized** the sound as a warning.
- #2 prepositional phrase opener: By contrast.
- MC: his **uncle seemed** undaunted or perhaps oblivious to the noise.

Style

If desired, have students identify the strongest of the vocabulary dress-ups from this week. Discuss their answers. Suggestions:

- **Strong verbs.** compensated, bounded.
- **Quality adjectives.** quick-witted, agile, watchful, creditable, undaunted, oblivious.
- **-ly adverbs.** erratically, wildly.

STUDENT REWRITE

Quick-witted and agile, Robert compensated for his limitation by an eagerness to please and to learn. Ever watchful of the king, he had sought opportunities to serve or aid his uncle.

"Now, they were riding through the royal forest with Robert's beloved hound Hrothgar by his side. The lad had raised Hrothgar and trained him well. As they passed through a cedar grove, Hrothgar erratically bounded ahead and out of sight. Robert could hear him barking wildly in the distance, which surprised him since his hound never barked without a creditable reason. Even though he did not know what was troubling Hrothgar, he recognized the sound as a warning. By contrast, his uncle seemed undaunted or perhaps oblivious to the noise.

Week 27

Commas with -ing Participial Phrases

LEARN IT

You have learned that you should use commas after introductory -ing participial phrases, even if they are short.

- **Sobbing,** Dorinda wished someone would retrieve her ball.

- **Jumping into the cold water and lugging the ball back up,** the frog rescued Dorinda's favorite bauble.

When an -ing (participial) phrase occurs later in the sentence, a comma is usually needed because the phrase is usually nonessential. Remember, *nonessential* does not mean unimportant; it only means that the sentence could make sense without it.

- Dorinda fled the garden with her ball in hand**, ignoring the pleas of the creature behind her**.

- Dorinda entered the palace**, bolting the door behind her**.

Page 56, *Fix It! Grammar: Frog Prince, or Just Deserts*, Student Book 3

Institute for Excellence in Writing

DAY 1

#4   *DC*   *S*   *V*   *MC*   *S*   *V*

¶ "kneeling at the foot of the cliff, (where tiny drops of water trickled down), [king arthur had cupped his

#1
    MC   *S*   *V*   *MC*   *S*   *V*   *V*

hands for a drink]. [it was a mere dribble of water], and [the king had developed a **potent** thirst].

Fixes

INDENT because of a new topic, King Arthur's attempt to get water.

CAPITALIZATION. Kneeling, King Arthur, It. Lowercase: the king.

ADVANCED. TENSE. We use past perfect tense ("had" plus a past participle) to indicate the earlier of two past times: **had cupped** *his hands*; **had developed** *a thirst*. Last week's final passage was in past tense (Robert recognized the sound as a warning). Past perfect here shows that *before* Robert's recognition, his uncle *had been doing* these things.

COMMAS AND OTHER PUNCTUATION.

- **ADVANCED. Quotations.** The last paragraph closes with no quotations to indicate that Arthur was not finished speaking. This paragraph opens with quotations to remind us that someone is still speaking: "Kneeling … . No close quotes because he is not finished.

- **#4 -ing openers** take a comma just before the MC at the end of all the openers. Fix: **Kneeling at the foot of the cliff, where tiny drops of water trickled down,** King Arthur had cupped his hands for a drink. *See* ♡.

- **Run-on sentence** (fused sentence MC MC). Ask students to find, explain, and correct the fused sentence.

  Two main clauses meet after *drink* with no punctuation to hold them together. A period is the best fix. Fix: *King Arthur had cupped his hands for a drink. It was a mere dribble of water.*

- **MC, cc MC.** Use commas before cc's when they join main clauses. Fix: *It was a mere dribble of water,* **and** *the king had developed a potent thirst.*

Grammar Notations

PREPOSITIONAL PHRASES. at the foot; of the cliff; of water; for a drink; of water.

Down is an adverb going with the verb: trickled down. Since there is no noun after it, it cannot be a preposition.

CLAUSES, PHRASES, AND OPENERS.

- **#4 -ing participial phrase opener:** Kneeling at the foot of the cliff.
- **DC (www clause):** where tiny **drops** of water **trickled** down.

  If students mark *water* as the subject, explain that *water* follows a preposition. It is the object of the preposition (noun at the end of that phrase), not the subject of the clause. Nouns cannot be both subjects and objects.

- **MC: King Arthur had cupped** his hands for a drink.
- **#1 subject opener and MC: It was** a mere dribble of water.

  If students mark this as a #6 vss, ask them to count the number of words. A sentence is a vss only if it has two to five words, no more.

- **MC: the king had developed** a potent thirst.

potent: powerful; mighty

♡ **Grammar lovers.** *Where* starts an adjective clause because it modifies the noun *cliff*. It is nonessential (takes commas) because it does not specify further where he was kneeling but just adds description. However, this concept of www words starting clauses other than adverb clauses is too advanced for this level.

DAY 2

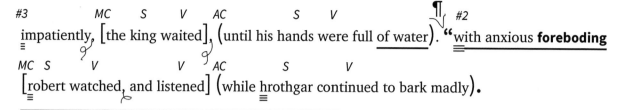

Fixes

INDENT the second sentence because of a new topic, turning back to Robert.

CAPITALIZATION. Impatiently, With, Robert, Hrothgar. Lowercase: the king.

COMMAS AND OTHER PUNCTUATION.

- **#3 -ly adverb openers.** Use the pause test. Since we do not need a pause, leave the comma out.

  ADVANCED. Commas are unneeded after -ly adverb openers when they modify the verb (the king waited impatiently), not the whole sentence.

- **Mid-sentence adverb clauses** do not take commas (twice). Rule: MC AC.

  Fix: the king waited **until his hands were full of water.** In the second sentence, the original is correct: Robert watched and listened **while Hrothgar continued to bark madly.**

- **Quotations.** The first sentence continues the story in the same paragraph, so no new quotes. The second sentence begins a new paragraph, so it starts with quotations to remind us that someone is still speaking. No close quotes because Arthur has not finished.

- **Short #2 prepositional openers** (under five words) do not require commas unless a strong pause is helpful. A comma is not wrong, but it is better without.

- **Items in a series.** No comma before cc's that join compound verbs: MC cc 2nd verb. Fix: Robert **watched and listened.**

Grammar Notations

PREPOSITIONAL PHRASES. of water; With anxious foreboding.

CLAUSES, PHRASES, AND OPENERS.

- #3 -ly adverb opener: Impatiently.
- MC: the **king waited.**
- AC (adverb clause dress-up): until his **hands were** full of water.
- #2 prepositional phrase opener: With anxious foreboding.
- MC: **Robert watched** and **listened.** Did students mark both verbs?
- AC (adverb clause dress-up): while **Hrothgar continued** to bark madly.

  If students mark *bark* as a verb, explain that it is formed from one but does not function as a verb because it does not have a subject with it. Contrast "he barked madly." It is an infinitive: to bark.

foreboding: a sense of coming evil or misfortune

DAY 3

#5 AC   S   V   DC   S   V   V   MC S   V

(although he feared) (that something in the water might be **noxious**), being mute, [robert was

                  #1

                  MC S   V   DC S   V   V

unable to warn his uncle]. [he took the only ~~coarse~~/course of action (he could envision) to

accomplish his objective swiftly].

Fixes

noxious: poisonous; harmful to health

CAPITALIZATION. Although, Robert, He.

HOMOPHONE. course of action. *Coarse* means rough or harsh.

COMMAS AND OTHER PUNCTUATION.

- **Quotation.** This continues the story in the same paragraph, so no new quotes.
- *That* **clauses** do not take commas. The original is correct: Although he feared **that something in the water might be noxious.**
- **Multiple openers.** Add a comma after both the #5 clausal opener and the participial opener. Fix: **Although he feared that something in the water might be noxious, being mute,** Robert was unable to warn his uncle.

  ADVANCED. Usually have only one comma at the end of all the openers, but since -ing participial phrases are nonessential, *being mute* needs commas on both sides.
- **ADVANCED. Infinitive phrases** are not set off with commas. If your students ask, it is correct without a comma before *to accomplish his objective.*

Grammar Notations

PREPOSITIONAL PHRASES. in the water; of action.

CLAUSES, PHRASES, AND OPENERS.

- #5 clausal opener and AC: Although **he feared.**
- DC: that **something** in the water **might be** noxious. *See* ♡.
- -ing participial phrase (students do not have to label): being mute.
- MC: **Robert was** unable to warn his uncle.
- #1 subject opener and MC: **He took** the only course of action (he could envision) to accomplish his objective swiftly.
- **ADVANCED.** DC (*which* or *that* is implied): **he could envision.**

♡ **Grammar lovers.** This is a noun clause, which follows a verb and answers the question *what*. He feared what? That something might be noxious.

DAY 4

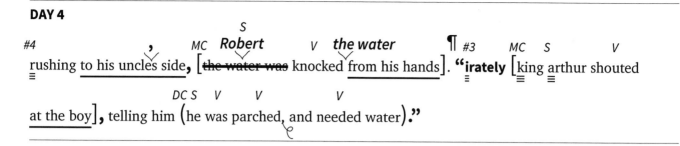

Fixes

irately: angrily

CAPITALIZATION. Rushing, Robert (in revision), Irately, King Arthur.

INDENT second sentence because of a new topic, the king's response.

COMMAS AND OTHER PUNCTUATION.

- **Quotations.** The first paragraph opens and closes with no quotes to indicate continued speech. The second paragraph opens and closes with quotes to remind us that someone is still speaking and to signal the end of Arthur's speech. Fix: "Irately … water."

- **Apostrophes** for possession: his **uncle's** side.

- **#4 -ing openers** take commas. Fix: **Rushing to his uncle's side,** the water was knocked from his hands.

  Ask: Is the subject after the comma the one doing the -inging? Answer: No! It is not the water that rushed to his uncle's side but Robert. This is an illegal #4, a.k.a. dangling modifier.

  Make *Robert,* the one doing the -inging, the new subject after the comma. If this is difficult for students, show them how instead of asking them to do it. Fix: Rushing to his uncle's side, **Robert knocked the water from his hands.**

- **#3 -ly adverb openers** do not need commas when no pause is required. *Irately* is correct both ways but no comma is better.

  ADVANCED. *Irately* modifies the verb only (*shouted irately*), not the whole main clause, so the comma is optional.

- **-ing participial phrases** take commas. Fix: King Arthur shouted at the boy, **telling him he was parched and needed water.**

  ADVANCED. This participial phrase is nonessential because it does not change the meaning of the rest of the sentence if removed; King Arthur still shouted at his nephew.

- **Items in a series.** Remove the comma before the cc *and* since it joins only two verbs: MC cc 2nd verb. Fix: he was **parched and needed** water.

Grammar Notations

PREPOSITIONAL PHRASES. to his uncle's side; from his hands; at the boy.

CLAUSES, PHRASES, AND OPENERS.

- #4 -ing participial phrase opener: Rushing to his uncle's side.
- MC: **Robert knocked** the water from his hands.
- #3 -ly adverb opener: Irately.
- MC: **King Arthur shouted** at the boy.
- **ADVANCED.** DC: **he was parched** and **needed** water.

  This is a hidden noun clause with *that* understood, which makes it dependent. Help students see that there are two verbs.

Style

If desired, have students identify the strongest of the vocabulary dress-ups from this week. Discuss their answers. Suggestions:

- **Strong verbs.** trickled, cupped, envision, parched.
- **Quality adjectives.** mere, potent, noxious.
- **-ly adverbs.** madly, swiftly.

STUDENT REWRITE

"Kneeling at the foot of the cliff, where tiny drops of water trickled down, King Arthur had cupped his hands for a drink. It was a mere dribble of water, and the king had developed a potent thirst. Impatiently the king waited until his hands were full of water.

"With anxious foreboding Robert watched and listened while Hrothgar continued to bark madly. Although he feared that something in the water might be noxious, being mute, Robert was unable to warn his uncle. He took the only course of action he could envision to accomplish his objective swiftly. Rushing to his uncle's side, Robert knocked the water from his hands.

"Irately King Arthur shouted at the boy, telling him he was parched and needed water."

Week 28

Review

LEARN IT

There are no new concepts this week. Test your grammar knowledge with these questions. Check your grammar cards if you cannot remember.

1. What are the four reasons for indenting a sentence?

2. What numbers should be written out?

3. Name the *be* verbs.

Do you remember what these vocabulary words mean? If not, look them up in your vocabulary list in the back of your notebook.

- poised
- ignobly
- futilely
- prominent
- snickered
- conspicuous
- repulsive
- requisition
- sanguine
- rummaged

✏ Teacher's note. Remember to keep the discussion light and fun—make it a game.

Teacher's answers

1. new speaker, new topic, new place, new time

2. ones that can be expressed in one or two words

3. *am, is, are, was, were, be, being, been*

Page 58, *Fix It! Grammar: Frog Prince, or Just Deserts,* **Student Book 3**

DAY 1

¶ "well, [that seems a **flimsy** excuse to bother his uncle]," [dorinda interrupted]. "[the poor man

just wanted a drink of water], . [why did robert trust his dog over his uncle]?"

Fixes

INDENT ¶ because of a new speaker.

CAPITALIZATION. Well, Dorinda, The, Why, Robert.

COMMAS AND OTHER PUNCTUATION.

- **Quotations.** "Well … uncle," Dorinda interrupted. "The … uncle?"
  Rules:
  - ◆ Enclose speech in quotes and add a comma when a speaking verb (*interrupted*) sets up a quote.
  - ◆ Keep the period after *interrupted* because Dorinda starts a new thought afterward. *See* ✎.
  - ◆ Dorinda's last statement is a question so takes a question mark inside the closing quotes.
- **Introductory transitions** take commas. Fix: **Well,** that seems a flimsy excuse.
- **Run-on sentence** (comma splice MC, MC). Ask students to find, explain, and correct the comma splice.

  Answer: The comma after *water* should be a period because the two MCs express different ideas; the first is a statement and the second a question. Fix: "The poor man just wanted a drink of water. Why did Robert trust his dog over his uncle?"

Grammar Notations

PREPOSITIONAL PHRASES. of water; over his uncle.

CLAUSES, PHRASES, AND OPENERS.

- #T transitional opener: Well.
- MC: **that seems** a flimsy excuse to bother his uncle.

  If students do not see that the pronoun *that* is the subject of this clause, ask them who or what is doing the action of *seems*. Remind them that pronouns can function as subjects, just as nouns can. It may also help to explain that *that* does not always start a dependent clause.
- MC: **Dorinda interrupted.**
- MC: The poor **man** just **wanted** a drink of water!
- #Q (question) and MC: Why **did Robert trust** his dog over his uncle?

flimsy: weak; inadequate; not convincing

✎ **Teacher's note.**
This is a comma splice, but you have to look just at the spoken words to tell. What she says needs more than just a comma between her main clauses.

DAY 2

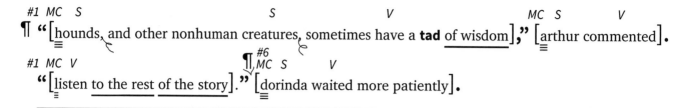

#1 MC S   *S*   *V*   *MC S*   *V*

¶ "[hounds, and other nonhuman creatures, sometimes have a **tad** of wisdom]," [arthur commented].

#1 MC V   ¶*#6* *MC S*   *V*

"[listen to the rest of the story]." [dorinda waited more patiently].

Fixes

tad: a small amount; a bit

INDENT. 1) new speaker; 2) new topic, Dorinda's response.

CAPITALIZATION. Hounds, Arthur, Listen, Dorinda.

COMMAS AND OTHER PUNCTUATION.

- **Quotations.** Fix: "Hounds … wisdom," Arthur commented. "Listen … story."

  Rules: 1) Enclose speech in quotes. 2) Interruption: Add a comma when a speaking verb (*commented*) sets up a quote. See Run-on sentence below for the reason for the period after the attribution. 3) Close his second sentence with a period inside the closing quotes.

- **Items in a series.** Ask: What does the cc *and* join? Answer: *hounds* and *other nonhuman creatures*, two nouns. Ask: What is the rule? Answer: a and b, no comma when a cc joins just two items. Fix: **Hounds and other nonhuman creatures** sometimes have a tad of wisdom.

  - 🖉 **Teacher's note.** Sometimes students put two commas around the second of two items in a series to emphasize it, but there is no reason to dramatize *and other nonhuman creatures*.

- **Run-on sentence.** Ask students to find, explain, and correct the fused sentence (MC MC). Tip: Have them look at what is inside the quotations.

  Solution: Arthur makes two statements (two MCs), needing a period between them. Since *Arthur commented* goes with the first, put a period after *commented*. To help, show students his two statements without the interrupter: *Hounds and other nonhuman creatures sometimes have a tad of wisdom listen to the rest of the story.*

  Fix: "*Hounds and other nonhuman creatures sometimes have a tad of wisdom,*" Arthur commented. "*Listen to the rest of the story.*"

Grammar Notations

PREPOSITIONAL PHRASES. of wisdom; to the rest; of the story.

CLAUSES, PHRASES, AND OPENERS.

- #1 subject opener and MC: **Hounds** and other nonhuman **creatures** sometimes **have** a tad of wisdom.
- MC: **Arthur commented.**
- #1 subject opener and MC: **Listen** to the rest of the story. This is in the imperative (request or command) mood with the subject, *you*, understood: *You* listen to the story.
- #6 vss and MC: **Dorinda waited** more patiently.

DAY 3

MC   S   V

#4 [*King Arthur collected*   #T

¶ "cupping his hands again, more of the precious liquid]. ~~was collected in king arthur's hands~~, again,

MC S   V   ,   DC   S   V   V

[robert **jiggled** his uncles hands], signaling (that they should check the source before drinking).

jiggled: moved with short, quick jerks

Fixes

INDENT because of a new topic, the continuation of the story.

CAPITALIZATION. Cupping, King Arthur, Again, Robert.

COMMAS AND OTHER PUNCTUATION.

- **Quotations.** Quotes at the beginning for new speech but not the end because Arthur is not finished: "Cupping … drinking.
- **#4 -ing openers** take commas. Fix: **Cupping his hands again,** more of the precious liquid was collected in King Arthur's hands.

  Ask: Is the subject after the comma doing the -inging? Answer: No, it is not the liquid that is cupping his hands but King Arthur! This is an illegal #4 opener (a dangling modifier). Guide students to change the subject after the comma to *King Arthur.*

  Fix: Cupping his hands again, **King Arthur collected more of the precious liquid.** We can drop *in his hands* since the opener conveys that.
- **Transitional openers** take commas. Fix: **Again,** Robert jiggled his uncle's hands.
- **Apostrophes.** Use apostrophes to show possession: his **uncle's** hands.
- **Nonessential elements** (participial phrases) take commas. This -ing phrase adds information but does not alter the fact that he jiggled his uncle's hands, so it is nonessential. Fix: Robert jiggled his uncle's hands, **signaling that they should check the source before drinking.**
- **Run-on sentence** (comma splice MC, MC). Ask students to find and correct the comma splice. Answer: We need a period instead of a comma after *liquid* (revised version) because a comma is not strong enough to hold two MCs together. Fix: King Arthur collected more of the precious liquid. Again, Robert jiggled his uncle's hands.

Grammar Notations

PREPOSITIONAL PHRASES. of the precious liquid; before drinking. See ✎.

CLAUSES, PHRASES, AND OPENERS.

- #4 -ing participial phrase opener: Cupping his hands again.
- MC: **King Arthur collected** more of the precious liquid.
- #T transitional opener: Again.
- MC: **Robert jiggled** his uncle's hands.
- **ADVANCED.** DC: that **they should check** the source before drinking. *See* ♡.

✎ **Teacher's note.** Show advanced students that -ing words do not always function as verbs. *Drinking* is the object of the preposition *before* so is functioning as a noun (called a gerund and not a participle).

♡ **Grammar lovers.** This is a noun clause because it answers the question "What?" after *signaling.* Students do not need to mark *signaling,* but it may help to know that it starts a participial phrase with the *that* clause inside it.

DAY 4

#T   MC   S   V   ¶   #2 *third*   MC   S   V

<u>again</u>, [the king ignored his nephew], **callously** pushing him away. "for a ~~3rd~~ time, [hrothgar came

to his rescue], jumping up against the king, and, spilling the water.

Fixes

callously: unfeelingly; insensitively

INDENT second sentence because of a new topic, the third incident.

CAPITALIZATION. Again, For, Hrothgar. Lowercase: king (title not used with a name).

NUMBERS. Spell out ordinal numbers: for a **third** time.

COMMAS AND OTHER PUNCTUATION.

- **Quotations** are correct in the student version. In continued speech with a new topic, end the first paragraph with no quotes (shows the speaker is not finished) and start the new paragraph with quotes (shows that someone is still speaking).
- **Introductory transitions** take commas. Fix: **Again,** the king ignored.
- **Nonessential participial phrases** take commas. 1) the king ignored his nephew, **callously pushing him away.** 2) Hrothgar came to his rescue, **jumping up against the king and spilling the water.**
- **Short #2 prepositional openers** (under five words) take commas if a pause is needed. *For a third time* does not require a pause, so drop the comma. It is not incorrect but better without.
- **Items in a series.** Ask: What words is the cc *and* joining? Answer: two -ing words. Ask: Does *and* need a comma? Answer: No—never one after a cc, and none before cc's that join just two items.

Grammar Notations

PREPOSITIONAL PHRASES. For a third time; to his rescue; against the king.

CLAUSES, PHRASES, AND OPENERS.

- #T transitional opener: Again.
- MC: the **king ignored** his nephew.
- -ing participial phrases (students do not label): callously pushing him away. Just identify this construction for your students.

   ADVANCED. Remember, -ing words are not verbs unless coupled with a subject and helping verb. Contrast "the *king was pushing* him away."
- #2 prepositional phrase opener: For a third time.
- MC: **Hrothgar came** to his rescue.
- -ing participial phrases: jumping up against the king and spilling the water.

   ADVANCED. These participles function as adjectives describing the dog, just as *pushing* describes the king.

Style

If desired, have students identify the strongest of the vocabulary dress-ups from this week. Discuss their answers. Suggestions:

- **Strong verbs.** interrupted, jiggled, signaling (a verbal).
- **Quality adjectives.** flimsy, precious.
- **-ly adverbs.** patiently, callously.

STUDENT REWRITE

"Well, that seems a flimsy excuse to bother his uncle," Dorinda interrupted. "The poor man just wanted a drink of water. Why did Robert trust his dog over his uncle?"

"Hounds and other nonhuman creatures sometimes have a tad of wisdom," Arthur commented. "Listen to the rest of the story."

Dorinda waited more patiently.

"Cupping his hands again, King Arthur collected more of the precious liquid. Again, Robert jiggled his uncle's hands, signaling that they should check the source before drinking. Again, the king ignored his nephew, callously pushing him away.

"For a third time Hrothgar came to his rescue, jumping up against the king and spilling the water.

Week 29

Overusing Coordinating Conjunctions (FANBOYS)

LEARN IT

You have learned that one way to fix a run-on sentence is to connect the two main clauses with a comma + coordinating conjunction, a handy pattern to use in your own writing: MC, cc MC.

Sometimes, however, we overuse this pattern. It works well when the chosen cc properly links the two ideas, but when it does not, either separate them into two sentences or subordinate one of the clauses instead. *And* is the major culprit in overused MC, cc MC sentences.

Examples:

- With all the food he could want and no inclement weather or flies, *Arthur rather enjoyed his enforced vacation in the infirmary*, and *he especially looked forward to Dorinda's visits.*

  These are two separate ideas, which *and* does not connect well. Connecting these two main clauses (italicized) in one sentence also weakens both of them because the ideas do not stand out.

  Better: With all the food he could want and no inclement weather or flies, *Arthur rather enjoyed his enforced vacation in the infirmary. He especially looked forward to Dorinda's visits.*

- Arthur savored his VIP treatment. *The orderly brought him a steaming bowl of fly soup,* and *the maids fluffed the pillows under his broken leg.*

  This time *and* is an effective connector since it joins two clauses doing the same sort of thing: the orderly serving him in one way and the maids in another.

If certain concepts have become easy for your students, then you do not need to address them in your conversation.

Page 60, *Fix It! Grammar: Frog Prince, or Just Deserts,* **Student Book 3**

DAY 1

¶ #6 *MC* *S* *V* *patience* #1 *MC* *S* *V* *V* *MC S* *V*
" [king arthur lost all ~~patients~~] . ' [that hound dog is forever banished from my kingdom] !' [he snapped

#1
MC S *V* *V* *V*
at his nephew] . ' [you must quit camelot, and return to your home for such **insubordination**] .'

Fixes

insubordination: defiance of authority

INDENT because of a new topic, the king's response. All this may go in one paragraph since his losing patience sets up his speech. If students want a new paragraph at "That hound dog," that works, too. It would then need double and single quotes: "'That … .'

CAPITALIZATION. King Arthur, That, You, Camelot.

HOMOPHONE. King Arthur is not a doctor. It is his patience (even temper, peace of mind) that he has lost, not his patients (people under medical care)!

COMMAS AND OTHER PUNCTUATION.

- **Quotations.** Fix: "King Arthur lost all patience. 'That hound dog … kingdom!' he snapped at his nephew. 'You … insubordination.'
  Rules:
  - Start a new paragraph in continued quotes with quotations.
  - Since the quote is not set up by a speaking verb, add a period after *patience*.
  - Use single quotes for his speech (quotes within quotes).
  - *Snapped* implies strong emotion, so add an exclamation after *kingdom*.
  - Keep *he* lowercase since *he snapped at his nephew* sets up the quote before it and is therefore in the same sentence.
  - When the king speaks again, he starts a new thought, so end the interruption with a period and start the new sentence with a capital letter (*You*).
  - If the story ended here, it would end with single (for the king) and double (for Arthur the frog) quotes: "' … insubordination.'" Since only the king is finished speaking, close with single quotes alone.
- **Items in a series.** No comma before the cc *and* because it joins two verbs to one subject (compound verbs): MC cc 2nd verb. Fix: You **must quit** Camelot **and return** to your home.

Grammar Notations

PREPOSITIONAL PHRASES. from my kingdom; at his nephew; to your home; for such insubordination.

CLAUSES AND SENTENCE OPENERS.

- #6 vss and MC: **King Arthur lost** all patience.
- #1 subject opener and MC: That **hound dog is** forever **banished** from my kingdom. Did students mark both the helping verb *is* and the action verb *banished*?
- MC: **he snapped** at his nephew.
- #1 subject opener and MC: **You must quit** Camelot and **return** to your home for such insubordination. Did students mark both action verbs? The helping verb *must* helps out both of them: *must quit* and *must return*.

DAY 2

#3   MC S   V   #2   MC S

¶ "grievingly [robert turned away], signaling hrothgar to his side,. ~~and~~ through the woods [he

V

wound his way back to the castle], anxious in his heart, for his uncles safety yet **discerning**

DC   V   S   DC S   V   V

(there ~~their/they're~~ was nothing) (he could do)."

discerning: recognizing; perceiving

Fixes

INDENT ¶ because of a new topic, Robert's leaving the woods.

HOMOPHONE. there was nothing he could do.

COMMAS AND OTHER PUNCTUATION.

- **Quotations.** Start new paragraphs in a continued quotation with quotes; close with a period and quotations. Fix: "Grievingly … . could do."
- **#3 -ly adverb opener.** The comma after *Grievingly* is optional. Let the pause test be your guide. See ✎ **1**.
- **Nonessential -ing participial phrases** take commas. Fix: Robert turned away, **signaling Hrothgar to his side.**
- **cc overuse.** Coordinating conjunctions can be useful transitions, but often students overuse the MC, cc MC pattern, especially with *and*. When the MCs express different ideas, they should be in different sentences. Fix: Robert turned away, signaling Hrothgar to his side. Through the woods he wound his way back to the castle. See ✎ **2**.
- **ADVANCED. Nonessential phrases** take commas. The original is correct: he wound his way back to the castle, **anxious in his heart.**
- **Mid-sentence prepositional phrases** do not take commas. Fix: anxious in his heart **for his uncle's safety.**
- **Apostrophes** for possession: his **uncle's** safety.
- **Items in a series.** If students put a comma before *yet*, guide them to see why a comma is incorrect. When cc's join just two items in a series (two adjectives here), there is no comma. The original is correct: **anxious** … yet **discerning**.

Grammar Notations

Prepositional phrases. to his side; Through the woods; to the castle (*back* is an adverb); in his heart; for his uncle's safety. See ✎ **3**.

CLAUSES, PHRASES, AND OPENERS.

- #3 -ly adverb opener: Grievingly.
- MC: **Robert turned** away.
- **ADVANCED.** -ing participial phrase (not required but helpful to understand): signaling Hrothgar to his side. Remember, -ing words are not verbs unless coupled with a subject and helping verb, as in *Robert was signaling Hrothgar.*
- #2 prepositional phrase opener: Through the woods.
- MC: **he wound** his way back to the castle.

✎ **1. Teacher's note.** When the -ly opener modifies just the verb (he *grievingly turned* away), the comma is optional but generally unneeded.

✎ **2. Teacher's note.** Although technically the punctuation is correct, the MC, cc MC pattern in this passage is a grammar error dealing with sentence sense.

✎ **3. Teacher's note.** Ask how these phrases fit the pattern: preposition + noun, no verb. Remind students that words often function as different parts of speech, but not at the same time, and this can affect punctuation. E.g., When *for* is a cc joining MCs, it needs a comma; when it is a preposition, as here, no comma.

- **ADVANCED.** Adjective phrase (not required but helpful to understand): anxious in his heart for his uncle's safety yet discerning (there was nothing (he could do)). This has two hidden dependent clauses inside it.
- **ADVANCED.** DC (noun clause with *that* implied): there **was nothing**.
- **ADVANCED.** DC (adjective clause with *that* implied): **he could do**.

DAY 3

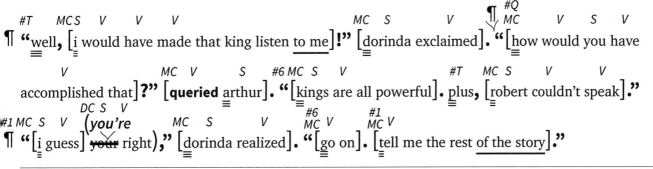

Fixes

INDENT three times because of new speakers.

CAPITALIZATION. Well, I, Dorinda, How, Arthur, Kings, Plus, Robert, I, Dorinda, Go, Tell.

HOMOPHONES. Use the contraction *you're* for *you are*, not the possessive *your*: **you're** right.

COMMAS AND OTHER PUNCTUATION.

- **Run-on sentences.** Start by checking the nine missing end marks in this passage. If students do not catch them all, just tell them the answer and a brief explanation; then move on! Fixes:
    - Exclamation ending the sentence she exclaimed: I would have made that king listen to me!
    - Period after attribution: Dorinda exclaimed.
    - Question mark after his question: How would you have accomplished that?
    - Period after second attribution to separate Arthur's second thought from his first: queried Arthur.
    - Period between his next two sentences: Kings are all powerful. Plus, Robert …
    - Period ending his speech: Plus, Robert couldn't speak. *See* ✐.
    - Period after the third attribution: Dorinda realized.
    - Period between her next two sentences: Go on. Tell me the rest …
    - Period after her final sentence: Tell me the rest of the story.
- **Quotations and end marks.** Fix: "Well … me!" "How … that?" queried Arthur. "Kings … speak." "I … right," Dorinda realized. "Go on … story." Rules:
    - Enclose speech in quotes.
    - Keep *queried* lowercase because it is part of the same sentence as the quotation it sets up.
    - Quotation + comma + speaking verb: "I guess you're right," Dorinda **realized**.
    - Check that commas and periods are inside closing quotations.
- **Introductory transitions** take commas. Fixes: 1) **Well,** I would have made. 2) **Plus,** Robert couldn't speak.

queried: asked; inquired about

✐ **Teacher's note.** When you add words like *plus* (conjunctive adverbs) to a main clause, you still have a main clause, so *Plus, Robert couldn't speak* must have a period separating it from MCs before and after.

Grammar Notations

PREPOSITIONAL PHRASES. to me; of the story.

CLAUSES, PHRASES, AND OPENERS.

- #T transitional opener: Well.
- MC: **I would have made** that king listen to me.
- MC: **Dorinda exclaimed.**
- #Q (question) and MC: How **would you have accomplished** that?
- MC: **queried Arthur.**
- #6 vss and MC: **Kings are** all powerful.
- #T transitional opener OR #6 vss, and MC: Plus, **Robert could**n't **speak.** Students may count this as a #T or a #6.
- #1 subject opener and MC: **I guess.**
- **ADVANCED.** DC (noun clause with invisible *that*): **you're** right. Remind students that some verbs, especially *be* verbs, are often buried in contractions.
- MC: **Dorinda realized.**
- #6 vss and MC: **Go** on. The subject, *you*, is understood.
- #1 subject opener and MC: **Tell** me the rest of the story. The subject, *you*, is understood.

DAY 4

¶ "frustrated, [king arthur decided to climb to the top of the cliff], (where he could drink from the pool of water collected above). and with one hand reaching over the other, [he made the **laborious** climb].

Fixes

INDENT because of a new topic, more of the story.

CAPITALIZATION. Frustrated, King Arthur, With.

COMMAS AND OTHER PUNCTUATION.

- **Quotation.** Begin the passage with quotes because Arthur is speaking again. No close quotes because he is not finished. Fix: "Frustrated … climb.
- **#4 -ing openers** take commas. Fix: **Frustrated,** King Arthur decided to climb. *See* ✏ **1.**
- **cc overuse.** The clauses in this MC, cc MC pattern express different ideas so need to be in separate sentences.

  Fix, with MCs italicized: *King Arthur decided to climb to the top of the cliff,* where he could drink from the pool of water collected above. With one hand reaching over the other, *he made the laborious climb.*

- **Long #2 prepositional openers** take commas: **With one hand reaching over the other,** he made the laborious climb.

laborious: requiring much work and effort

✏ **1. Teacher's note.** If students did not catch this, read the sentence with and without the comma. Without a comma, *frustrated* is a simple adjective modifying *King Arthur* and the sentence a #1 subject opener, but it sounds silly to say "frustrated King Arthur" did this. With the comma, *being* is implied, and the sentence is saying, "Being frustrated, King Arthur did this."

Grammar Notations

PREPOSITIONAL PHRASES. to the top; of the cliff; from the pool; of water; With one hand; over the other.

CLAUSES, PHRASES, AND OPENERS.

- #4 invisible -ing opener with *being* implied: Frustrated.
- MC: **King Arthur decided** to climb to the top of the cliff.
- DC (www clause): where **he could drink** from the pool of water collected above. *See* ♡ **1.**
- #2 prepositional phrase opener: With one hand reaching over the other. *See* ♡ **2.**
- MC: **he made** the laborious climb.

Style

If desired, have students identify the strongest of the vocabulary dress-ups from this week. Discuss their answers. Suggestions:

- **Strong verbs.** banished, snapped, quit, wound (rhymes with *sound*), queried.
- **Quality adjectives.** anxious, discerning, laborious.
  - ✏ **Teacher's note.** *Discerning* functions as an adjective in the Day 2 passage instead of a verb (no subject plus helping verb with it). If students mark it as a verb, decide whether they are ready to understand this concept.
- **-ly adverbs.** None to choose from.

♡ **1. Grammar lovers.** This is an adjective clause because *where* follows the noun (*cliff*) that it also describes. It is nonessential (commas) because even though it adds information, it does not specify *top of the cliff* any further so is not required for the rest of the sentence to make sense.

Also, the -ed past participle *collected* is simply an adjective describing *water*, not a verb.

♡ **2. Grammar lovers.** This -ing present participle, *reaching*, is another adjective, not a verb. It describes *hand*.

STUDENT REWRITE

"King Arthur lost all patience. 'That hound dog is forever banished from my kingdom!' he snapped at his nephew. 'You must quit Camelot and return to your home for such insubordination.'

"Grievingly Robert turned away, signaling Hrothgar to his side. Through the woods he wound his way back to the castle, anxious in his heart for his uncle's safety yet discerning there was nothing he could do."

"Well, I would have made that king listen to me!" Dorinda exclaimed.

"How would you have accomplished that?" queried Arthur. "Kings are all powerful. Plus, Robert couldn't speak."

"I guess you're right," Dorinda realized. "Go on. Tell me the rest of the story."

"Frustrated, King Arthur decided to climb to the top of the cliff, where he could drink from the pool of water collected above. With one hand reaching over the other, he made the laborious climb.

Week 30

Review

LEARN IT

There are no new concepts this week. Test your grammar knowledge with these questions. Check your grammar cards if you cannot remember.

1. Which of these mid-sentence elements take commas?
   a) interrupters
   b) mid-sentence prepositional phrases
   c) mid-sentence adverb clauses (usually)
   d) NDAs

2. Which of the following need commas?
   a) a cc connecting two main clauses
   b) a cc connecting two items in a series
   c) a cc connecting a MC and a second verb
   d) a cc connecting three items in a series

3. What is important about the kinds of things that cc's connect?

Do you remember what these vocabulary words mean? If not, look them up in your vocabulary list in the back of your notebook.

- inadvertently
- allay
- brandishing
- revulsion
- forlorn
- erratically
- undaunted
- potent
- noxious
- flimsy

Teacher's answers

1. a and d

2. a and d

3. must be the same kind (i.e., parallel): two or more clauses, two or more verbs, two or more adjectives, etc.

Page 62, *Fix It! Grammar: Frog Prince, or Just Deserts*, **Student Book 3**

Institute for Excellence in Writing

DAY 1

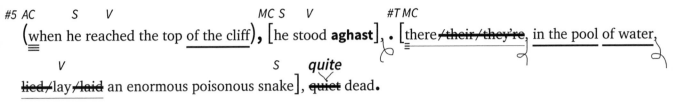

#5 AC · · S · · · V · MC S · · · V · · · · · · · · · #T MC

(when he reached the top of the cliff), [he stood **aghast**] . [there ~~their/they're~~ in the pool of water,

· · · · · · V · S · · · · · · *quite*

~~lied~~/lay/~~laid~~ an enormous poisonous snake], ~~quiet~~ dead.

Fixes

CAPITALIZATION. When, There.

HOMOPHONES AND SPELLING.

- Use *there*, meaning in that place: **there** lay an enormous snake.
- Use *to lie* when the subject is lying himself down. The past tense of *to lie* is *lay*: There **lay** an enormous snake.
- The snake is **quite** dead, that is, very dead, not *quietly* dead (not making a sound). Had the second meaning been intended, it would require the adverb *quietly*, not the adjective *quiet*, to modify an adjective (*dead*). It would also be silly to say that anything is quietly dead! What would noisily dead sound like?

COMMAS AND OTHER PUNCTUATION.

- **#5 clausal openers** take a comma at the end of the clause. Fix: **When he reached the top of the cliff,** he stood aghast.
- **Run-on sentence.** Ask students to find, explain, and correct the comma splice (MC, MC). Answer: The comma after *aghast* is not strong enough to hold the two MCs together. Change to a period. Fix (with MCs italicized): When he reached the top of the cliff, *he stood aghast. There* in the pool of water *lay an enormous poisonous snake.*

  ADVANCED. Discuss alternatives students propose, such as connecting the clauses with a *comma + for* or with *because*. It is more stylish with a period since the first MC already has an adverb clause in front of it.
- **Mid-sentence prepositional phrases** do not take commas: There **in the pool of water** lay an enormous poisonous snake. *See* 🖊 **1.**
- **Adjectives before a noun.** Ask if *enormous* and *poisonous* are coordinate (comma) or cumulative (no comma). Try the two tests: 1) *a poisonous, enormous snake* sounds strange; 2) *an enormous and poisonous snake* sounds awkward. Since both tests fail, these are cumulative adjectives, so no comma. *See* 🖊 **2.**
- **ADVANCED. Nonessential elements** take commas. The comma setting off *quite dead* is correct since this is a nonessential adjective phrase.

Grammar Notations

PREPOSITIONAL PHRASES. of the cliff; in the pool; of water.

CLAUSES, PHRASES, AND OPENERS.

- **#5 clausal opener and AC:** When **he reached** the top of the cliff.
- **MC: he stood** aghast.
- **#T or #2 prepositional opener:** There in the pool of water. Transition: There; #2: in the pool of water.
- **MC: There … lay** an enormous poisonous **snake.** *See* 🖊 **3.**
- **ADVANCED. Invisible *which*** (students do not label): quite dead. Students who use IEW writing may recognize this as an invisible *which*. It is not a true clause but an adjective phrase.

aghast: struck with horror or shock

Since it follows a linking verb, *aghast* is a subject complement, in this case an adjective. This matters only because students are allowed to identify it as a quality adjective dress-up but may not realize it is an adjective.

🖊 **1. Teacher's note.** *There* is fine with or without a comma. It is transitional, but it does not require a strong pause.

🖊 **2. Teacher's note.** With cumulative adjectives, the first adjective modifies both the second adjective and noun together: it is an enormous snake that is poisonous. The two adjectives do not separately modify *snake.*

🖊 **3. Teacher's note.** Many students will have trouble identifying the subject, thinking it is either the adverb *there* or the prepositional objects *pool* or *water.* Ask what is doing the action of lying: Is it the pool, the water, or the snake that lay there? Answer: The snake lay in the pool of water, so *snake* is the subject.

DAY 2

#1 MC   S   V   V   #1 MC   S   S   V   V   V

[the poison had contaminated the water]. [hrothgar, and robert, had been trying to save his life all

MC S   V   V   #6
*   MC   S   V   **deeply***

along], but [he had been ~~to/two/~~too **cavalier** to listen to <u>them</u>], • [their loyalty affected him ~~deep~~].

---

cavalier (adjective): showing haughty disregard of others; disdainful; arrogant

Fixes

CAPITALIZATION. The, Hrothgar, Robert, Their.

HOMOPHONES AND USAGE.

- Use *too*, meaning excessively (too much): He had been **too** cavalier to listen.
- *Affected* is correct: Their loyalty **affected** him. *Effect* is the noun, *affect* the verb.
- Use adverbs to modify verbs: Their loyalty affected him **deeply**. *Deeply* modifies the verb *affected*: it deeply affected him.

COMMAS AND OTHER PUNCTUATION.

- **Quotations.** Arthur is still speaking and there is no new topic, so students should continue writing in the same paragraph with no quotes.

- **Items in a series.**

  The cc *and* is joining only two items, the compound subject *Hrothgar and Robert*. Do not put commas around the cc + second of two items. Fix: Hrothgar **and Robert** had been trying to save his life.

  The cc *but* needs a comma because it joins two main clauses. Rule: MC, cc MC. Fix: Hrothgar and Robert had been trying to save his life all along, **but** he had been too cavalier to listen to them.

- **Run-on sentence.** Ask students to find, explain, and correct the comma splice (two MCs joined with only a comma). Answer: The comma after *them* is not strong enough to hold these two MCs together. Change to a period. Fix: he had been too cavalier to listen to them. Their loyalty affected him deeply.

Grammar Notations

PREPOSITIONAL PHRASES. to them.

CLAUSES, PHRASES, AND OPENERS.

- #1 subject opener and MC: The **poison had contaminated** the water.
- #1 subject opener and MC: **Hrothgar** and **Robert had been trying** to save his life all along. Did students mark the compound subject, both helping verbs, and the action verb?
- MC: **he had been** too cavalier to listen to them. *See* ♡.
- #6 vss and MC: Their **loyalty affected** him deeply.

♡ **Grammar lovers.** *Had* is a helping verb and *been* a linking verb connecting the subject to its subject complement (a.k.a. predicate adjective), *cavalier*.

DAY 3

#5 AC   S V   MC S V   #4

¶ "(when the king returned to the castle), [he sought his nephew, without delay]. ~~and~~ finding robert in

             MC S   V *himself*

his room with his servant, [arthur humbled ~~him~~ contritely].

Fixes

contritely: with genuine regret or sorrow

INDENT because it is a new scene.

CAPITALIZATION. When, Finding, Robert, Arthur.

PRONOUN USAGE. *Arthur humbled him* means the king humbled Robert. The true meaning is that Arthur humbled **himself**. Use reflexive pronouns like *himself* to refer back to the subject of the same sentence.

COMMAS AND OTHER PUNCTUATION.

- **Quotations.** Start new paragraphs in continued speech with quotations. Since the story is not yet over, do not close with quotations, just the period. Fix: "When … contritely.

- **#5 clausal openers** take commas. Fix: **When the king returned to the castle,** he sought his nephew.

- **Mid-sentence prepositional phrases** do not take commas. Fix: he sought his nephew **without delay.**

- **cc overuse.** The MCs in this MC, cc MC pattern express different ideas so need to be in separate sentences. A full stop allows the main ideas to sink in better.

  Fix: When the king returned to the castle, *he sought his nephew without delay*. **Finding** Robert in his room with his servant, *Arthur humbled himself contritely*.

- **#4 -ing openers** take commas. Fix: **Finding Robert in his room with his servant,** Arthur humbled himself contritely.

  Ask: Is the subject after the comma the one doing the -inging? Answer: Yes, Arthur is both humbling himself and finding Robert. This is therefore a legal #4.

Grammar Notations

PREPOSITIONAL PHRASES. to the castle; without delay; in his room, with his servant.

CLAUSES, PHRASES, AND OPENERS.

- #5 clausal opener and AC: When the **king returned** to the castle.
- MC: **he sought** his nephew without delay.
- #4 -ing participial phrase opener: Finding Robert in his room with his servant. *See* ♡.
- MC: **Arthur humbled** himself contritely.

♡ **Grammar lovers.**
Finding functions as an adjective and modifies the subject after the comma, *Arthur*.

DAY 4

¶ "'[can you forgive me], nephew?' [he began]. '[you were ~~rite~~ all along, and wise to act on your instincts]. (while you **astutely** trusted your beloved hrothgar), [i depended on no one, except I].

#Q MC V   S   V   MC S   V   #1 MC S   V   right   #5 AC   S   V   MC S   V   myself

Fixes

INDENT ¶ because of a new speaker.

CAPITALIZATION. Can, You, While, Hrothgar, I. Keep *he* lowercase because its verb (*began*) sets up the quote before.

HOMOPHONE. You were **right**, meaning correct.

Pronoun usage. Use reflexive pronouns to refer back to the subject in the same sentence. Fix: I depended on no one except **myself**. *See* ♡ **1**.

COMMAS AND OTHER PUNCTUATION.

- **Quotations.** Fix: "'Can you forgive me, nephew?' he began. 'You … myself.

  Start a new paragraph in continued speech with quotations. Use single quotes for the king's words (quote within a quote). Since he is not finished speaking, no close quotes.

  Add a question mark after his question inside the closing quotes. The attribution begins with a lowercase letter (*he*) because it sets up the quote before. When the king speaks again (*You* …), he is starting a new sentence, so end the attribution with a period and capitalize *You*.

- **NDAs take commas.** Fix: Can you forgive me, **nephew**? *See* ✏ **1**.

- **Run-on sentence.** Ask students to find, explain, and correct the comma splice (MC, MC). To help, ask them first to figure out whether the *while* clause goes with the MC before or after it. Answer: After, so the problem is the comma after *instincts*, which is not strong enough to hold the two MCs together. Use a period instead.

  Fix (with MCs italicized): *You were right all along and wise to act on your instincts.* While you astutely trusted your beloved Hrothgar, *I depended on no one except myself.*

- **Items in a series.** Do not put commas before cc's that join only two adjectives: You were **right** all along **and wise**.

- **#5 clausal openers** take commas: **While you astutely trusted your beloved Hrothgar**, I depended on no one.

- **Mid-sentence prepositional phrases** do not take commas. Fix: no one **except myself**.

Grammar Notations

PREPOSITIONAL PHRASES. on your instincts; on no one; except myself. *See* ✏ **2**.

CLAUSES, PHRASES, AND OPENERS.

- #Q (question) and MC: **Can you forgive** me?
- MC: **he began.**
- #1 subject opener and MC: **You were** right all along and wise to act on your instincts. *See* ♡ **2**.
- #5 clausal opener and AC: While **you** astutely **trusted** your beloved Hrothgar.
- MC: **I depended** on no one except myself.

astutely: wisely; perceptively

♡ **1. Grammar lovers.** *I* should never follow a preposition: it is a subjective pronoun, and the object of a preposition should be an objective pronoun or a reflexive one, as here.

✏ **1. Teacher's note.** Students often confuse nouns of direct address with appositives (nouns that rename the noun before them), so ask them to explain how *nephew* works in this sentence to check their understanding.

✏ **2. Teacher's note.** If students do not catch *on no one*, explain that *no one* is a noun so can be the object of a preposition. If they do not catch *except myself*, ask them to pull out their list of prepositions and look for one of the prepositions in the middle column.

♡ **2. Grammar lovers.** The adjectives *right* and *wise* are subject complements (a.k.a. predicate adjectives) describing the subject, *you*.

Style

If desired, have students identify the strongest of the vocabulary dress-ups from this week. Discuss their answers. Suggestions:

- **Strong verbs.** contaminated, humbled.
- **Quality adjectives.** aghast, cavalier, beloved.
- **-ly adverbs.** contritely, astutely.

STUDENT REWRITE

When he reached the top of the cliff, he stood aghast. There in the pool of water lay an enormous poisonous snake, quite dead. The poison had contaminated the water. Hrothgar and Robert had been trying to save his life all along, but he had been too cavalier to listen to them. Their loyalty affected him deeply.

"When the king returned to the castle, he sought his nephew without delay. Finding Robert in his room with his servant, Arthur humbled himself contritely.

"'Can you forgive me, nephew?' he began. 'You were right all along and wise to act on your instincts. While you astutely trusted your beloved Hrothgar, I depended on no one except myself.

Week 31

Review

LEARN IT

Word lists help you identify parts of the sentence quickly, which aids in choosing the correct punctuation. Since there are no new concepts this week, answer these questions. Use your grammar cards if you have forgotten.

1. List the *be* verbs. (verb card)

2. List the words that often start dependent clauses. (clause card)

3. Name the coordinating conjunctions. Hint: FANBOYS. (the front of the coordinating conjunctions card)

Do you remember what these vocabulary words mean? If not, look them up in your vocabulary list in the back of your notebook.

- drivel
- folderol
- inarticulately
- fastidiousness
- abject
- consternation
- fretted
- twaddle
- inquisitiveness
- stipulation

> **Teacher's answers**
>
> **1.** *am, is, are, was, were, be, being, been*
>
> **2.** www.asia.b: *when, while, where, as, since, if, although, because* and *who, which, that*
>
> **3.** FANBOYS: *for, and, nor, but, or, yet, so*

Page 64, *Fix It! Grammar: Frog Prince, or Just Deserts,* **Student Book 3**

DAY 1

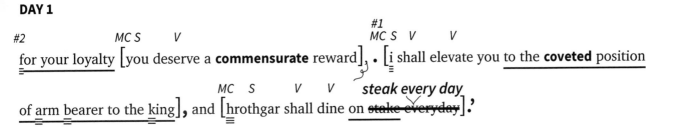

for your loyalty [you deserve a **commensurate** reward]. [i shall elevate you to the **coveted** position

of arm bearer to the king], and [hrothgar shall dine on ~~stake everyday~~ *steak every day*].'

Fixes

CAPITALIZATION. For, I, Arm Bearer to the King (honorific title for a single person, so proper noun), Hrothgar.

> **Titles:** Do not capitalize minor words that are not the first or last word: Arm Bearer to the King.

HOMOPHONES AND SPELLING.

- A stake is a stick you put in the ground. Hrothgar would much prefer **steak**!
- *Everyday* is one word only as an adjective before a noun. Here, it is two words: Hrothgar shall dine on **steak every day**, that is, each day.

COMMAS AND OTHER PUNCTUATION.

- **Quotations.** Fix: For your loyalty … . every day.' Rules: 1) No open quotes because the king is still speaking and this is the same paragraph. 2) Close with single quotes only (quote within a quote) since King Arthur is now finished but the frog Arthur is not.
- **Short #2 prepositional openers** (under five words): commas are optional. *For your loyalty* is correct with or without a comma.
- **Run-on sentence.** Ask students to find, explain, and correct the comma splice (MC, MC). Answer: The comma after *reward* is not strong enough to hold these main clauses together. Change to a period. Fix: For your loyalty you deserve a commensurate reward. I shall elevate you to the coveted position of Arm Bearer to the King.
- **MC, cc MC.** Use commas before cc's that join main clauses: I *shall elevate you to the coveted position of Arm Bearer to the King,* **and** *Hrothgar shall dine on steak every day.*

  This is a case where *MC, and MC* is an effective way to connect main clauses because the king is listing the two rewards he is giving Robert. *And* makes sense as a connector.

commensurate: corresponding in magnitude or degree

coveted: greatly desired

Grammar Notations

PREPOSITIONAL PHRASES. For your loyalty; to the coveted position; of Arm Bearer to the King; on steak.

> ✏ **Teacher's note.** The object of the preposition *of* is the whole title *Arm Bearer to the King*. The title has another prepositional phrase inside it, but you do not need to explain this unless students are curious.

CLAUSES, PHRASES, AND OPENERS.

- #2 prepositional phrase opener: For your loyalty.
- MC: **you deserve** a commensurate reward.
- #1 subject opener and MC: **I shall elevate** you to the coveted position of Arm Bearer to the King.
- MC: **Hrothgar shall dine** on steak every day.

DAY 2

¶ "modestly [robert signed a reply to his servant], (who translated his words): '[your safety is all] (that matters). [i am pleased to be of service to my **liege** lord], and [i shall do everything (i can) to be worthy of this position] (entrusted to me).'"

(Labels above text: #3 MC S V over "modestly robert signed a reply to his servant"; DC S V over "who translated his words"; MC S V over "your safety is all"; DC S V #1 MC S V over "that matters. i am pleased to be of service to my liege lord"; MC S V V over "and i shall do everything i can"; DC S V over "to be worthy of this position"; DC V over "entrusted to me")

Fixes

INDENT because of a new speaker.

CAPITALIZATION. Modestly, Robert, Your, I, I, I. Lowercase: lord (no name with it).

COMMAS AND OTHER PUNCTUATION.

- **Quotations.** "Modestly … his words: 'Your safety … entrusted to me.'" Rules: 1) Start a new paragraph in a continued quote with quotations. 2) Use single quotations for quotes within quotes. 3) End the passage with single and double quotations because both are finished speaking. 4) Did students add a period inside both close quotes?
- **#3 -ly adverb openers:** commas optional unless a pause is needed. See ✏ **1.**
- **Nonessential elements** take commas. Fix: Robert signed a reply to his servant, **who translated his words.** This *who* clause is nonessential because it only adds information but does not change the fact that he signed a reply to his servant.
- **ADVANCED. Colon.** The colon is correct because it follows a MC and sets up the quote that follows it. Since there is no speaking verb, we use a colon instead of a comma.
- **Run-on sentence.** Ask students to find and correct the fused sentence (MC MC). Answer: Add a period after *matters* since Robert's second sentence includes two MCs. Other solutions lose the impact of his first statement. Fix: Your safety is all that matters. I am pleased to be of service to my liege lord.
- **MC, cc MC.** Coordinating conjunctions are not strong enough to hold two MCs together; a comma plus cc is. Fix: I am pleased to be of service to my liege lord, **and** I shall do everything I can to be worthy of this position.

Grammar Notations

PREPOSITIONAL PHRASES. to his servant; of service; to my liege lord; of this position; to me.

CLAUSES, PHRASES, AND OPENERS.

- #3 -ly adverb opener: Modestly.
- MC: **Robert signed** a reply to his servant.
- DC (*who-which* clause): **who translated** his words.
- MC: Your **safety is** all. See ✏ **2.**
- **ADVANCED.** DC (*that* clause): **that matters.** *That* substitutes for *which* in this essential adjective clause.
- #1 subject opener and MC: **I am** pleased to be of service to my liege lord. See ✏ **3** and ♡.
- MC: **I shall do** everything (I can) to be worthy of this position.
- **ADVANCED.** DC (invisible *that*): **I can.**
- **ADVANCED.** DC (invisible *which*): **entrusted** to me.

liege: entitled to the loyalty and services of subjects

✏ **1. Teacher's note.** When #3 openers describe the verb only instead of the entire main clause, as here (Robert signed a reply in a modest manner), they are not needed.

✏ **2. Teacher's note.** Since this quotation is part of the sentence beginning with *modestly*, do not label it as a sentence opener.

✏ **3. Teacher's note.** If students mark *pleased* as part of the verb, that is fine.

♡ **Grammar lovers.** *Pleased* is a subject complement, in this case a predicate adjective following the linking verb and describing the subject, *I*.

DAY 3

#2   MC   S   V   #3   MC   S   V

¶ at that moment [dorinda realized the message of the simple story]. deeply [she felt the injury

                                  #4   ,   MC S   V

committed, yet **poignantly** forgiven]. struck by the boys kindness, [she examined her own heart].

Fixes

INDENT because of a new topic.

CAPITALIZATION. At, Dorinda, Deeply, Struck.

COMMAS AND OTHER PUNCTUATION.

- **Short #2 prepositional openers** (under five words): comma optional but discouraged. Keep *At that moment* without a comma.
- **#3 -ly adverb openers.** The comma is optional but generally discouraged after #3 openers that do not require a pause: **Deeply** she felt the injury.

  ADVANCED. This adverb does not require a pause because it modifies the verb rather than the whole sentence: she *deeply felt*.
- **Items in a series.** Do not put commas before cc's (*yet*) that join only two items in a series: she felt the injury **committed yet** poignantly **forgiven**.

  If students miss this one, ask them to tell you what *yet* joins. Answer: two adjectives, *committed* and *forgiven*. Since it is only two items in a series instead of three or more, no comma.
- **#4 -ing openers** take commas. The original is correct: **Struck by the boy's kindness,** she examined her own heart. Ask: Is this a legal #4? Answer: Yes. The subject after the comma (*she*) is the -inger, the one being struck by his kindness.
- **Apostrophes** for possession: the **boy's** kindness.
- **Run-on sentence.** Ask students to find, explain, and correct the comma splice (MC, MC). Answer: The comma after *story* is not strong enough to hold together the two MCs and should be a period instead. Fix: Dorinda realized the message of the simple story. Deeply she felt the injury committed yet poignantly forgiven.

poignantly:
touchingly; in a profoundly moving way

Grammar Notations

PREPOSITIONAL PHRASES. At that moment; of the simple story; by the boy's kindness.

CLAUSES, PHRASES, AND OPENERS.

- #2 prepositional phrase opener: At that moment.
- MC: **Dorinda realized** the message of the simple story.
- #3 -ly adverb opener: Deeply.
- MC: **she felt** the injury committed yet poignantly forgiven.
- Invisible #4 invisible -ing opener with *being* implied: Struck by the boy's kindness.
- MC: **she examined** her own heart.

DAY 4

#Q MC   V S   V   DC   S   V   V #1 MC

[why had she not recognized] (how **abhorrent** her own behavior to arthur had been)? [a mere

   S   V   DC S V V   #2   MC S V   V   AC

promise to befriend him was all] (he had asked). in truth, [she had treated him] as dreadfully, (as the

  S   V   V

king had treated his faithful nephew), robert.

Fixes

abhorrent: hateful; loathsome; detestable

CAPITALIZATION. Why, Arthur, A, In, Robert.

COMMAS AND OTHER PUNCTUATION.

- **Run-on sentence.** Ask students to find and correct the fused sentence (MC MC). Answer: The first sentence is a question so needs a question mark. Fix: Why had she not recognized how abhorrent her own behavior to Arthur had been? A mere promise to befriend him was all he had asked.
- **Transitional #2 prepositional openers** (under five words) require commas. Since *In truth* works transitionally, it needs a comma even though it is short. Fix: **In truth,** she had treated him dreadfully.
- **Random commas.** Do not separate the idiom *as ... as* with a comma: she had treated him **as dreadfully as** the king had treated his faithful nephew.
- **ADVANCED. Nonessential elements** take commas. The original is correct: his faithful nephew, **Robert.** This is a nonessential appositive (a noun that renames the noun right before it) because we do not need Robert's name to specify which is his faithful nephew.

Grammar Notations

PREPOSITIONAL PHRASES. to Arthur; In truth.

CLAUSES, PHRASES, AND OPENERS.

- #Q question opener and MC: Why **had she** not **recognized**.
- **ADVANCED.** DC: how abhorrent her own **behavior** to Arthur **had been**.
- #1 subject opener and MC: A mere **promise** to befriend him **was** all.
- **ADVANCED.** DC (invisible *that*): **he had asked**.
- #2 prepositional phrase opener: In truth.
- MC: **she had treated** him.
- AC (adverb clause): as the **king had treated** his faithful nephew. Note that *as ... as* is an idiom.

Style

If desired, have students identify the strongest of the vocabulary dress-ups from this week. Discuss their answers. Suggestions:

- **Strong verbs.** elevate, befriend.
- **Quality adjectives.** coveted, liege, worthy, entrusted, abhorrent, faithful.

   If students mark *entrusted* from Day 2 as a verb, that is fine, but you might want to point out that it is not a verb because there is no subject and helping verb with it. It is an adjective describing *position*.

- **-ly adverbs.** poignantly, dreadfully.

STUDENT REWRITE

For your loyalty you deserve a commensurate reward. I shall elevate you to the coveted position of Arm Bearer to the King, and Hrothgar shall dine on steak every day.'

   "Modestly Robert signed a reply to his servant, who translated his words: 'Your safety is all that matters. I am pleased to be of service to my liege lord, and I shall do everything I can to be worthy of this position entrusted to me.'"

   At that moment Dorinda realized the message of the simple story. Deeply she felt the injury committed yet poignantly forgiven. Struck by the boy's kindness, she examined her own heart. Why had she not recognized how abhorrent her own behavior to Arthur had been? A mere promise to befriend him was all he had asked. In truth, she had treated him as dreadfully as the king had treated his faithful nephew, Robert.

Week 32

Then Versus *Than*

LEARN IT

Students often confuse *then* and *than*. The term *then* means immediately afterward, or next. The term *than* is used for comparing things.

Examples:

- Dorinda despised golf more **than** any other sport.
- She could hit the ball squarely, but the ball would hook left and **then** drop into the lake.

When you see *then* or *than* in the passages, check that it is used correctly.

DAY 1

#2

with heartfelt tears, and **remorse** for her appalling behavior to him, [princess dorinda kissed him

MC   S   V

on his cheek] . and [she now new] , (that kindness to others was far more rewarding, then nurturing

#1 MC S   knew   DC   S   V   than

ones selfish interests).

Fixes

remorse: deep regret for wrongdoing

CAPITALIZATION. With, Princess Dorinda (title used with name), She.

HOMOPHONES AND USAGE. 1) She now **knew**, not the adjective *new*. 2) Use *than* for comparisons: more rewarding **than** nurturing.

COMMAS AND OTHER PUNCTUATION.

- **Long #2 prepositional openers** (five or more words) take commas. Save the comma for the end of all these phrases: **With heartfelt tears and remorse for her appalling behavior to him,** Princess Dorinda kissed him.

- **cc overuse.** The clauses in this MC, cc MC pattern express different ideas so need to be in separate sentences. *And* does not make sense connecting these ideas; the cc *for* would make more sense, but a full stop allows the main ideas to sink in better.

  Fix: With heartfelt tears and remorse for her appalling behavior to him, *Princess Dorinda kissed him on his cheek. She now knew that kindness to others was far more rewarding than nurturing one's selfish interests.*

- ***That* clauses** do not take commas. Fix: She now knew **that kindness to others was far more rewarding than nurturing one's selfish interests**. *See* ♡.

- **Random commas.** Do not separate *more ... than* with a comma. Fix: far **more rewarding than** nurturing.

- **Run-on sentence.** Ask students to find and correct the comma splice (MC, MC). Answer: Replace the comma after *cheek* with a period to hold the two MCs together. Fix: Princess Dorinda kissed him on his cheek. She now knew that kindness to others was far more rewarding than nurturing one's selfish interests.

- **Apostrophes** for possession. Fix: **one's** selfish interests.

♡ **Grammar lovers.** This is a noun clause because it follows a verb and answers the question *what* after the verb. It functions as the direct object of *knew*.

Grammar Notations

PREPOSITIONAL PHRASES. With heartfelt tears and remorse (two objects of this preposition); for her appalling behavior; to him; on his cheek; to others.

CLAUSES, PHRASES, AND OPENERS.

- #2 prepositional phrase opener: With heartfelt tears and remorse for her appalling behavior to him.
- MC: **Princess Dorinda kissed** him on his cheek.
- #1 subject opener and MC: **She** now **knew**.
- DC (noun clause): that **kindness** to others **was** far more rewarding than nurturing one's selfish interests.

DAY 2

#Q MC   V   S   V   DC   S   V   #1
                                                  MC   S   V
¶ [what do you think (arthur did) after that kiss],? [he kissed her back], of course—the only **sensible**

                                          S
                        DC who   V   grown
action for this self-respecting frog, (~~which~~ had secretly ~~groan~~ fond of the princess).

Fixes

INDENT because of a new topic.

CAPITALIZATION. What, Arthur, He.

WHO VERSUS WHICH. Use *who* for animals in stories who act like people. Fix: frog, **who** had grown fond.

SPELLING. Not *groan* (a mournful sound) but *grown* (past of *to grow*): **grown** fond of.

COMMAS AND OTHER PUNCTUATION.

- **Run-on sentence.** Ask students to find and correct the comma splice (MC, MC). Answer: The first sentence is a question so needs a question mark. Fix: What do you think Arthur did after that kiss? He kissed her back.
- **Transitional expressions** take commas: He kissed her back, **of course**.
- **ADVANCED. Em dash.** Ask: Is this em dash used 1) to draw attention to something, or 2) to show an interruption to the train of thought? Answer: To draw attention.

  This is an invisible *which* clause (*which was the only sensible action*), which normally would take a comma but can use a dash instead to draw attention to what follows. The original is correct: He kissed her back, of course—**the only sensible action for this self-respecting frog.**
- **Nonessential elements** take commas. *This self-respecting frog* can only refer to Arthur, so while the *who* clause adds important information, it does not further specify which character is meant and is therefore nonessential. Fix: this self-respecting frog, **who had secretly grown fond of the princess.**

sensible: showing good sense or sound judgment

Grammar Notations

PREPOSITIONAL PHRASES. after that kiss; for this self-respecting frog; of the princess.

CLAUSES, PHRASES, AND OPENERS.

- #Q question opener and MC: What **do you think** (Arthur did) after that kiss?
- **ADVANCED.** DC (noun clause with implied *that*): **Arthur did.**
- #1 subject opener and MC: **He kissed** her back.
- DC (*who-which* clause): **who had** secretly **grown** fond of the princess.

  Fond is an adjective, not part of the verb, but it is not critical that students understand this.

DAY 3

              V   #6

Q MC   S *occurred* MC S   V   #3   MC S   V   V

¶ [then what ~~occured~~],? [you guessed it]. poof! instantly [both were restored into the prince

             DC S   V   V   #1 MC S   V

and princess] (they were meant to be),. ~~and~~ [both breathed a **colossal** sigh of relief], delighting

    their

in ~~they're~~ transformation.

Fixes

colossal: huge; gigantic

INDENT because of a new topic.

CAPITALIZATION. Then, You, Poof, Instantly, Both.

HOMOPHONES AND SPELLING. 1) **Occurred** has two *r's* as well as two *c's*. 2) Use the possessive *their*: delighting in **their** transformation.

COMMAS AND OTHER PUNCTUATION.

- **Run-on sentences.** Ask students to identify and fix the comma splice (MC, MC). Answer: The comma after *occurred* should be a question mark. Fix: Then what occurred? You guessed it.
- **Interjections** expressing strong emotions take an exclamation mark. Fix: **Poof!**
- **#3 -ly adverb openers.** The comma after *instantly* is optional since no strong pause is needed.

  ADVANCED. *Instantly* modifies the verb (*both were instantly restored*), not the entire sentence, so the comma is unneeded.

- **cc overuse.** *And* only lamely connects these ideas. A full stop gives more attention to each MC and accentuates the parallel structure (*both ... both*). A semicolon would also work.

  Fix: Instantly both were restored into the prince and princess they were meant to be. Both breathed a colossal sigh of relief.

- **Nonessential elements** (participial phrases) take commas. Fix: Both breathed a colossal sigh of relief, **delighting in their transformation.**

Grammar Notations

PREPOSITIONAL PHRASES. into the prince and princess; of relief; in their transformation.

CLAUSES, PHRASES, AND OPENERS.

- #6 vss or #Q question opener (choose either) and MC: Then **what occurred**?
- #6 vss and MC: **You guessed** it.
- No marking: Poof! This is not a #6 very strong *sentence* since it is not a sentence at all—no subject or verb. *Poof* is an exclamatory interjection.
- #3 -ly adverb opener: Instantly.
- MC: **both were restored** into the prince and princess.
- **ADVANCED.** DC (invisible *who*): **they were meant** to be.
- #1 subject opener and MC: **Both breathed** a colossal sigh of relief.

DAY 4

#1   *MC*   *S*   *V*   *DC*   *S*   *V*   *V*

[the only noticeable change, was] (that dorinda had **fortuitously** lost her beauty mark), along with

¶ #4

all the other warts. free at last of the magicians spell, [arthur revealed to dorinda the truth about

        MC S   *V*

past

his ~~passed~~].

Fixes

fortuitously: luckily; fortunately, though by chance

CAPITALIZATION. The, Dorinda, Free, Arthur, Dorinda.

INDENT the second sentence because of a new topic.

HOMOPHONE. Use the noun *past*, not the verb *passed*. Fix: the truth about his **past**.

COMMAS AND OTHER PUNCTUATION.

- **Random commas.** Do not place commas between subjects (*change*) and their verbs (*was*). Fix: The only noticeable **change was** that Dorinda had fortuitously lost her beauty mark.

- **ADVANCED. Nonessential phrases** take commas. Phrases like *along with* and *as well as* are considered nonessential and are set off with commas, so the original is correct: Dorinda had fortuitously lost her beauty mark, **along with all the other warts.**

  Phrases like *along with* and *as well as* are considered nonessential and are set off with commas, so the original is correct: Dorinda had fortuitously lost her beauty mark, **along with all the other warts.**

- **#4 -ing openers** take commas. Fix: **Free at last of the magician's spell,** Arthur revealed to Dorinda the truth.

  Ask: Is the subject after the comma doing the -inging? Answer: Yes, Arthur is the one free of the spell who is also revealing his past, so this is a legal #4.

- **Apostrophes** for possession. Fix: the **magician's** spell.

Grammar Notations

PREPOSITIONAL PHRASES. with all the other warts; at last; of the magician's spell; to Dorinda; about his past.

CLAUSES, PHRASES, AND OPENERS.

- #1 subject opener and MC: The only noticeable **change was**.
- DC (noun clause): that **Dorinda had** fortuitously **lost** her beauty mark.
- Invisible #4 -ing participial phrase opener: Free at last of the magician's spell.
- MC: **Arthur revealed** to Dorinda the truth about his past.

Style

If desired, have students identify the strongest of the vocabulary dress-ups from this week. Discuss their answers. Suggestions:

- **Strong verbs.** breathed.
- **Quality adjectives.** heartfelt, appalling, sensible, self-respecting, colossal, noticeable.
- **-ly adverbs.** secretly, fortuitously.

STUDENT REWRITE

With heartfelt tears and remorse for her appalling behavior to him, Princess Dorinda kissed him on his cheek. She now knew that kindness to others was far more rewarding than nurturing one's selfish interests.

What do you think Arthur did after that kiss? He kissed her back, of course—the only sensible action for this self-respecting frog, who had secretly grown fond of the princess.

Then what occurred? You guessed it. Poof! Instantly both were restored into the prince and princess they were meant to be. Both breathed a colossal sigh of relief, delighting in their transformation. The only noticeable change was that Dorinda had fortuitously lost her beauty mark, along with all the other warts.

Free at last of the magician's spell, Arthur revealed to Dorinda the truth about his past.

Week 33

Review

LEARN IT

This is it: your last week! Do your best to catch the last of the fixes and show your teacher all that you have learned.

Since there are no new concepts this week, test your grammar knowledge with these questions. Check your grammar cards if you cannot remember.

1. What is the comma rule for mid-sentence prepositional phrases?

2. What is the comma rule for mid-sentence adverb clauses?

3. What is the comma rule for *that* clauses?

Do you remember what these vocabulary words mean? If not, look them up in your vocabulary list in the back of your notebook.

- aphorism
- callously
- laborious
- discerning
- queried
- cavalier
- contritely
- astutely
- poignantly
- sensible

Teacher's answers

1. Mid-sentence prepositional phrases do not take commas.

2. Mid-sentence adverb clauses do not take commas.

3. *That* clauses do not take commas.

Page 68, *Fix It! Grammar: Frog Prince, or Just Deserts*, **Student Book 3**

Institute for Excellence in Writing

DAY 1

1 MC S   V   DC   S   ♂   V   V
[he told her], (that the real secret to his kindness, was learning humility in the guise of a frog), .

#4   MC S   V   *knowledgeable*
~~so~~ recognizing his wisdom, [~~dorinda's head nodded~~ in **fervent,** ~~knowledgeable~~ agreement].

                                                                                Dorinda nodded her head

fervent: intensely felt; showing great emotion

Fixes

CAPITALIZATION. He, Recognizing, Dorinda.

SPELLING. Knowledgeable is spelled *knowledge* + *able*. Keep the *e* before *able*.

COMMAS AND OTHER PUNCTUATION.

- *That* **clauses** do not take commas on either end of the clause. Fix: He told her **that the real secret to his kindness** was learning humility.

- **cc overuse.** The clauses in this MC, cc MC pattern express different ideas so need to be in separate sentences. A full stop gives clear attention to the MCs.

  Fix: *He told her that the real secret to his kindness was learning humility in the guise of a frog. Recognizing his wisdom, Dorinda nodded her head in fervent, knowledgeable agreement.*

- **#4 -ing openers** take commas. Fix: Recognizing his wisdom, Dorinda's head nodded.

  Ask: Is the subject after the comma doing the -inging? Answer: No, it is not her head that recognizes his wisdom but Dorinda herself. Fix by changing the subject to *Dorinda.* Fix: Recognizing his wisdom, **Dorinda nodded her head.**

- **Adjectives before a noun.** Ask if *fervent* and *knowledgeable* are coordinate (comma) or cumulative (no comma) adjectives.

  Apply the two tests: 1) *knowledgeable, fervent agreement* sounds right; 2) *knowledgeable and fervent agreement* also works. Therefore, these are coordinate adjectives and need a comma. Fix: in **fervent, knowledgeable** agreement.

Grammar Notations

PREPOSITIONAL PHRASES. to his kindness; in the guise; of a frog; in fervent, knowledgeable agreement.

CLAUSES, PHRASES, AND OPENERS.

- #1 subject opener and MC: **He told** her.
- DC (noun clause): that the real **secret** to his kindness **was learning** humility in the guise of a frog.
- #4 -ing participial phrase opener: Recognizing his wisdom.
- MC: **Dorinda nodded** her head in fervent, knowledgeable agreement.

DAY 2

#5 AC   S   V   V   AC S   V   V   MC   S

¶ (when he was asked) (if he would permit them to marry), [king morton uncharacteristically

        V   ¶ #2   MC S   V

replied, "sweet.!"] with joy [he gave them his blessing], **indebted** to arthur and the fairy for

restoring dorinda to her lovable self.

Fixes

INDENT twice because of a new speaker and then a new topic.

CAPITALIZATION. When, King Morton, Sweet, With, Arthur, Dorinda.

COMMAS AND OTHER PUNCTUATION.

- **#5 clausal openers** take commas, but save the comma for the end of both adverb clauses. Fix: **When he was asked if he would permit them to marry,** King Morton uncharacteristically replied.

- **Quotations.** Fix: … replied, "Sweet!" Rules: 1) Add a comma after the speaking verb *replied* to set up the quote. 2) Capitalize *Sweet*, follow it with an exclamation since it is exclamatory, and surround it with quotes.

- **Short #2 prepositional openers** (under five words) have optional commas. Since no pause is needed, the original is best: **With joy** he gave them his blessing.

- **ADVANCED. Nonessential elements** (participial phrases) take commas. The original is correct: With joy he gave them his blessing, **indebted to Arthur and the fairy for restoring Dorinda to her lovable self.** *See* ♡.

Grammar Notations

PREPOSITIONAL PHRASES. With joy; to Arthur and the fairy (two objects of the preposition); for restoring; to her lovable self.

> **ADVANCED.** *Restoring* is the object of the preposition *for*, so it acts as a noun (known as a gerund). If students do not mark this prepositional phrase, that is fine.

CLAUSES, PHRASES, AND OPENERS.

- #5 clausal opener and AC: When **he was asked**.
- AC (adverb clause dress-up): if **he would permit** them to marry.
- MC: **King Morton** uncharacteristically **replied**, "Sweet!"
- #2 prepositional phrase opener: With joy.
- MC: **he gave** them his blessing.

indebted: obligated for kindness or favors received

♡ **Grammar lovers.** *Indebted* is a past participle functioning as an adjective modifying *he*.

DAY 3

¶ epilogue. [the wedding was triumphant] despite the fact (that dorinda, true to form, tripped, and dropped her crown in the new sturgeon pond), . [it simply gave arthur a chance to fish it out]—a little **déjà vu**!

Fixes

INDENT because of a new scene and time.

CAPITALIZATION. Epilogue, The, Dorinda, It, Arthur.

COMMAS AND OTHER PUNCTUATION.

- **Mid-sentence prepositional phrases** do not take commas. The original is correct: The wedding was triumphant **despite the fact** that Dorinda tripped and dropped her crown.
- **Transitions** that interrupt the flow of the sentence take commas. Fix: Dorinda, **true to form,** tripped. It is equally valid to explain this as a nonessential phrase.
- **Items in a series.** Do not use a comma before cc's that join two verbs to one subject: MC cc 2nd verb. Fix: Dorinda ... **tripped and dropped** her crown.
- **Run-on sentence.** Ask students to explain and correct the comma splice (MC, MC). Answer: The comma after *pond* is not strong enough to hold the MCs together.

  Fix, with MCs italicized: *The wedding was triumphant* despite the fact that Dorinda, true to form, tripped and dropped her crown in the new sturgeon pond. *It simply gave Arthur a chance to fish it out.*

  ADVANCED. If students argue for a different fix, such as *because* before the second main clause, ask which sounds better. *Because* is a logical connector but weak structurally. There are too many words between the idea that *because* explains—*The wedding was triumphant*—and the *because* clause—*because it simply gave Arthur a chance to fish it out*—for the connection to be clear.

- **ADVANCED. Em dash.** Ask: Is this em dash used 1) to draw attention to something, or 2) to show an interruption to the train of thought? Answer: To show an interruption.

Grammar Notations

PREPOSITIONAL PHRASES. despite the fact; to form; in the new sturgeon pond.

  If students do not mark *despite the fact*, guide them to find *despite* on the preposition card from Week 1.

CLAUSES, PHRASES, AND OPENERS.

- #1 subject opener and MC: The **wedding was** triumphant.
- DC: that **Dorinda** ... **tripped** and **dropped** her crown in the new sturgeon pond.
- #1 subject opener and MC: **It** simply **gave** Arthur a chance to fish it out.

epilogue: an afterward. The epilogue tells what happened after the main events of the story.

déjà vu: the feeling that a new situation had happened before

Remind students that the whole conflict began when Dorinda dropped her golden ball in the well.

DAY 4

#2 ~~*six-tier*~~ *MC* *S* *V*
¶ atop the ~~6-tier~~ wedding cake**,** [the iron chef fashioned a frog and toad anticipating joyous

#T *MC* *S* *S* *V*
matrimony]**.** later that evening at the wedding feast**,** [the **erstwhile** frog and toad skipped the main

V *desserts*
course of sturgeon roe soufflé**,** and enjoyed just ~~deserts~~].

Fixes

erstwhile: former; of times past

INDENT because of a new topic. The second sentence takes place later the same day but can go in the same paragraph because it is all about the wedding.

CAPITALIZATION. Atop, Iron Chef, Later.

NUMBERS AND HYPHENS. Spell out numbers that can be written in one or two words: **six.** Hyphenate compound adjectives before a noun: the **six-tier** wedding cake.

SPELLING. The final words pick up the pun in the subtitle and draw attention to two homophones: *just deserts* means one's deserved reward; **just desserts** means only dessert, which is the meaning here but with the implication that Dorinda and Arthur have finally received their just deserts as well. *See* ✏ **1.**

COMMAS AND OTHER PUNCTUATION.

- **Long #2 prepositional openers** of five or more words take commas (twice). Fixes:

  Atop the six-tier wedding cake, the Iron Chef fashioned a frog and toad.

  Later that evening at the wedding feast, the erstwhile frog and toad skipped the main course. Although this is labeled a #T opener, the other phrases before the MC need a comma since they count as a long #2. *See* ✏ **2.**

- **Run-on sentence.** Ask students to explain and correct the comma splice (MC, MC). Answer: The comma after *matrimony* is not strong enough to hold the MCs together. Fix, with MCs italicized: *the Iron Chef fashioned a frog and toad anticipating joyous matrimony. Later that evening at the wedding feast, the erstwhile frog and toad skipped the main course of sturgeon roe soufflé and enjoyed just desserts.*

- **Items in a series.** Remove the comma before the cc *and* because it joins two verbs to the same subject: MC cc 2nd verb. Fix: the erstwhile frog and toad **skipped** the main course of sturgeon roe soufflé **and enjoyed** just desserts.

Grammar Notations

PREPOSITIONAL PHRASES. Atop the six-tier wedding cake; at the wedding feast; of sturgeon roe soufflé.

CLAUSES, PHRASES, AND OPENERS.

- #2 prepositional phrase opener: Atop the six-tier wedding cake.
- MC: the **Iron Chef fashioned** a frog and toad anticipating joyous matrimony. *See* ✏ **3.**
- #T: Later that evening. *That evening* is an invisible #2 with *during* implied.
- MC: the erstwhile **frog** and **toad skipped** the main course of sturgeon roe soufflé and **enjoyed** just desserts. *See* ✏ **4.**

✏ **1. Teacher's note.** If your students are using IEW in their writing, point out that this final sentence follows the title-clincher rule. It works effectively in stories as well as academic papers!

✏ **2. Teacher's note.** Words before the main clause are punctuated like openers.

✏ **3. Teacher's note.** *Anticipating* is not a verb because it does not have a helping verb; it is an adjective modifying *frog* and *toad*. Contrast this: The **frog** and **toad were anticipating** matrimony.

✏ **4. Teacher's note.** Check that students marked the two subjects and two verbs. Both subjects perform both verb actions.

Style

If desired, have students identify the strongest of the vocabulary dress-ups from this week. Discuss their answers. Suggestions:

- **Strong verbs.** fashioned, skipped.
- **Quality adjectives.** fervent, indebted, lovable, triumphant, joyous, erstwhile.
- **-ly adverbs.** uncharacteristically.

STUDENT REWRITE

He told her that the real secret to his kindness was learning humility in the guise of a frog. Recognizing his wisdom, Dorinda nodded her head in fervent, knowledgeable agreement.

When he was asked if he would permit them to marry, King Morton uncharacteristically replied, "Sweet!"

With joy he gave them his blessing, indebted to Arthur and the fairy for restoring Dorinda to her lovable self.

Epilogue. The wedding was triumphant despite the fact that Dorinda, true to form, tripped and dropped her crown in the new sturgeon pond. It simply gave Arthur a chance to fish it out—a little déjà vu!

Atop the six-tier wedding cake, the Iron Chef fashioned a frog and toad anticipating joyous matrimony. Later that evening at the wedding feast, the erstwhile frog and toad skipped the main course of sturgeon roe soufflé and enjoyed just desserts.

Week	Parts of Sentences	Punctuation	Style	Other Concepts	Vocabulary
1	Subjects and verbs Prepositional phrases	End marks Apostrophes Commas with prepositional phrases		Indents Capitalization Homophones Usage Comparative and superlative adjectives	decorous drivel folderol vehemently
2	Clauses Main clause (MC) Dependent clause (DC)	Commas with coordinating conjunctions (cc's), a.k.a. items in a series		FANBOYS (cc's—for, and, nor, but, or, yet, so) who, which, that www.asia.b words	inarticulately obstinate courtiers prestigious
3		Commas with #2, #4, and #5 openers Commas with mid-sentence adverb clauses	#1 subject #2 prepositional #4 -ing #5 clausal #6 vss		mortification queasiness sever diplomatic
4	Run-on sentences (comma splices and fused sentences)	Commas with #3 openers Commas with adjectives before a noun	#3 -ly adverb	"Be" verbs	pompadour lamentably fastidiousness abject consternation
5		Transitional expressions Interjections	#T transitional		tractable gratify prodigality blemished
6		Commas with multiple openers	Multiple openers		minuscule fretted haven trepidation
7	Sentence fragments				twaddle meandered transpired copiously benefactor
8		Commas with NDAs Hyphens			throaty tendered inquisitiveness salvage
9				*Affect* versus *effect*	benevolent stipulation dexterity curtly
10	Different ways to fix run-ons				wheezed sumptuously forbearing hospitably

Week	Parts of Sentences	Punctuation	Style	Other Concepts	Vocabulary
11			#Q opener		deficiencies rejoinder expediently piteously histrionics
12			Illegal #4 -ing openers (dangling modifiers)		audibly resplendent unstintingly surmised
13		No commas with *that* clauses	Alliteration (advanced)		pretentious desolate oblivious plummeting
14			Additional clausal starters		bestows sequestered conjectured unceremoniously
15			Invisible #2s		savory fare delectable peremptorily substantial
16				Imperative mood	inadvertently feigned convalescence recumbent
17			Transitional #2s	Review *be* verbs	infirmary propitious apropos nefariously
18		Essential and nonessential *who, which, that*			poised germane allay proximate fowler
19		Semicolons			aphorism ignobly futilely palsied
20		Review quotation marks			querulously brandishing prominent gallant
21				Personal pronouns and their antecedents	inherent bona fide snickered testily
22				Review questions: capitalization and adjectives	toady trump card conspicuous repulsive

Week	Parts of Sentences	Punctuation	Style	Other Concepts	Vocabulary
23				Review questions: run-ons	revulsion snubbed involuntarily pattered requisition forlorn
24				Rules for punctuating titles	humane regaled orderly (person) chastise
25				Review questions: sentence openers	sanguine empathy albeit rummaged mute
26			Invisible #4s		compensated erratically creditable undaunted
27		Commas with -ing participial phrases			potent foreboding noxious irately
28				Review questions: indents, numbers, *be* verbs	flimsy tad jiggled callously
29				Overusing cc's	insubordination discerning queried laborious
30				Review questions: comma rules	aghast cavalier contritely astutely
31				Review questions: www words and FANBOYS	commensurate coveted liege poignantly abhorrent
32				*then* vs. *than*	remorse sensible colossal fortuitously
33				Review questions: comma rules	fervent indebted epilogue déjà vu erstwhile

Fix It!
Grammar

Glossary

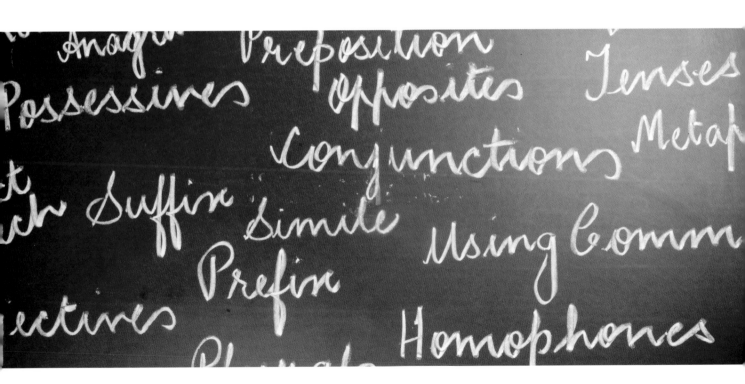

Pamela White

Institute for
Excellence in
Writing

Listen. Speak. Read. Write. Think!

Fix It!
Grammar

Glossary

Pamela White

THIRD EDITION

Contents

Making grammar friendly

This glossary is available for reference if you wish to refresh your memory or would like more information about a specific rule.

One goal of the Institute for Excellence in Writing is to make grammar friendly for younger students and beginning writers. Thus, the terms used in the early *Fix It! Grammar* books are layman's terms, such as *-ing opener* instead of participle and *who-which* instead of adjective clause.

However, grammar terms are useful to the teacher and the student over time, so they are gradually incorporated into the books as well as defined in the glossary.

With the repetition provided in the Fix Its, your students will learn the elements and rules of grammar in manageable increments.

Editing Marks

indent	¶
capitalize	
	≡
lowercase	/
delete	ℓ
insert	∨
space	#
close up	‿

Parts of Speech

Many words can be used as different parts of speech. You have to look at how they are used in the sentence to determine their parts of speech. To see how these parts of speech are used as IEW dress-ups and sentence openers, see the Stylistic Techniques section beginning on page G-35.

Articles (ar)

Articles are the words *a, an, the.*

Articles always set up a noun, so when students see an article, they should know that a noun will follow soon after. Sometimes adjectives come between the article and its noun: *a tall stranger; the reluctant, timid soldier.*

Nouns (n)

Nouns are objects (things), people, animals, places, and ideas.

To determine if a word is a noun, apply these two tests, which work best for objects and animals:

    1. Is it countable? *two* _____

    2. Can an article come in front of it? *the* _____ *; a/an* _____ .

Common and Proper Nouns

Common nouns name general things and are not capitalized.

Proper nouns are capitalized and name specific people, places, animals, and sometimes objects with a name unique to that specific person, place, or animal. *The king* is a common noun, but *King James* is proper. A *beagle* is a common noun, but the name of my pet beagle *Benji* is proper.

Compound Nouns

These are two or more words combined to form a single noun. They can be written as separate words (*apple tree; shooting match*), as hyphenated words (*lady-in-waiting*), or as one word (*marksman; wintertime*). To spell compound words correctly, consult a dictionary.

Students may be confused how to use something like *apple tree* in key word outlines or in marking nouns. A compound noun is not an adjective + noun or two nouns but just a single noun. These are nouns that could have been written as a single word because they express a single thing.

Noun Functions

The two functions of nouns and pronouns that are most useful to understand are the subject and the object of a preposition.

Subjects are nouns or pronouns that perform a verb action. Identify subjects by finding the verb first and then asking, "Who or what is doing this action?" That is the subject.

Saying that a noun is a subject identifies how it functions or behaves in that sentence; it is different from the part of speech (noun or pronoun).

Subject-verb agreement means that the subject and its verb should agree in number. If the subject is singular, the verb should be singular; if the subject is plural, the verb should be plural. Students occasionally find it confusing that a singular verb often ends in *s* and a plural verb does not: *she walks* but *they walk*.

The **object of a preposition** is the noun or pronoun that is the last word in a prepositional phrase. See under Parts of Speech: Prepositions, page G-11; and Stylistic Techniques: Sentence Openers: #2 Prepositional Opener, page G-39.

Other Noun Functions (Advanced)

Direct and **indirect objects** are important mainly as they relate to pronoun usage (*The soldier treated him graciously*, not *The soldier treated he graciously*). Since these are objects, they must use objective pronouns (see under Pronouns on the next page).

Direct objects follow a verb and answer the question *what* or *who*. Example: *The third soldier built a fire*. Built what? *a fire* (direct object).

Indirect objects are rarer and appear only when there is a direct object. They usually come between the verb and direct object and tell who or what received the direct object. Example: *The little man gave the second soldier a purse*. Gave what? *the purse* (direct object). Who received it? *the soldier* (indirect object).

The difficulty is that indirect objects also seem to answer the question *who* or *what* (gave who? *the soldier*). Tip: To tell the difference, you should be able to insert *to* in front of the indirect object: *gave a purse to the second soldier*. He is not giving the soldier to someone else.

Subject complements, a.k.a. predicate nouns, are important for the same pronoun usage problem (*It was she*, not *It was her*). These are nouns that follow a linking verb and point back to the subject, so they *complement* the subject.

Subject complements use subjective, not objective, pronouns (see under Pronouns on the next page), which is the only reason to teach these to older students. Note: Adjectives can also be subject complements.

Appositives are nouns that rename the noun that comes before them. They are important because they are punctuated with commas if nonessential (*Robin Hood, the archer*) and without commas if essential (*the archer Robin Hood*).

Imperative mood is used to issue commands. The subject, *you*, is implied.

Example: *Tarry for me here*. Robin Hood is addressing his men, asking them to wait for him. *You* is the implied subject.

Pronouns (pr)

Personal pronouns refer back to a person or thing recently mentioned and substitute for that person or thing. They should agree in case, person, and number with the noun they refer to. Begin with having students identify basic pronouns and later work on pronoun agreement.

There are three cases:

Subjective case pronouns are used as the subject (or, infrequently, subject complements).

Objective case pronouns are used as objects of verbs or prepositions.

Possessive case pronouns show ownership. These do not have an apostrophe.

	Subjective pronouns	Objective pronouns	Possessive pronouns
1st person singular	I	me	my/mine
2nd person singular	you	you	your/yours
3rd person singular	he, she, it	him, her, it	his, her/hers, its
1st person plural	we	us	our/ours
2nd person plural	you	you	your/yours
3rd person plural	they	them	their/theirs
	who	whom	whose

Pronoun agreement: To agree in person means that first person pronouns should not shift suddenly to second or third. To agree in number means that a singular pronoun should refer back to a singular noun and a plural pronoun should refer to a plural noun.

There are several different categories of pronouns in addition to personal pronouns (relative, demonstrative, interrogative, indefinite, reflexive), but in practice, teach them only as they become relevant in writing.

Reflexive pronouns end in *self* or *selves* and refer back to a noun or pronoun in the same sentence.

Examples:

Princess Dorinda fancied *herself* quite chic.

The fish allowed *themselves* to be stroked.

Verbs (vb)

Verbs are words that express either action or a state of being. There are three types: action, linking, and helping verbs.

Action Verbs

Action verbs express action (as in *chop, budge, confide*) or ownership (as in *have, possess, own*).

Verb + Adverb (Advanced)

In identifying parts of speech, some students are confused by what look like prepositions after a verb but without the usual noun afterward. In this case, these words do not function as prepositions but as adverbs that must be coupled with that verb.

Examples: *Robin Hood set off; the Merry Men rose up; they cavorted about; stand back.*

Helping Verbs

Helping verbs appear with action verbs to help them along. Picture the helping verb as a Boy Scout who helps an elderly lady cross the street. One helps the other along!

Examples: *The magical purse would always refill with gold. Would* helps *refill. She had played him a trick. Had* helps out *played.*

Tip: Helping verbs communicate possibility (*can, could, might*, etc.) or time (*was, did, has*, etc.).

Helping verbs:

> *am, is, are, was, were, be, being, been* (*be* verbs, which can also be linking verbs)
>
> *have, has, had*
>
> *do, does, did*
>
> *may, might, must, ought to*
>
> *would, will, could, can, should, shall*

Linking Verbs

Linking verbs connect the subject to a noun or adjective that renames or describes it and is called the **subject complement** (a.k.a. predicate noun and predicate adjective).

Examples: *Robin Hood was* (linking verb) *an outlaw* (subject complement). *The combatants seemed* (linking verb) *weary* (subject complement). *The princess was* (linking verb) *artful and cunning* (subject complements).

Common linking verbs:

> *am, is, are, was, were, be, being, been* (*be* verbs, which can also be helping verbs)
>
> *seem, become* (always linking verbs)
>
> *appear, grow, remain, continue*
>
> *taste, sound, smell, feel, look* (verbs dealing with the senses)

Some of these verbs can also be action verbs. Tip: If you can substitute *seem* for the verb, it is probably a linking verb.

Be Verbs

Be verbs often stump students when identifying parts of speech because they do not show action. Since they dominate our language and perform important functions as helping and linking verbs, it is important students can recognize that they are verbs.

Ask students to memorize the *be* verbs: *am, is, are, was, were, be, being, been.*

Verbals: Infinitives, Participles, Gerunds (Advanced)

Verbals are words formed from a verb, but they usually do not function as a verb.

You do not have to teach students to identify whether a particular verbal is functioning as a noun or adjective or adverb. There is little point to drilling this harder concept except to mention that verbals are not verbs. Learning what function they take will not affect punctuation or help most students understand grammar, nor will it show up on the SAT or ACT.

As a strong verb dress-up? If students want to label a verbal as a strong verb, decide whether it is too advanced to direct them toward basic action verbs instead.

It helps older students to have a basic understanding of these verbals:

> **1. Infinitives** are verbals formed by placing *to* in front of the simple present form of a verb (like *to sneeze*). Infinitives function as adjectives, adverbs, and nouns but never as verbs.

> **2. Participles** often function as adjectives and come in two forms: present (-ing words) and past participles (-ed words). However, when participles are coupled with a subject and a helping verb, they function as verbs, as in *He **was splashing**, which frightened the fish. For years, she **had longed** to visit the world above the sea.*

>> **a.** Sometimes these participle-adjectives appear directly before the noun: *hunting skills; a botched case.*

>> **b.** Sometimes they are an -ing or -ed phrase coming before or after a main clause and modifying the subject of the main clause: *Springing to his feet, Robin Hood confronted the challenger.* (*Springing* describes *Robin Hood*, the subject after the comma.) See under Stylistic Techniques: Sentence Openers: #4 -ing Participial Phrase Opener, page G-41.

> **3. Gerunds** are -ing words that function as nouns. Examples: *His splashing frightened the fish.* (*Splashing* is the subject of the sentence and therefore a noun.) *The fish were frightened by his splashing.* (*Splashing* is the object of the preposition *by* and therefore a noun.)

Split infinitives

A concern more of the past than the present, *split infinitives* are worth teaching advanced writers. To split one's infinitive is to insert one or more adverbs between "to" and the verb, as in "to foolishly insert."

Generally, split infinitives are acceptable but formerly frowned on, so avoid them when it is just as smooth to place the intervening adverb somewhere else.

Adjectives (adj)

Adjectives are words that describe or modify nouns and pronouns. Usually they come before the noun they modify, as in *the crowded room* or *covetous princess*.

Sometimes adjectives come after a linking verb, as in *the princess was **thrilled**; the soldiers were **penniless** and **forlorn***.

Comparative and Superlative Adjectives

Comparative adjectives (ending in *-er*) and superlative adjectives (ending in *-est*) are forms of adjectives comparing two or more nouns. Students sometimes have trouble recognizing that words ending in *-er* or *-est* can be adjectives. Have them drop the ending and ask if the word remaining is an adjective.

Example: *The noblest buck is the most noble buck.* Drop the ending and ask if *noble* can describe a noun. It can, so *noble* and *noblest* are both adjectives.

Some words form irregular comparatives and superlatives. The most common of these are *good* and *bad*:

> good, better, best

> bad, worse, worst

Caution students against using *more* or *most* with a comparative or superlative adjective. Not *more prouder* but *prouder*. Most one-syllable adjectives form the comparative and superlative by adding the suffix. Adjectives of three or more syllables form the comparative with *more* and the superlative with *most* in front of the regular adjective. Two-syllable adjectives have more complex rules, but usually whichever sounds better is correct.

Adverbs (adv)

Adverbs usually modify verbs or adjectives and answer the questions *how, when,* or *where*. Encourage students to identify what part of speech the adverbs modify.

Example: *The princess stoutly denied that she possessed stolen goods. Stoutly* tells us how she denied, so it is the adverb, and it comes right before the verb it describes.

Many adverbs end in *-ly*. See Stylistic Techniques: Dress-Ups: -ly Adverb, page G-35; and Sentence Openers: #3 -ly Adverb Opener, page G-40.

Imposter -ly's: Some -ly words are adjectives like *chilly, ghastly, ugly,* and *friendly*. If the word describes an object or person (*the ugly duckling*), it is an adjective and not an adverb.

Advanced: Adverbs can also modify other adverbs, but this is rare and usually awkward in the hands of young writers, giving such unhelpful constructions as *she spoke extremely quickly*.

Advanced: Comparative adverbs are usually formed by adding *more* or *most* in front of the adverb. If the adverb is short, sometimes the suffix is used, as in *deadliest*. If in doubt, students should check a dictionary.

Tip: When adjectives come after a linking verb, they are known as **subject complements** or **predicate adjectives**. See Parts of Speech: Verbs: Linking Verbs, page G-8.

Prepositions (prep)

Prepositions start phrases that usually show some relationship dealing with space (*on the branch*) or time (*in the morning*). If it is something a frog can do with a log or a squirrel with a tree, it is probably a prepositional phrase: *climbs on the log, sits in the branches, runs around the tree.*

A prepositional phrase always follows this pattern:

preposition + noun (no verb)

It begins with a preposition, ends with a noun, and does not have a verb in it. Since there is not a subject + verb, it is a phrase, not a clause. There may be other words in between the preposition and noun, but there will never be a verb: *in the act; by a great baron; of strong and goodhearted yeomen.*

First learning parts of speech helps students accurately identify prepositional phrases. Until the concept is mastered, guide them to see that the phrase begins with a preposition, ends with a noun, and has no verb in it.

The most common prepositions:

aboard	at	despite	near	throughout
about	because of	down	of	to
above	before	during	off	toward
according to	behind	except	on, onto	under
across	below	for	opposite	underneath
after	beneath	from	out	unlike
against	beside	in	outside	until
along	besides	inside	over	unto
amid	between	instead of	past	up, upon
among	beyond	into	regarding	with
around	by	like	since	within
as	concerning	minus	through	without

In the first stories of *Fix It!* students are asked to identify prepositional phrases. Removing prepositional phrases helps students see the underlying structure of their sentences better, which is the basis for being able to punctuate correctly.

Doubling as other parts of speech: A few words in the preposition list are sometimes another part of speech, so guide students to determine this based on the pattern. The two most important examples:

1. Adverbs that follow a verb but do not start a prepositional phrase (*warded **off**; cried **out***).

2. Subordinating conjunctions that start dependent clauses: *since, as, until, after, before.* See under Stylistic Techniques: Sentence Openers: #5 Clausal Opener, page G-42.

Younger students do not need to count the preposition *to* in an infinitive, as in *to float*, since infinitives work a little differently from prepositional phrases.

On not ending sentences with prepositions: This is a carryover from Latin and not a true rule in English. Andrew Pudewa quips that Winston Churchill gave the definitive answer to this problem when he remarked, "That is a rule up with which I will not put!"

If the sentence is more awkward to revise with the preposition placed earlier, it is better to have it at the end. Example: *I have only a plain blackthorn staff to meet you with.* The alternative is this stilted construction: *I have only a plain blackthorn staff with which to meet you.*

Misplaced prepositional phrases: The later stories deal with the problem of dangling prepositional phrases where misplaced prepositional phrases distort the meaning, often humorously.

Example: ***King Arthur declared on special days*** *he would not feast until someone narrated a bizarre tale that he could trust.* The king did not make this declaration on special days; instead, he declared he would not feast on them.

Revise by moving the prepositional phrase: *King Arthur declared **he would not feast on special days** until someone narrated a bizarre tale that he could trust.*

Coordinating Conjunctions (cc)

Coordinating conjunctions connect parts of speech, phrases, and clauses. Whatever they connect needs to be the same thing grammatically: two or more nouns, two or more present participles, two or more dependent clauses, two or more main clauses, and so forth.

Have students memorize the seven basic coordinating conjunctions using the mnemonic device FANBOYS, an acronym for the cc's: *for, and, nor, but, or, yet, so.*

Punctuation: The main problem with cc's is that sometimes they have a comma in front of them and sometimes they do not. See Punctuation: Commas, page G-21.

The principles to keep in mind:

   1. Use commas before cc's when they join

   a. two main clauses. Pattern: **MC, cc MC.** Example: *Usually Robin towered over others,* **but** *the stranger was taller by a head and a neck.*

   b. three or more items in a series. Pattern: **a, b, and c.** Example: *He ran to the window, opened it,* **and** *vaulted out.*

   2. Do not use commas before cc's when they join two items in a series unless those are MCs. Example: *fine gardens* **and** *wide lawns.*

   This applies to two verbs (a compound verb) with one subject. Pattern: **MC cc 2nd verb** (notice there is no comma). Example: *He bowed* **and** *walked away.*

Train students to locate cc's and then determine what same parts of speech or constructions they are joining. This matters because it shows whether or not the commas will be necessary: comma if three or more; no comma if only two unless MCs. It also matters because it helps students identify faulty parallelism. See sidebar.

Starting sentences with cc's: Strict grammarians forbid this on the basis that the job of cc's is to connect things of equal grammatical rank. Generally, encourage this avoidance, especially in academic papers, but it is not a hard and fast rule.

One clear exception is in dialogue, which can mimic real speech patterns. We often start our thoughts with *and* or *but.*

Faulty parallelism

Coordinating conjunctions should join parts of speech, phrases, or clauses of equal grammatical rank. When they do not, it is known as faulty parallelism, a concept middle and high school students should learn. It means that the items in a series are not parallel, that is, not the same part of speech, type of phrase, or type of clause.

Example: Once she **stole** into the throne room, **swinging** on the chandeliers, and **landed** at the feet of the scandalized courtiers.

Problem: The sentence sets up a parallel construction but is not consistent with its items in a series (bolded).

Corrected: Once she **stole** into the throne room, **swung** on the chandeliers, and **landed** at the feet of the scandalized courtiers.

Subordinating Conjunctions

In IEW's stylistic techniques, we begin by teaching students the because clause, then seven more common clause starters using the acronym **www.asia.b** for the words that can start dependent clauses:

> when, while, where, as, since, if, although, because

Later we add three more:

> until, whereas, unless

These are all subordinating conjunctions, so named because they start subordinate clauses, an older term for dependent clauses. There is no special need to teach the terminology (subordinating conjunction) except that it is important to distinguish these types of words from coordinating conjunctions (cc). For simplicity's sake, students can mark these clause starters with a *cl*.

The main difference is that when coordinating conjunctions (*for, and, nor, but, or, yet, and so*) are added to a main clause, we still have a main clause. When subordinating conjunctions (*when, while, where,* etc.) are added to a main clause, they turn it into a dependent clause. The punctuation changes too. See under Stylistic Techniques: Dress-ups: Clause Starters, page G-38; and Sentence Openers: #5 Clausal Opener, page G-42.

Advanced: Confusingly, *since, until,* and *as* sometimes function as prepositions, and *because of* is also a preposition. See tips for distinguishing them under Stylistic Techniques: Sentence Openers: #5 Clausal Opener, page G-42.

Advanced: Also confusingly, *as, where, when, while* and *whereas* sometimes start adjective clauses or function as coordinating conjunctions. See Sentences, Clauses, and Phrases: Clauses: Dependent Clauses (Advanced), page G-17; and Stylistic Techniques: Sentence Openers: #5 Clausal Opener, page G-42.

Conjunctive Adverbs (Advanced)

These words are a writer's plague—albeit an important group of words!—because they are often confused with subordinating conjunctions but need different punctuation.

Some common conjunctive adverbs: *however, therefore, then, moreover, consequently, otherwise, nevertheless, thus, furthermore, instead, otherwise.*

Learn this principle: When you add a conjunctive adverb to a main clause, it is still a main clause, which is not the case with subordinating conjunctions.

How this matters:

1. If conjunctive adverbs start a sentence, usually follow them with a comma as you would any transitional word or expression. The exception is short conjunctive adverbs like *then*, which do not require a pause.

Examples: ***Then*** *they dropped it when we were older.* ***Moreover****, didn't they realize cell phones were for emergencies only?*

2. If a conjunctive adverb falls between two main clauses that belong together in one sentence, put a semicolon before it and comma after: **MC; ca, MC.**

Example: *Years of indulgence had spoiled her beyond recognition;* ***however****, Lady Constance recalled a time in Dorinda's childhood when she had been a lovable child.*

If the main clauses express two different ideas, separate them with a period.

The lady bent down and awarded Gawain a kiss. **Then** *she appealed to him to rhapsodize about the tribulations and treasures of true love.*

3. If conjunctive adverbs fall in the middle of a sentence, however, use two commas or none, depending on whether you need a clear pause around them.

Examples: *Chanticleer ignored her advice,* **however.** *Pertelote* **therefore** *argued more vehemently for laxatives from the garden. Chanticleer* **then** *countered with another round of dire dreams, which* **nevertheless** *failed to convince Pertelote.*

Interjections

Interjections are words that express a strong emotion, such as *ow, oh, ugh, whew.* They usually are set off with commas, but if they have a strong exclamatory message, you may put an exclamation mark after them. Alone, they do not count as a sentence.

"Oops! I do believe I've broken your leg."

"Oh, yes, benevolent frog!"

"Yuck! I won't touch another bite!"

Sentences, Clauses, and Phrases

Sentences

A sentence expresses one complete thought. To do so, it must have at least one main clause.

Sentence sense. Writers often string together more than one main clause in a sentence, often with the coordinating conjunction *and*, when those main clauses would be more powerful as separate sentences. When students are ready to understand the concept, discourage this practice.

Sentence fragments. A fragment is an error in which a sentence has phrases and/or dependent clauses but no main clause.

Servants came forth, attending to his horse. Welcoming the warrior. The second part is an unacceptable fragment.

In fiction and even in academic writing for some teachers, fragments that do not leave the reader hanging and that fit the flow of the paragraph are dramatic and effective. *Fix It!* stories permit such fragments, especially in dialogue when complete sentences would sound unnatural. The key is whether or not the fragment leaves the reader feeling as if something more is needed.

"Would you like me to rescue your ball?"

"Oh, yes!" (acceptable fragment)

Because students often use fragments ineffectively in formal writing, many teachers forbid the use of any fragment. Discuss which fragments in the *Fix It!* stories work well and which ones do not in order to arm students with the practice of recognizing sentence fragments. This will also help them distinguish phrases and dependent clauses from main, or independent, clauses.

Clauses and Phrases

Failure to recognize the basic clauses and phrases that form the underlying structure of sentences is at the heart of most students' inability to punctuate their sentences properly.

When older students struggle with knowing where to place their commas, this, along with knowing basic parts of speech, is most likely the root problem. They cannot recognize a main clause if they do not know what a subject-verb pair is, and they cannot know this if they do not distinguish nouns, pronouns, and verbs from other parts of speech.

The different levels of *Fix It!* teach grammar progressively in this way: beginning with basic parts of speech, then identifying phrases and clauses, and gradually adding in punctuation. Once students understand the basic structure of their sentences, they will know how to apply the punctuation rules.

Phrases

A phrase is a group of related words that does not have both a subject and a verb.

Prepositional phrases. Practically speaking, these are the only phrases worth teaching. Finding prepositional phrases helps get the "noise" out of the sentence and makes it easier for students to see their clauses. It also helps them properly identify #2 sentence openers. See Parts of Speech: Prepositions, page G-11; and Stylistic Techniques: Sentence Openers: #2 Prepositional Opener, page G-39.

Appositive. A convenient word for a simple concept, an appositive is a noun that renames the noun that comes right before it. Example: *Robin Hood,* **the archer.** The only reason appositives are worth flagging is that they usually are set off with commas but sometimes not. See under Punctuation: Commas: Rule 15: Essential-Nonessential Elements, page G-24.

Clauses

A clause is a group of related words that must have both a subject and a verb.

Main Clauses (MC)

These are clauses that can stand alone as a sentence.

a. *Main clause* is abbreviated *MC* in *Fix It!* The MC is also known as an independent clause or strong clause.

b. MCs usually start with a subject or with an article (*a, an, the*) and/or adjectives plus subject. Example: *The poor soldiers returned* follows the pattern of "Article (*The*) adjective (*poor*) subject (*soldiers*) verb (*returned*)."

Sometimes the subject-verb will be inverted, with the verb coming before the subject. Examples: *There gathered around him displaced countrymen.* subject-verb = countrymen gathered. *Up rose his Merry Men.* subject-verb = Merry Men are. These are still MCs.

c. When identifying MCs, include prepositional phrases in the middle or at the end of the clause but not ones that come before MCs. Follow common sense in determining which words must group with the basic subject and verb of the main clause.

d. Sometimes dependent clauses (like *who-which*'s) are included in a MC and needed for it to make sense. Example: *I have never met a man who could topple me off a bridge.* The MC includes the dependent who clause and does not makes sense as just *I have never met a man.*

Dependent Clauses (DC)

These are clauses that cannot stand alone as a sentence.

a. *Dependent clause* is abbreviated *DC* in *Fix It!* It is also known as a subordinate clause or weak clause.

b. DCs are basically main clauses with another word or words in front that turn the main clause into something that leaves us hanging, that cannot stand alone as a sentence.

For practical purposes, it is enough for younger students to recognize the dependent clause starters *who, which, that,* and the subordinating conjunctions, the www.asia. buwu words *when, while, where, as, since, if, although, because, until, whereas, unless.*

As an example, start with a main clause: *The foresters discovered them in the act.* Now add a www word: *Although the foresters discovered them in the act.* There is still a subject and verb, so this is a clause and not a phrase. However, the second version leaves us hanging. Although this is true, something else must also be true.

DCs (Dependent Clauses) must be attached to a MC (Main Clause) to be a legal sentence.

c. To simplify grammar, focus on teaching just two types of DCs: 1. *who-which* clauses, and 2. www.asia.b clauses. In *Fix It!* adverb clauses that begin with one of the www words are abbreviated as *AC.*

See Stylistic Techniques: Dress-Ups: *Who-Which* Clause, page G-36, and Clause Starters (www.asia.b), page G-38; and Stylistic Techniques: Sentence Openers: #5 Clausal Opener, page G-42.

Tip: Conjunctive adverbs like *however, therefore, then* and coordinating conjunctions like *and, or, but* do not turn a MC into a DC.

Dependent Clauses (Advanced)

Understanding DCs well and punctuating them perfectly every time can get complex. The amount of time it would take to teach most students these finer points of grammar is not always worth it, but it may help teachers to understand the following.

Dependent clauses function in different ways, which can affect their punctuation.

1. Adverb clauses, a.k.a. adverbial clauses (AC)

Most of the time, a clause starter from the www word list will start an adverb clause. It should not be set off with a comma if it falls in the middle or at the end of a sentence (**MC AC**), but it takes a comma after the clause if it is an opener (**AC, MC**).

2. Adjective clauses

This usually starts with a relative pronoun, mainly *who, which,* or *that.* Adjective clauses usually follow nouns or pronouns and describe the nouns they follow: *the **arrow that** Robin shot...; the **princess, who** was artful and cunning....*

Adjective clauses are set off with commas if they are nonessential to the rest of the sentence but not set off with commas if they are essential. See under Punctuation: Commas: Rule 15: Essential-Nonessential Elements, page G-24.

Unfortunately—and this is one of the areas where grammar gets messy—three of the subordinating conjunctions that are in the clause starter list, *as, where,* and *when,* sometimes start adjective clauses and thus act as relative pronouns. This matters because adverb clauses in the middle or end of sentences never take commas, but adjective clauses take commas when they are nonessential.

Contrast these examples:

> *The roof is formed of shells, which open and close **as** the water flows over them. As* is a subordinating conjunction meaning *while;* it starts an adverb clause, so no comma.

> *The outcome of joy is invariably woe, **as** all creatures know. As* is a relative pronoun meaning *a fact that;* it starts a nonessential clause and needs a comma.

Other messy exceptions are *while* and *whereas*, which can be subordinating conjunctions (no comma before them) or coordinating conjunctions (comma before them when they join main clauses).

Contrast these sentences:

> *The second soldier took the road to the right* **while** *he thought about his next plan of action.* No comma because *while* is a subordinating conjunction starting an adverb clause, and adverb clause dress-ups are not set off with commas. *While* means "at the same time that" here.

> *The second soldier took the path to the right,* **while** *the other two determined to travel down the road to the left.* Comma because *while* is a coordinating conjunction joining two main clauses (**MC, cc MC**). As a cc, *while* and *whereas* convey a contrast.

3. Noun clauses

These function as nouns. Most often, they follow a verb and begin with *that*, one of the words that confusingly can also begin an adjective clause. You can tell the difference because *that* adjective clauses follow a noun while *that* noun clauses follow a verb. Example: *People felt that Robin Hood was like them. That* follows the verb *felt* so starts a noun clause.

Tip: A clause is a noun clause if you can substitute a pronoun for it. Example: *People felt* **that** *Robin Hood was like them. People felt* **it***.* Makes sense! But: *Robin returned to the town* **that** *he had left. Robin returned to the town* **it***?* This does not make sense, so this *that* starts an adjective, not a noun, clause.

Where grammar gets even muddier is that *when, where, who* and other words sometimes start noun clauses. However, students will not run into these situations enough in marking dress-ups and openers to make it worth spending the time to teach noun clauses. Fortunately, students rarely have trouble punctuating noun clauses, so learning about them becomes a moot issue.

Punctuation

End Marks . ? !

A sentence may end with a **period**, **question mark**, or **exclamation mark**.

Do not double punctuate. Not *"You're sure?!"* or *"Hah!," he said.* But *"You're sure?"* and *"Hah!" he said.*

Rule 1. Use periods at the end of statements and in abbreviations.

He bowed and walked away.

Advanced: Comma splices and **fused sentences** occur when students join main clauses with only commas or with no punctuation. MCs need something stronger to hold them together, often a period. See under Semicolons, page G-26.

Rule 2. Periods (and commas) go inside closing quotation marks.

"The better man should cross first."

Rule 3. Use question marks after direct questions.

Did you ever hear the story of the three poor soldiers?

Rule 4. Use exclamation marks when the statement expresses strong emotion, but do not overuse them. When a character is said to exclaim something, the context begs for an exclamation mark.

"No one calls me a coward!"

"Hah!" the other exclaimed.

Quotations " "

Rule 1. Use quotation marks to enclose direct quotations but not indirect speech, which usually begins with *that*. Quotation marks should "hug" the words they enclose—that is, there should not be a space between the quotation mark and the word or punctuation it encloses.

"It's no wonder that child has turned out so blemished," clucked Lady Constance. (direct)

Secretly he thought that in beauty she surpassed Queen Guinevere herself. (indirect)

Rule 2. The attribution is the narrative that sets up a quotation with a speaking verb (*he said*). Set attributions off from quotations with commas. The attribution can come before, after, or in the middle of the quotation.

When using your computer, be sure you are creating *curly quotes* (" ") and not *straight quotes* (" ").

Straight quotes should be reserved for measurements, and only when the format is very tight, such as 6" 2' for six feet, two inches.

Patterns: **speaking verb, "quote"** or **"quote," speaking verb**

> He *answered,* "Hand me a stout bow and straight arrow."

> "I will join your band," *announced* the stranger.

> "You stand back," *responded* his adversary, "since I am the better man."

Rule 3. Commas and periods always go inside closing quotations (unless they are followed by parentheses, in which case they go after the parentheses).

> "It's gold, you know."

Rule 4. Exclamation marks and question marks go inside closing quotations when they are part of the material quoted; otherwise, they go outside. Also, use only one ending mark of punctuation—the stronger—with quotation marks, em dashes excepted.

> "If only I could have my ball back, I would bestow a handsome reward on my benefactor!"

> "Dorinda, who was at the door?" King Morton inquired.

Rule 5. If a quotation ends in an exclamation mark or question but is followed by an attribution, use a lowercase letter at the beginning of the attribution (unless it starts with a proper noun) because the attribution is part of the same sentence as the quotation.

> "Have at him!" cried Will Stutely.

Rule 6. When a spoken sentence is interrupted, close the first part and begin the second with quotation marks. Do not capitalize the first letter of the continuation.

> "By the great yew bow of Saint Withold," cried the stranger, "that is a shot indeed!"

Rule 7. When typing, place thoughts in italics instead of in quotation marks.

> *It's time she was humbled a little,* thought the wise soldier.

When handwriting, use quotation marks.

Rule 8. Use italics or place quotation marks around words referred to as words. Trick: Insert "the word(s)" or "the name" before the word in question to tell if this rule applies.

> Since "Little" is indeed your true name…. (Since the name "Little"…)

> He would have none of this recent drivel of dropping "sir" and "madam" when addressing one's elders. (dropping the words "sir" and "madam")

Rule 9. Use single quotation marks for quotations within quotations. This is the only time to use single quotations.

> "She also insisted on stripping the top coverlets from all the mattresses because, as she put it, 'They might be unclean.'"

Rule 10. In conversation, if someone is speaking and changes topic, start a new paragraph. However, close his first paragraph without a quotation mark and open his new paragraph with a quotation mark.

The missing quotation mark at the end of the first paragraph signals that he has not finished speaking. The opening quotation mark in the next paragraph reminds us that someone is still speaking.

> Robin accepted the challenge. "I will stoop to you as I never stooped to man before.

> ¶ "Friend Stutely, cut down a white piece of bark four fingers tall and wide."

Apostrophes '

Rule 1. Use an apostrophe with contractions, placing it where the letter(s) have been removed. Note that in formal writing contractions should be avoided, but they are acceptable in fiction, especially in dialogue.

"I'll figure out how to trick them."

"It's too bad, but we'd better go our separate ways."

Rule 2. Use an apostrophe to show possession. To form plural possessives, make the noun plural first; then add an apostrophe. An exception is irregular plural possessives like *children's* and *women's*.

the second soldier's turn

the soldiers' last night at the palace (the last night of all three soldiers)

Rule 3. Never use an apostrophe with possessive pronouns (*his, hers, its, theirs, ours, yours*) since they already show possession. Teach students the differences in these tricky pairs:

Possessive Pronoun	Contraction
its	it's (it is; remember by it's)
whose	who's (who is)
theirs	there's (there is)

> Just like with quotation marks, when using your computer, be sure you are using *curly apostrophes* (') and not *straight apostrophes* (').

Commas ,

Rule 1. Adjectives before a noun

Use commas to separate two or more coordinate adjectives before a noun. **Coordinate adjectives** each independently describe the noun, as in *dewy, silent leaves*.

Do not use commas to separate **cumulative adjectives**, in which the first adjective modifies both the second adjective and the noun, as in *one fair morning*. The adjectives are cumulative if the last one deals with time, age, or color *or* if it forms a compound noun with the noun (*apple tree*).

Two tricks help distinguish coordinate from cumulative, but these are just tricks that depend on a quick response, not rules. If you think about it too long, it is harder to tell.

Adjectives are coordinate and need a comma if you can

1. reverse their order.

2. add *and* between them.

Examples: With *pointed, protruding nose*, it sounds right to say both *protruding, pointed nose* and *pointed and protruding nose*, so the adjectives are coordinate and the comma is necessary.

With *stout oak staff*, it sounds awkward to say either *oak stout staff* or *stout and oak staff*, so the adjectives are cumulative and should not have a comma.

Occasionally students will put a comma between an adjective and the noun it modifies, as in *the pointed, protruding, nose*. Be on the lookout for this and squash this habit if it forms!

Rule 2. Quotations

Use a comma with a verb of speaking that introduces a direct quotation, whether the verb comes before or after the quotation.

> Older students who do not correctly punctuate their sentences rarely learn by memorizing punctuation rules. The problem goes back to understanding the underlying sentence structure. See under Sentences, Clauses, and Phrases: Clauses and Phrases, page G-15.
>
> Students with weak understanding of when to punctuate should start with the first story of *Fix It!*

"King Mel loathes courtly balls," Lord Ashton *protested*.

Lord Ashton *protested*, "King Mel loathes courtly balls."

Rule 3. Nouns of Direct Address (NDAs)

Set off nouns of direct address (NDAs) with commas.

"*Fool*, you have killed the king's deer."

"For fourteen days we have enjoyed no sport, *my friends*."

Rule 4. Items in a series

Pattern: a, b, and c. Use commas to separate three or more items in a series. These items must be the same part of speech or same grammatical construction, such as phrases or clauses. The last two items are usually connected by a coordinating conjunction.

Robin was *mature*, *strong*, and *dauntless*. (three adjectives)

He *accepted* the match, *grabbed* his bow and arrow, and *started* off from Locksley. (three verbs)

The Oxford comma. Current trend is to keep the Oxford comma, which is the comma before the coordinating conjunction in three or more items in a series. Although the Oxford comma is optional if there is no danger of misreading, writers do not always recognize potential confusion. It is never wrong to include the Oxford comma, so it is easier to include it always.

Example: *To his hens, Chanticleer gave fine gifts, the pleasure of his singing and corn.* Ambiguity: Are "the pleasure of his singing and corn" the actual gifts, or are these three separate items? The Oxford comma clarifies that these are three separate items: *Chanticleer gave fine gifts, the pleasure of his singing, and corn.*

Pattern: a and b. Do not use commas with only two items in a series unless those items are main clauses.

You shall enjoy succulent *venison* and the stoutest tasting *ale*. (two nouns)

He will receive a *trouncing* and a *ducking* himself. (two -ing words)

Rule 5. Compound verb. Pattern: MC cc 2nd verb.

Do not use a comma before a coordinating conjunction that joins two verbs (a compound verb) with the same subject. It helps to think of this as joining only two items (two verbs) in a series. You will not see a second subject after the coordinating conjunction.

They *built* great fires and *roasted* the does. (two verbs)

He also *had* the little man in the red jacket for his guest and *treated* him graciously.

Rule 6. Main clauses with a coordinating conjunction. Pattern: MC, cc MC

Use a comma before a coordinating conjunction that joins two main clauses. You will see a subject and verb after the coordinating conjunction.

"*He is* of diminished princely stature, *and he doesn't care* for polo."

They had fought well in the wars, *but* now *they were* out of work and destitute.

Rule 7. Introductory prepositional phrases (#2 sentence openers)

Use commas after introductory prepositional phrases of five or more words. The comma is optional with fewer than five words. With short prepositional openers, let the pause test be your guide: If it sounds better with a pause, include a comma; if it does not need a pause, leave it out.

For advanced writers, emphasize that this is the only situation when quotations are set up with a comma. In research, quotations are often worked into the text with no punctuation or with a colon when they follow a main clause that they also illustrate.

Technically, the comma in the MC, cc MC pattern is optional when the clauses are short and there is no danger of misreading.

However, since it can cause confusion to omit it, it is easier to include it always.

On his journey north Gawain encountered few obstacles. (comma optional)

From stone *to* stone they cavorted about. (comma optional)

"*By* the faith *of* my heart, never have I been called a craven in all my life!"

With a string of opening introductory prepositional phrases, save the comma for the end of all of them, even if one of them is long.

Not: During the long and arduous weeks, of preparation, for the ball, Mel was shuffled off to the hunting lodge.

But: During the long and arduous weeks of preparation for the ball, Mel was shuffled off to the hunting lodge.

Advanced: When the introductory prepositional phrase is followed by a verb instead of noun or pronoun, do not add the comma.

Behind them close on their heels *bounded* the cow and the calf.

Rule 8. Mid-sentence prepositional phrases

Prepositional phrases in the middle of sentences are not set off with commas.

The stranger shot *at the small white square* fixed to its front.

Rule 9. Transitional expressions and interjections

Use a comma after introductory transitional expressions and interjections. Usually include commas on both sides of interrupting words or phrases that appear elsewhere in a sentence.

Meanwhile, Robin's men lay off to the side of the prodigious oak.

Moreover, didn't they realize cell phones were intended for emergencies only?

The palace accountant ordered them a new HDTV, complete with a surround system, *too*.

As grown-up girls, *however,* they could go when they pleased.

When an interjection expresses a strong emotion, use an exclamation mark instead.

Alas! In an ox's stall this night I shall be murdered where I lie.

Rule 10. Introductory adverb clauses (#5 sentence openers). Pattern: AC, MC

Use commas after introductory #5 adverb clause sentence openers, even if they are short. An adverb clause is a type of dependent clause. See Stylistic Techniques: Sentence Openers: #5 Clausal Opener, page G-42.

Although the foresters discovered them in the act, they narrowly escaped.

Since the problem was obvious, he continued after a pause.

When he finished, they thanked their old friend heartily for his kindness.

Because the Sheriff of Nottingham was related to the slain forester, he had a vendetta to catch Robin Hood.

Rule 11. Adverb clause dress-up. Pattern: MC AC

Do not use a comma with mid-sentence adverb clauses. See Stylistic Techniques: Dress-Ups: www.asia.b words, page G-38. See exceptions in Rules 13 and 15 below.

Robin observed him *as* he trimmed his staff.

"Remain on the other side *while* I quickly make a staff."

"I will tan your hide *until* it's as many colors as a beggar's cloak *if* you touch your bow."

Rule 12. Comparisons.

Do not use a comma to separate parts of a comparison.

O disconsolate hens, louder was your keening *than* that of senators' wives in Rome.

Rule 13. Contrasting elements.

Use commas to separate contrasting parts of a sentence.

The ideas in this story are the cock's thoughts, not mine.

This is especially confusing with the www words *although*, *while*, and *whereas*. When they contrast the main clause before them, set them off with a comma, despite the more common rule **MC AC**.

"Now you flinch for fear, *although* you have felt no harm."

"Whatever I win in the woods I will award you in the evening, *while* all that you have gained you must bestow on me."

This sometimes applies to the cc *but* when it presents a strong contrast, even when it is joining only two items in a series that are not main clauses and therefore normally do not take a comma.

"Dreams are often a portent not just of joy, *but* of tribulations to come."

Rule 14. Participial Phrases (#4 sentence openers)

Use commas after introductory -ing participial phrases, even if they are short.

Excusing herself from the table, Dorinda hastened away.

Participial phrases in the middle or at the end of sentences are usually nonessential and therefore set off with commas.

Her sisters rose from the depths, *singing plaintively*.

Rule 15. Essential-Nonessential elements (a.k.a. restrictive-nonrestrictive)

Set off *who-which* clauses, appositives, participial phrases, and adjective clauses with commas if they are nonessential. Do not put commas around them if they are essential.

If the clause or phrase is necessary to the meaning of the rest of the sentence or if it specifies which one of something is being discussed, it is essential and should not be enclosed in commas.

If it does not alter the meaning of the rest of the sentence or if the person or thing is adequately identified, it is nonessential and needs commas, even though it may be adding important information. *Nonessential* should not be taken to mean unimportant.

Tricks to test:

1. Mentally remove the clause or phrase from the sentence to see if it alters the information in the rest of the sentence or specifies who or what is meant. If it does not, the element is nonessential and should be set off with commas.

2. Put parentheses around the clause or phrase. If the sentence still seems to work, the clause or phrase is probably nonessential.

Importantly, often whether or not you use commas changes the meaning. For example, it is correct to punctuate the following who clause as essential or nonessential: *Even the footmen, who once toadied to her, snubbed her.* With commas, it is saying that all footmen

Tip: Sometimes it is not crystal clear whether a clause or phrase is essential or nonessential. Ask these questions:

Does it affect the meaning of the rest of the sentence?

Does it specify which particular noun is intended?

Then use your best guess. Grammarians will not always agree on particular examples!

Tip: The concept of essential and nonessential elements does not apply to sentence openers, which have separate rules of punctuation. Test this out only on phrases and clauses in the middle or at the end of sentences.

snubbed her, and, incidentally, all once toadied to her. Without commas it is saying that only those footmen who used to toady to her now snubbed her: *Even the footmen who once toadied to her snubbed her.*

Examples:

"Be ready to heed my call, *which will sound as three short blasts upon the bugle horn.*" (nonessential which clause)

> If we remove the which clause from the sentence, the main clause meaning does not change: the speaker still wants them to be ready to heed his call. The which clause is therefore nonessential, even though it adds important information, and should be set off with commas.

He had shot a deer *that the king reserved for his own table.* (essential that clause, so no comma)

> This clause is essential because it specifies which particular deer. He did not shoot just any deer but one reserved for the king.

"It was agreed that the poor soldier *who had already suffered from the power of the apple* should undertake the task." (essential who clause)

> The who clause specifies which soldier—the one who had already suffered from the apple's power—so is needed in the sentence and therefore not set off with commas. It restricts the information to that particular soldier, which is why these are sometimes called restrictive clauses.

She had confessed the truth to Lady Constance, *who now played her trump card.* (nonessential who clause)

> Lady Constance is already sufficiently identified. The who clause adds an important detail but does not alter the meaning of the rest of the sentence so is nonessential and needs a comma.

the archer *Robin Hood* (essential appositive)

> Without his name, we would not know which archer is intended, so this is an essential appositive and should not be set off with a comma.

Robin Hood, *the archer* (nonessential appositive)

> It adds information but does not restrict the information to a particular Robin Hood or change the meaning of the rest of the sentence.

Robin Hood rose, *needing a change.* (nonessential participial phrase)

> He still rose, regardless of whether or not he needed a change. The participial phrase adds information but does not alter the meaning of the main clause.

Advanced: Sometimes *when, as,* and *where* start adjective clauses instead of adverb clauses. When they do, they can be essential or nonessential. This next example illustrates a nonessential adjective clause (*where*) and a nonessential participial phrase (*frightened*).

> Robin waded to the bank, *where* the little fish scattered and fled, *frightened* at his splashing.

Tip: The word *that* can replace *which* in essential clauses.

Tip: Most participial phrases are nonessential.

Semicolons ;

Rule 1. Use semicolons to join main clauses when they are so intricately linked they belong in the same sentence. Otherwise, use a period. Pattern: **MC; MC**

> "He sounds like just my type; he sounds just like me!"

Advanced: Conjunctive adverbs (words like *therefore, however, nevertheless, moreover, furthermore*) do not turn a main clause into a dependent one; therefore, use a semicolon before the conjunctive adverb if it joins two main clauses that belong in one sentence. Use a period if the main clauses should be two sentences.

Run-ons. A **comma splice** is the error caused by joining two main clauses with only a comma when they need to be joined with something stronger, such as a semicolon, a period, or a comma plus a coordinating conjunction. A **fused sentence** is the error of joining two main clauses with no punctuation or coordinating conjunction.

> Comma splice: *Gawain glanced up, the great ax descended.* Something stronger than a comma is needed to join these two main clauses.

There are four common solutions to run-ons, which work better or worse depending on the sentence:

1. Period: Gawain glanced up. The great ax descended.

2. Semicolon: Gawain glanced up; the great ax descended.

> **a.** Use a semicolon only when the two clauses are so inextricably linked (and often parallel in construction) that they are expressing one idea and need to go together in one sentence.

> **b.** A semicolon is more effective than a period here because it shows there is a link between these two ideas, but solutions 3 and 4 are better still.

3. Comma + cc: Gawain glanced up, *and* the great ax descended.

4. Adverb clause: Subordinate one of the clauses by starting it with one of the www.asia.b words:

> **a.** As Gawain glanced up, the great ax descended. (Comma needed after the introductory adverb clause: **AC, MC.**)

> **b.** Gawain glanced up as the great ax descended. (No comma needed with adverb clause dress-up: **MC AC.**)

> This is the best solution to this comma splice because the subordinating conjunction *as* explains how the two clauses are related: Gawain happened to glance up at the same time that the Green Knight lowered his ax.

A period is usually the easiest and often the best solution for run-ons, especially for younger students.

Advanced: Rule 2. Use semicolons to separate items in a series when the items contain internal commas. (Rare)

> Highborn women lamented when Troy, that noble city celebrated by Homer, fell through trickery; when Pyrrhus, ancient Greek ruler, seized King Priam by the beard; and when the Romans, ruthless and crazed, torched Carthage to the ground.

Colons :

Rule 1. Use a colon after a main clause to introduce an explanation or a list when a phrase like *for example* or *that is* is not included. Lists take no punctuation if there is not a main clause setting them up.

"Yet one other boon I ask: please accept this simple souvenir from me."

Advanced: High school students will benefit from this pattern when they make a point and want to use a quotation to support that point. The colon is the perfect mark of punctuation to join the main clause to the quotation that illustrates it. Think of colons as meaning *see what follows* or *an example follows*.

Rule 2. In business or technical writing, use colons after subheads or words like *example* to set up what follows. Rarely use this in academic papers.

To: Example:
Fix: Dear Sir or Madam:

Rule 3. Use a colon to separate the hour and minutes when specifying time of day.

"We have a manicure scheduled for 10:15."

Hyphens -

Rule 1. Use hyphens in some compound nouns, such as *lady-in-waiting*. Consult a dictionary to check whether the compound noun should be written as one word (*marksman*), two words (*apple tree*), or hyphenated words.

Rule 2. Use hyphens with compound adjectives in front of a noun but usually not after a noun: jewel-encrusted crown, nineteenth-century author, well-attired people. Her crown was jewel encrusted. He lived in the nineteenth century. The people were well attired.

Rule 3. Use hyphens with compound numbers from *twenty-one* to *ninety-nine* and with spelled out fractions like *one-fourth*.

Rule 4. Use hyphens in phone numbers: 555-1212.

Em Dashes and Parentheses — ( )

Although em dashes and parentheses should be used sparingly, especially in academic writing, they can be effective tools when used properly. Distinguish between the **hyphen** (-), which joins things like compound words, and the **em dash**, which is longer (—).

Rule 1. Use em dashes in place of commas when you want to emphasize or draw attention to something. Use **parentheses** in place of commas to minimize the importance of something or to offer an aside. Em dashes are loud, parentheses quiet.

Chanticleer would raise his beak high on a fine summer evening and sing—to the jealousy of neighboring roosters for miles around—such ecstasy had he in his crowing.

(Notice that in fairy tales, characters don't have great curiosity about such oddities as talking frogs.)

Rule 2. Use em dashes to indicate an interruption in speech or a sudden break in thought.

His younger daughter—now there was another topic that brought red to his face.

Rule 3. Use em dashes to set off nonessential elements that have commas inside them.

The poor widow owned a few farm animals—three hefty sows, three cows, and a sheep dubbed Molly—with which she attempted to eke out a living.

Rule 4. Use parentheses for area codes in phone numbers: (260) 555-1212.

Pattern: **MC: illustrating list, example, or quotation**.

Remember, a main clause must come before a colon.

Advanced: When a main clause follows the colon, use a capital letter under two circumstances:

1) The colon introduces more than one sentence (rare).

2) It introduces a formal statement or quotation.

Example:
Charlemagne stated the dual boon of herbs: "An herb is the friend of physicians and the praise of cooks."

Em dashes get their name from the fact that they are roughly the width of the upper-case M in the alphabet.

There is no key for a em dash on your keyboard, but there are shortcuts:

On a PC, type **ctrl-alt-minus sign**: specifically, the minus sign on the numeric keypad on the far right of the keyboard.

On a Mac, type **option-shift-hyphen**.

Ellipsis Points ...

Rule 1. Use ellipsis points to signal hesitation or a reflective pause, especially in dialogue in fiction. Rarely use them in formal papers for this reason.

> "Ahem..." Lord Ashton cleared his throat conspicuously.

> "Um... certainly... the mattress test."

Rule 2. In composition or academic writing, use three spaced periods (the ellipsis mark) to indicate an omission in a quotation. It is not necessary to use the ellipsis mark at the beginning or end of an excerpted passage.

Rule 3. In quoting another source, if the part you leave out spans more than one sentence, use four ellipsis points. The fourth one is actually a period.

Additional Rules and Concepts

Indentation Rules

Indent at the beginning of appropriate sentences to start new paragraphs. On the student pages, mark sentences that need indenting with the editing notation for a paragraph, which looks like a backwards P: ¶.

In copy work, indent by doing two things: 1. start on the next line, and 2. start writing ½ inch from the left margin.

Begin a new paragraph with the following:

1. A new speaker.

a. Start the paragraph at the beginning of the sentence in which someone is speaking, even if the quotation appears later in the sentence. Example: *She cried out with great force, "Thieves!"*

b. If a narrative sentence sets up the quotation, it can go in the same paragraph as the quoted sentence. Example: *The stranger came right to the point. "It is cowardly to stand there with a lethal arrow aimed at my heart."*

c. If narrative follows a quotation in a separate sentence but points directly back to the quotation, it can also go in the same paragraph. Example: *"It is cowardly to stand there with a lethal arrow aimed at my heart." The stranger did not mince words.*

2. A new topic.

a. This is the fuzziest to determine. Generally, if the narrator or a character switches topic or the focus, start a new paragraph.

b. The problem is that topics are a bit like a camera lens: they can sweep a broad scene or zoom in on details. If not much time is devoted to any of the details, you can safely combine different but related points in one paragraph, just as a photograph of the ocean—which takes in the water, sky, beach, swimmers, and even distant ships—can be as harmonious as one of a single shell on shore.

3. A new place.

a. Start a new paragraph when the story switches to a new scene.

b. If several switches are made in quick succession, such as a character's journey to find something, it may be less choppy to keep in one paragraph. Encourage older students to be flexible in making these choices, but if students are more comfortable with a stricter interpretation (hence more paragraphs), that is fine.

You may have noticed that this book does not follow this indentation format. These rules are perfect for students, though, because they typically do not have the typographic tools that book designers have, such as being able to control the space between paragraphs.

4. A new time.

> **a.** Same principles as with place: start a new paragraph with a new time unless there are several time shifts in close succession that make sense together in a single paragraph.

The rules for new paragraphs in fiction are less rigid than they are in academic writing. Do not get hung up on the details, but try to follow the main principles and aim for some consistency. If students make a reasonable case based on these principles for something other than what the book suggests, let them choose. In practice, paragraph divisions are clearer and more critical in academic writing, so we can be more flexible with fiction.

Capitalization Rules

Rule 1. Capitalize the first word of a sentence and of a quoted sentence, even when it does not begin the full sentence.

> The stranger responded, "You joke like a numbskull!"

Rule 2. Use lowercase to continue interrupted quotations.

> "Princess," he began, "you have a visitor at the door."

Rule 3. Capitalize proper nouns and words derived from proper nouns.

> Sherwood Forest; Robin Hood; Arthurian; Spartan

Rule 4. Capitalize people's titles when used with a name or as a substitute for a name in a noun of direct address. Do not capitalize titles when used without a name. Do not capitalize family members unless used as a substitute for a name or with a name.

An exception to Rule 4 is *sir* or *madam* as a noun of direct address: *"Stand back, sir," demanded Robin.*

> The Sheriff of Nottingham was related to the forester whom Robin Hood killed.

> The sheriff was related to the forester whom Robin Hood killed.

> "Can you clean the bullet from his wound, Doctor?"

> He succeeded his father as king.

Rule 5. Capitalize calendar names (days of the week and months) but not seasons.

> the month of June; in the spring; on Wednesday

Rule 6. Capitalize compass directions only when they refer to specific geographic regions, such as the South, or are part of a proper noun, such as North Carolina or New South Wales.

> On his journey north Gawain encountered few obstacles. (He is heading in a northward direction but not traveling to a region known as the North.)

Rule 7. Capitalize the first and last words of titles and subtitles and all other words except articles, coordinating conjunctions, and prepositions.

> A shy, small girl recited "Mary Had a Little Lamb."

> Your Knights of the Round Table are reputed superior in courtesy and arms.

> Note: Titles of long works like books, magazines, and movies should be italicized. Titles of short works like poems, short stories, and articles in magazines should be in quotation marks.

When writing longhand, it is customary to underline words that you will want to italicize.

Numbers Rules

Different style guides give different rules about how to write numbers. These simplified rules follow the principles of the Chicago Manual of Style.

Rule 1. Spell out numbers that can be expressed in one or two words; use figures for other numbers.

> The younger of his two daughters had racked up one thousand text messages on her cell phone in a single month!

Rule 2. Spell out ordinal numbers.

> In another year the second sister was permitted to rise to the surface.

Rule 3. Use numerals with dates.

> Exiting the hall, the stranger called back, "Meet me at the Green Chapel in one year and one day on January 1, 1400."

Rule 4. When numbers are mixed with symbols, use figures.

> "We can expect at least 40% of those invited to attend, or 238 guests."

Homophones and Usage

Homophones are words that sound alike but are spelled differently and have different meanings. Usage errors occur when students use one word when another is meant, often with words that are spelled similarly.

Encourage students to start a list of troublesome words to consult whenever they write.

Some common errors:

1. *there, their, they're; your, you're*

    a. *There* is the adverb pointing to a place or point: *over there; there is the spot.*

    b. *Their* and *your* are possessive pronouns: *their journey; your weapon.*

    c. *They're* and *you're* are contractions meanings *they are* and *you are: they're finished; you're spying.*

2. *to, two, too*

    a. *To* is the preposition: *to the soldiers' aid; to the right. To* is also used in infinitives, the "to + verb" form of a verb: *to rush; to seize.*

    b. *Two* is the number.

    c. *Too* means either *also* or *to an excessive degree* or *too much.* It is easy to remember because it has one too many o's!

3. *its, it's*

    a. *Its* is the possessive: *its bark* (the bark of the tree).

    b. *It's* is the contraction *it is: It's too bad.* Teach the difference by explaining that the apostrophe in *it's* is like a little *i: it's.*

    c. *Its'* is always incorrect.

4. *then, than*

> Use *then* to mean *next* or *immediately afterward.* Use *than* for a comparison. *After Alice drank the potion, she was then shorter than she was a moment before.*

5. *lie, lay*

a. Simplify this problem pair by explaining that someone lies himself down but lays down an object.

b. The three main verb forms:

i. to lie: *lie, lay, lain* (present, past, past participle)

ii. to lay: *lay, laid, laid*

One reason students have trouble with these words is that the past tense of *to lie* is the same as the present tense of *to lay*.

c. For some students, memorizing a simple sentence can help with the confusing past tense forms: *Henny Hen lay down* (something she did to herself) *after she laid an egg* (something she did to an object).

6. *like, as*

a. Simple explanation: Use *like* when comparing two nouns; use *as* or *as if* when comparing a noun to an idea (subject + verb).

Not *She arranged her flowerbed as a whale* but *like a whale.*

Not *It looks like it will be a lengthy convalescence* but *It looks as if it will be a lengthy convalescence.*

b. When *as* means in the role, status or function of, it is a preposition.

Treat everything here as your own.

"Come to the Green Chapel or be known as a coward."

The word *like* is a preposition, not a conjunction, so it starts a prepositional phrase, which ends in a noun and does not have a verb. It should not start a clause.

To compare a noun to a clause, use *as, as if,* or *as though* instead of *like.*

7. *farther/farthest, further/furthest*

Use *farther* and *farthest* as the comparative and superlative forms of *far*, referring to physical distance, no matter how short or long. Use *further* and *furthest* for everything else. *Further* means *to a greater extent* or *additional/in addition.*

It is easy to remember the difference because *farther* and *farthest* derive from *far*, relating to distance. We do not say, "I am going fur down the road"!

She had earned a reputation for beauty reaching into the farthest kingdoms. (physical distance)

She swam out farther from the shore. (physical distance)

"I will no further descant on such matters." (to a greater extent)

Some dictionaries no longer distinguish these two, but most careful writers will.

8. *use to, used to*

Use to is substandard English. The correct form is *used to.*

She used to bring pictures she had drawn to Lady Constance.

9. *try and, try to*

Use *try to* when trying to do something. *She tried to sprint across the hill* means she attempted to accomplish this feat. *She tried and sprinted across the hill* does not make sense because *tried* needs an object, as in *she tried climbing.*

10. *affect, effect*

    a. *Affect* as a verb means *to influence, act on,* or *produce a change in. Effect* as a noun is the result of that change. Most of the times this is how we use these words.

    Years of indulgence had the obvious effect (noun meaning the result) *of spoiling Dorinda.*

    Maybe Dorinda was too self-centered for anyone else to affect (verb form meaning to influence) *her deeply.*

    b. *Affect* and *effect* both have a noun and verb meaning, which is one reason they are so confusing. As a noun, a person's affect is his emotional appearance, feeling or emotion. As a verb, *to effect* is to bring about or accomplish something.

11. *between, among*

    Use *between* when dealing with two items, *among* with three or more.

    She wandered among the exotic botanical species. (more than two different species of plants)

    Dorinda held the napkin between her thumb and first finger. (two fingers)

Idioms

An idiom is an expression that cannot be understood literally, word for word. Example: *We had better go our separate ways. Had better* is an idiom meaning *ought to.* No one *has,* or *possesses,* something called *better*!

Do not expect students to determine parts of speech of words in idioms because often this will not make sense. When sentences begin with idioms, they do not always have to be labeled as certain openers.

Passive versus Active Voice (Advanced)

In active voice, the subject of the sentence is doing the verb action. Most sentences are written in active voice. Example: *The soldier invited the dwarf to warm himself by the fire.*

In passive voice, we start with the person or thing being acted upon, in the example above, the dwarf, and make it the new subject of the sentence: ***The dwarf was invited by the soldier*** *to warm himself by the fire.*

Passive voice follows this pattern: **Person/thing being acted on + *be* verb + past participle + *by* someone or something** (either in the sentence or understood). *The dwarf* (person being acted on) *was* (be verb) *invited* (past participle) *by the soldier* (by someone) *to warm himself by the fire.* If the sentence does not have all four elements, it is not in passive voice. That is, not every *be* verb is passive.

In writing, discourage older students from misusing passive voice because it is usually wordy and dull. Do not teach the concept to younger students.

Understanding passive voice helps instructors and older students even at this level with one tricky part of speech identification. When -ed past participles (see Parts of Speech: Verbals, page G-9) follow a *be* verb, it is unclear whether they are subject complements after a linking verb or part of the verb phrase.

One way to tell is that they are verbs if the sentence is in passive voice.

    Example: *The castle would be **demolished** by the soldiers.* Test for passive voice: *The castle* (subject being acted upon) *would be* (be verb) *demolished* (past participle) *by the* *soldiers (by* someone). Since this sentence is in passive voice, *demolished* is a verb, not an adjective.

The men were famished. Test: *The men* (subject) *were* (be verb) *famished. Famished* ends in -ed, so can it be a past participle? No: there is no one *famishing* the men so no *by* someone phrase. This makes *famished* an adjective, not a verb.

Two hundred pounds would be rewarded to the man who delivered Robin Hood to the king. Test: *Two hundred pounds* (subject being acted upon) *would be* (be verb) *rewarded* (past participle) *to the man who delivered Robin Hood to the king.* There is also a *"by* someone" phrase that is understood: *by the king.* Since this is in passive voice, the past participle is part of the verb and not an adjective.

Past Perfect Tense (Advanced)

Use the past perfect when relating the earlier of two events that occurred in the past. The more recent event is couched in past tense, the earlier event in past perfect. Form past perfect with *had* + the past participle of the verb.

One such frightful deluge swept away (past tense) worthy King William, who *had reigned* (past perfect) in Flovenia for fourteen peaceful years.

Subjunctive Mood (Advanced)

Used infrequently, the subjunctive mood expresses contrary-to-fact conditions with wish or if statements in the third person followed by a *be* verb. For present tense, all subjects take *be*; for past, *were.* To test: Ask if the statement is literally true. If not, use subjunctive.

*Kissing his hand, the little mermaid felt as if her heart **were** already broken.* Her heart is *not* already broken, so the subjunctive is correct: "as if her heart were" rather than "as if her heart was."

*Fearing lest his name **be** tarnished, Gawain began to despair of ever finding his implacable enemy.* His name will not be tarnished, so the subjunctive is correct: not "Fearing lest his name *is* tarnished," but "Fearing lest it *be* tarnished."

Stylistic Techniques

Fix It! stories teach the stylistic techniques of the Institute for Excellence in Writing. The list below reviews these techniques and offers pointers about how dress-ups and sentence openers reinforce grammar.

Dress-Ups

Dress-ups are ways of dressing up writing style, either by using stronger vocabulary (-ly adverb; strong verb; quality adjective) or by making the sentence structure more complex (*who-which* clause; www.asia.b clause).

Generally, hold older students to a more rigorous standard than younger students, encouraging all students to use word lists like a thesaurus to build their vocabulary when they work on dress-ups in their own writing.

The words marked as vocabulary dress-ups in the book have varying levels of strength. It is up to teachers to decide whether to count some of these words as "dress-up quality" or to allow words the book does not mark. The goal is to encourage interesting and specific vocabulary.

Two of the dress-ups, -ly adverbs and www.asia.b clauses, can also be sentence openers if they start a sentence. Count them as dress-ups if they come later in the sentence but as sentence openers if they are the first word in the sentence.

-ly Adverbs

Found anywhere except the first word in a sentence, this dress-up enriches by adding color and detail. Like other adverbs, the -ly adverb describes or modifies adjectives or verbs. See Parts of Speech: Adverbs, page G-10.

> The palace accountant *vehemently* complained about the princess's excessive texting.

Count only -ly words that are adverbs, not imposter -ly's, which are adjectives, like *princely, lonely, ugly,* and *ghastly.*

When they are ready, direct students to distinguish true -ly adverbs from adjectives by understanding how these parts of speech work. Even younger students can be asked what part of speech follows the -ly word.

The easiest way to check if an -ly word is an adverb or adjective is to place it in front of a noun. If that makes sense, it must be an imposter -ly (an adjective) since only adjectives can describe nouns. Then check it by placing it in front of a verb. If it works, it is a legitimate -ly adverb.

Examples: *She **cleverly** masqueraded herself as a poor girl.* *Cleverly* comes before and describes a verb (*masqueraded*), so it must be an -ly adverb. It also answers the adverb question *how: She masqueraded. How did she masquerade? She cleverly masqueraded.*

*"What nonsense this **silly** frog is talking!"* *Silly* comes before and describes a noun (*frog*), so it must be an imposter -ly, an adjective and not an adverb. It also does not answer the adverb question *how*.

Who-Which Clauses

A *who-which* clause is a dependent clause that begins with *who* or *which*. These clauses deepen content by adding new information to the sentence or minimize choppiness by combining two short sentences. See also Sentences, Clauses, and Phrases: Clauses, page G-16.

Example: *Robin Hood cut straight a hefty staff,* **which** *measured six feet in length.*

To keep the *who* or *which* from stealing the main verb, remove the *who-which* clause from the sentence and confirm that a complete thought (a sentence) remains. If not, the *who* or *which* may have stolen the main verb.

Example: *A bedraggled young woman,* **who** *stood at the door.* If I remove my who clause, I am left with only *A bedraggled young woman,* which is not a complete thought. I need something more: *A bedraggled young woman, who stood at the door, dripped water into her shoes.*

Use *who* for people, *which* for things or institutions. Animals are a special category. If they are just animals, use *which*. If they are beloved pets or if they take on human characteristics like the frog in "The Frog Prince," use *who*.

Younger students should form *who-which* clauses by placing the *who* or *which* immediately after the noun it describes. Many *who-which* clauses take commas. For younger students, you could simply require that they put commas around them all and only later teach essential and nonessential *who-which* clauses.

Advanced *Who-Which* Clauses

Punctuation. *Who-which* clauses are set off with commas if they are **nonessential** but take no commas if they are **essential**.

Essential which clauses usually start with *that* instead of *which*, but do not count these as dress-ups because the dress-up is for practicing who and which clauses.

That starts an adjective clause when it follows a noun. If it follows a verb, it is a noun clause instead. See under Punctuation: Commas: Rule 15: Essential-Nonessential Elements, page G-24, for further information about this important concept. See also Stylistic Techniques: Advanced Style: Noun Clauses, page G-44.

Question. When *who* or *which* asks a question, it begins a full sentence (a main clause), so *who* or *which* starting a question is not a *who-which* adjective clause, which is a dependent clause. Example: "Who was at the door?" does not count as a dress-up.

Whose. *Whose* is the possessive pronoun, used with people or things.

Examples: There lived within the glades of Sherwood Forest a famous outlaw *whose* name was Robin Hood. The table *whose* legs were wobbly threatened to crash to the ground.

Who versus whom. Use *whom* instead of *who* when *whom* is the object of something (objective case), such as the object of a preposition or a direct object. Use *who* when it is

Who-which **clauses** are adjective clauses, which usually modify the noun they follow. Older students may write which clauses to modify the entire idea that comes before.

Example: You have killed the king's deer, which is a capital offense. It is not the deer that is the offense but killing it— the full idea expressed in the main clause.

Advanced: The pronouns *who, that,* and *which* become singular or plural according to the noun they modify. Since the clause modifies the noun right before it, the verb must agree in number with that noun.

Example: Gawain was one of the knights who honor courtesy. The verb honor agrees with knights, not with one.

Also, if you teach *who-which* clauses as a dependent clause, it may help to understand that who or which is usually the subject of the clause.

in the subjective case, functioning as the subject of the sentence or, rarely, as a subject complement. See Parts of Speech: Pronouns, page G-7.

Trick: *he/him* substitution. If you can revise the sentence and substitute *he* or *they*, use *who*; if *him* or *them*, use *whom*.

> *He bellowed his challenge, as if doubting* **who/whom** *in the hall held rule.* He held rule, so *who* is correct.

> *I am not he of* **who/whom** *you speak.* You speak of *him*, so *whom*. (object of preposition)

Invisible *who-which*. Who-which's followed by a *be* verb can be invisible for a more stylish sentence.

> Example: *Robin Hood started off from Locksley,* ~~which was~~ *the town where he lived. All had come to Sherwood Forest,* ~~which was~~ *a vast, uncharted wood.* In both cases, we could drop *which was* for a more elegant construction.

Strong Verbs

Teach younger students to recognize verbs by filling in these blanks with a form of the word in question: *yesterday he _____; today he _____; tomorrow he will _____.* (Yesterday he pitched; today he pitches; tomorrow he will pitch.)

As the most powerful part of speech, the verb can make or break a sentence. Challenge students to distinguish truly strong verbs from ordinary ones.

> Example: Compare ordinary: "It'll be the first thing I'll throw away when I make changes."

> versus strong: "It'll be the first thing I'll pitch when I redecorate."

Strong verb dress-ups should be action verbs, not helping or linking verbs. See Parts of Speech: Verbs, page G-8.

Quality Adjectives

Gradually teach students the difference between ordinary and quality adjectives. Quality adjectives are strong because they are more colorful, provide a stronger image or feeling, or add more detail and are more specific than ordinary adjectives. See also Parts of Speech: Adjectives, page G-10.

> Example: His advisers realized they had a *daunting* task.

Adjectives describe nouns. Teach how to locate adjectives with this simple test: The _____ person or object (thing).

> Examples: *the gurgling brook*. Is *brook* a person or thing? Yes, so *gurgling* is an adjective. Or *the confident stranger*. Is *stranger* a person or object? Yes, so *confident*, which describes the noun, must be an adjective.

www.asia.b Clauses

Initially, teach that dependent clauses may begin with one of these eight subordinating conjunctions: *when, while, where, as, since, if, although, because,* easy to learn by memorizing **www.asia.b**. IEW materials sometimes call these **the www words**. They usually start an adverb clause.

Eventually, students will learn that other words can start dependent clauses too, such as *until, whereas, wherever, whenever, as if, unless,* and sometimes *before* or *after.* See Sentences, Clauses, and Phrases: Clauses, page G-16, and Stylistic Techniques: Sentence Openers: #5 Clausal, page G-42.

A dependent clause cannot stand on its own as a sentence. It needs to be attached to a main clause to be a legal sentence.

Examples:

"Meet me *if* you dare."

"Your name, Little John, fits you ill *because* you are far from little!"

Robin Hood and his band guffawed loudly *until* the stranger began to grow enraged.

Remain on the other side *while* I quickly make a staff.

Most of the time, a www.asia.b word will begin an adverb clause. When an adverb clause occurs mid-sentence (the dress-up), it should not be set off with commas; when an adverb clause starts a sentence (the opener), it takes a comma after the clause. Teach simple patterns to help students remember these rules:

MC AC: no comma when an adverb clause falls in the middle or at the end of a sentence

AC, MC: comma at the end of a clause when the adverb clause comes before the main clause

Advanced: www.asia.b Words

The www words **since**, **as**, and **until** sometimes are prepositions instead of conjunctions. You can tell they do not start clauses if there is no subject and verb after them, as in *since childhood* or *as an archer* or *until the next day*. See under Sentence Openers: #5 Clausal Opener, page G-42, for tricks to tell the difference.

The www words **as**, **where**, and **when** can start adjective clauses instead of adverb clauses, usually when they follow and describe a noun. Adjective clauses can be essential (no commas) or nonessential (commas). See Punctuation: Commas: Rule 15: Essential-Nonessential Elements, page G-24.

Example: *King Arthur decided to climb to the top of the cliff, where he could drink from the pool of water collected above.* This *where* clause follows a noun that it also describes; since it is nonessential, it needs a comma.

While, although, and **whereas** sometimes need a comma before them because they present a contrast to the main clause in the sentence.

Examples: You stand there with a lethal bow to shoot at my heart, *while* I have only a plain blackthorn staff to meet you with.

Hrothgar and Robert had been trying to save his life all along, *whereas* he had been too foolish to listen to them.

www.asia.b

when
while
where
as
since
if
although
because

While and *whereas* technically function as coordinating conjunctions in this case and follow the punctuation pattern **MC, cc MC**, but it is easiest to explain this as needing a comma because of the contrast.

Sentence Openers

Sentence openers are the patterns that sentences begin with. Their obvious advantage is in encouraging more complex sentence structure and variety, which greatly improves the quality of student writing. A second advantage is that openers teach lots of grammar in a backdoor fashion. By teaching the patterns and punctuation that accompany the openers, you will help students master quite a bit of grammar in the context of writing.

#1 Subject Opener

Subject openers essentially begin with the subject of a main clause, although articles and/ or adjectives may precede it. If the sentence is shorter than six words, it can be counted as a #6 vss opener instead.

> Examples: *He became livid on the subject of modern gadgets.* The subject is *He.*
>
> *The convivial company congregated in the great hall.* The subject is *company*, but it is still a subject opener because *the* is an article and *convivial* an adjective.

Sometimes #1 sentences invert the usual word order, placing the verb or other word first. For this reason, it helps to explain that the #1 sentence starts with a main clause.

> Example: *There were blameless, loyal men at his side who rambled with him through the greenwood shades.* The actual subject is *men*, but the sentence begins with a main clause so is still a #1 subject opener.

#2 Prepositional Opener

Prepositions begin phrases that follow this pattern:

preposition + noun (no verb)

The phrase starts with a preposition and ends with a noun, with no verb inside. Other words may squeeze in between the preposition and noun but never a verb. See under #5 Clausal Opener, page G-42, for the trick to distinguish between #2s and #5s. See also Parts of Speech: Prepositions, page G-11.

Examples:

> *During* these reflections, King Morton shook his head in abject despair.
>
> *After* a pause she summed it up.

Younger students should practice finding prepositional phrases before identifying the #2 opener, showing how the phrase fits the pattern. Example: After (preposition) + a (article) + pause (noun). This phrase begins with a preposition, ends with a noun, and has no verb, which fits the pattern. Remind students that the lack of a verb means it must be a phrase and cannot be a clause.

Punctuation: Prepositional phrases of five or more words take a comma after them; with fewer than five, the comma is optional. Let the pause test be your guide for shorter prepositional phrases: use a comma if you need a pause, no comma if you do not.

When short prepositional openers work transitionally (as in *For example, In addition, On the other hand*), they will need a comma, just as any transitional opener should take a comma. Usually the pause test is sufficient to determine this.

Punctuation rule note: Grammar books express the punctuation rule more vaguely: long prepositional phrases take a comma; with short ones, the comma is optional.

For most students, a clear cutoff is more helpful than this general principle, and five or more words are usually long enough to warrant a comma.

Advanced Prepositional Phrase

Disguised #2. Sentences starting with some kind of time (*Wednesday; Two weeks ago; The evening of the ball; One night*) followed by the main clause begin with what is effectively a disguised #2, in which a preposition is implied but not stated, as in "One morning..." where "In," "On," or "During one morning" is implied. The sentence sounds better without the preposition, but the opener functions as if it were there and is punctuated the same way.

Infinitives. Although infinitives do not fit the usual pattern of prepositional phrases (**preposition + noun**), the *to* in them is still a preposition, used to mark the infinitive of a verb. Infinitives starting sentences may be counted as #2 openers. E.g., *To lend* credence to this claim, one of the most respected authors related a pertinent account.

#3 -ly Adverb Opener

The main difference between an -ly dress-up and -ly sentence opener is the flow of the sentence. Beginning the sentence with the -ly adverb gives a different kind of rhythm than placing it later in the sentence.

Advanced: -ly Adverb Punctuation. LY openers take a comma after them when they modify the sentence but do not need a comma when they modify the verb. The best way to tell what they modify is to put the sentence in two patterns that use the adjective form of the -ly adverb.

> Did the subject act in the [adjective] manner? **If so, the -ly modifies the verb: no comma.**
>
>> Example: *Resentfully the stranger answered him.* The stranger answered in a resentful manner, so this -ly modifies the verb and therefore does not take a comma.
>
> Is it [adjective] that the rest of the sentence is true? **If so, the -ly modifies the sentence: comma.**
>
>> Example: *Unfortunately, Queen Mary was traveling with him at the time.* It is unfortunate that she was traveling with him at the time, so this -ly modifies the whole sentence and needs a comma.

Sometimes, both the comma and no comma are correct but affect the meaning.

> *Sorrowfully Chanticleer acceded to the counsel of his wife.* He acceded, but he did so sorrowfully, with regret.

> *Sorrowfully, Chanticleer acceded to the counsel of his wife.* This opener is the narrator's warning that Chanticleer made a mistake in acceding to his wife's advice. It is sorrowful that Chanticleer acceded to his wife's counsel.

#4 -ing Participial Phrase Opener

Sentence opener #4 sounds easy but can be complicated grammatically. Teach this pattern:

-ing word/phrase + comma + subject/-inger + main verb

It begins with an -ing word (participle) or phrase, then a comma, then the subject of the main clause which is also doing the inging, then the main verb. Check that #4 openers have these four elements and teach students to ask this important question: Is the subject after the comma doing the inging?

Examples: *Gathering their three gifts, the soldiers set out on a journey to visit a neighboring king.* 1. *Gathering their three gifts* is an -ing phrase; 2. there is a comma; 3. the noun after the comma is both the subject of the main clause (*soldiers set out*) and the inger (*soldiers were gathering*); 4. *set out* is the verb. This follows the four steps and is therefore a legal, legitimate #4 opener.

Taking up his bow, Robin Hood shot with unparalleled skill. This also follows the four steps: Robin is both taking up his bow and shooting.

Advanced #4 Opener

There are two main ways students might mislabel #4s.

1. Illegal #4s look like #4s, only the person or thing after the comma is not the one doing the inging. This is known as a **dangling modifier**—an often humorous but still grammatically faulty sentence pattern.

Examples: *Hopping quickly to keep up, she let the frog traipse behind her to the resplendent dining hall.* It is not the princess but the frog that is supposed to be hopping!

Looming nearby in the harbor, she beheld a large ship. The mermaid is not looming nearby but the ship.

Scanning the noble assembly, the horse rode straight to the high dais. The horse is not the one doing the scanning but the Green Knight.

2. Imposter #4s begin with an -ing word so look like #4s but are actually #1 subject openers or #2 prepositional phrase openers. See also Parts of Speech: Verbals, page G-9.

#2s that look like #4s begin with one of these prepositions: *during, according to, regarding, concerning.* The four steps reveal that the pattern does not work.

Examples: *According to state history, the only indisputable test for real princess blood is the mattress test.* The subject after the comma is *test*, which is not doing the *according*, so this sentence does not fit the #4 pattern. It is actually a #2.

During the obligatory dance after dinner, she twirled him around. *She* is not doing the inging. In fact, nobody can "dure" because *during* is not a participle derived from a verb but a preposition.

#1s that look like #4s begin with an -ing word, but it functions as the subject of the sentence. (We call -ing nouns gerunds, not participles). These have no place for a comma and no person or thing mentioned doing the inging.

Examples: *Living at the splendid castle cheered the soldiers.* There is no comma or place for one, nor is there a subject that is doing the inging. The context makes it clear that the soldiers are living there, but the sentence does not use *soldiers* as the subject doing that action. The subject-verb pair is *Living cheered.*

Peering through the curtain left Gawain in wonder. Again, no comma or place for one. The subject-verb pair is *Peering left.*

Invisible #4s are sentences that follow the same pattern as regular #4s, but the -ing word is hidden. These sentences begin with an adjective or adjective phrase followed by a comma plus main clause, with the word *being, seeming,* or *appearing* implied at the beginning of the sentence. They are more elegant without the -ing participle but function and are punctuated just like a #4.

IEW instructors sometimes add a seventh opener for sentences starting with a past participle ending in -ed, but it is unnecessary to create a separate category for this since it follows the same pattern as an invisible -ing opener.

Examples: *Quick-witted and agile, Robert compensated for his limitation by an eagerness to please.* Implied: *Appearing* quick-witted and agile, Robert compensated for his limitation.

Relaxed and untroubled, the stranger genially waited for him. Implied: *Being* relaxed and untroubled, the stranger genially waited for him.

Energized by boyish blood, Arthur did not care to lounge at his ease. Implied: *Being* energized by boyish blood, Arthur did not care to lounge at his ease.

#5 Clausal Opener

This is the same as the dress-up and uses the same www words (subordinating conjunctions), except that now this dependent clause starts the sentence and needs a comma after it. Teach the simple pattern: **AC, MC**

Examples:

If possessions were plundered, the yeomen would recapture the goods and return them to the poor.

As he approached, Robin Hood noticed a tall stranger resolutely striding toward the bridge.

When he demanded it back, Dorinda mumbled something about not being able to locate it.

Advanced: #5s versus #2s. The problem with accurately identifying #5s, #2s, and www.asia.b dress-ups is that a few words might be either a preposition or a subordinating conjunction. *After, before, since, until* and *as* can function as either, and while *because* is a subordinating conjunction, *because of* is a preposition.

Two tricks help tell the difference, both bouncing off the fact that prepositional phrases never have a verb and clauses always do.

1. Drop the first word of the phrase or clause in question and look at what is left. If it is a sentence, the group of words is an adverb clause; if it is not, the words form a prepositional phrase.

2. Look for a verb: only #5s and adverb clause dress-ups can have a verb.

Example:

a. After supper, King Morton ordered Dorinda to prepare the Golden Guestroom.

b. After they finished supper, King Morton ordered Dorinda to prepare the Golden Guestroom.

Drop *After* and see what is left in the opener. Sentence *a* starts with a #2 prepositional opener because *supper* is not a complete sentence; sentence *b* starts with a #5 clausal opener because *they finished supper* is a complete sentence. Also, we know that sentence *b* starts with a #5 because the opener contains a verb (*finished*).

#6 vss, or Very Short Sentence

An occasional short sentence can pack a punch in paragraphs that otherwise have intricate and lengthy sentences.

Examples:

"Tarry for me here."

Robin Hood set off.

The blow inflamed him.

King Morton esteemed values.

The trick to #6s is that they must be short (two to five words) and they must be sentences (subject + verb and be able to stand alone).

They should also be strong: a vsss = Very Short Strong Sentence!

#T or Transitional Opener

#T works for sentences beginning with interjections, interrupters, or transitional words and expressions. Transitional openers are usually followed by a comma.

Common words and phrases in this class include the following: *however, therefore, then, thus, later, now, otherwise, indeed, first, next, also, moreover, hence, furthermore, henceforth, likewise.* Also included are interjections, such as *oh, ouch, wow, ha,* which can be followed by a comma or an exclamation mark.

> **Tip:** When you add one of these words or phrases to a main clause, the clause remains a main clause.

#T "Moreover, the august Macrobius explained that his dreams were clear portents." (transition)

#T Oh, how gladly she would have shaken off all this pomp and laid aside the heavy wreath! (interjection)

#T "Alas! For this, you have forfeited my heart and all my love." (exclamatory interjection)

#Q or Question

#Q takes care of sentences that ask questions. This teaches students not to mark questions beginning with *who* or *which* as their *who-which* dress-up or questions beginning with words like *when* or *where* as their clausal openers.

#Q Did you ever hear the story of the three poor soldiers?

#Q "What name do you go by, good fellow?"

#Q Where is fair Pertelote?

Advanced Style

Duals and Triples

Deliberate use of dual or triple adverbs, adjectives, or verbs, especially when the words add a different nuance, enriches prose and challenges students to be precise with words chosen. Classic writers of the past like Charles Dickens and persuasive essayists like Winston Churchill have used duals and triples to convey their meaning most powerfully.

Examples:

All who beheld her wondered at her *graceful, swaying* movements.

The ship glided away *smoothly and lightly* over the tranquil sea.

Noun Clauses

A noun clause is a dependent clause used as a noun. It can function in any of the ways that nouns function: subject, direct or indirect object, or object of a preposition. See also Sentences, Clauses, and Phrases: Clauses: Dependent Clauses (Advanced): Noun Clauses, page G-18.

Although noun clauses may begin with many words, those starting with *that* are the main ones highlighted in IEW because students sometimes confuse them with essential adjective clauses.

To tell the difference: If *that* begins an adjective clause, you can substitute *which* and it will still make sense. If *that* begins a noun clause, *which* does not work in its place. Also, noun clauses follow verbs and answer the question "What?" after a verb. Adjective clauses usually follow a noun and describe the noun they come immediately after.

Example:

"I know well that I am the weakest of these illustrious knights." Can you say, "I know well which I am the weakest of knights"? No, so it is not an adjective clause but a noun clause. It follows a verb (*know*) and answers the question "What?" E.g., *I know.* What does he know? That he is the weakest of these knights.

Invisible Noun Clause: This is a noun clause with the word *that* understood, not stated directly. Example: *He could tell [that] he was going to relish his palace stay.* Sometimes it is more elegant without *that*: *He could tell he was going to relish his palace stay.*

Decorations

Used sparingly, as an artist might add a splash of bright color to a nature painting, these stylistic techniques daringly or delicately decorate one's prose. You can introduce the decorations at any time when teaching IEW writing.

The six decorations are questions, conversation/quotation, 3sss (three short staccato sentences), dramatic opening-closing, simile/metaphor, and alliteration. In *Fix It! Grammar*, you will see the last two.

Similes and Metaphors

A simile is a comparison between two unlike things using the words *like* or *as*. A metaphor, harder to create, is a similar comparison but without the *like* or *as*.

Examples:

The ship dived like a swan between them. (simile)

The waves rose mountains high. (metaphor)

The key to recognizing these figures of speech is that they compare unlike things. For example, to say that a cat is like a tiger is a comparison but not a simile.

Alliteration

Alliteration is the repetition of the same initial consonant sounds in two or more words in close proximity. It adds flavor to writing when used judiciously.

Example: *Arthur was **seeking some** shady relief from the **sweltering sun**. Shady* is not part of the alliteration because it does not have the same initial sound as the other *s* words. It is not the letter that matters but the sound. Thus, *celery* and *sound* are alliterative, but *shady* and *sound* are not.

Stressed syllables in the middle of words that carry the same sound can contribute to the alliteration. Example: *I **will** a**ward** you **what** I **win** in the **woods***.

In academic writing, alliteration usually sounds awkward unless found in a title or the first or last sentence of a paper, where it can appropriately dramatize those parts.